W9-AEA-569

MESSAGE OF THE FATHERS OF THE CHURCH
General Editor: Thomas Halton

Volume 20

MESSAGE OF THE FATHERS OF THE CHURCH

SOCIAL THOUGHT

by

Peter C. Phan

Michael Glazier, Inc.
Wilmington, Delaware

ABOUT THE AUTHOR
PETER C. PHAN was born in Vietnam, did his undergraduate studies at the University of London and his graduate studies in Rome. He is a regular contributor to international journals on patristic and theological questions. He is Chairman of the Department of Theology at the University of Dallas.

First published in 1984 by Michael Glazier, Inc.
1723 Delaware Avenue, Wilmington, Delaware 19806

Library of Congress Catalog Card Number: 83-083156
International Standard Book Number:
  Message of the Fathers of the Church series:
    (0-89453-312-6, Paper; 0-89435-340-1, Cloth)
  SOCIAL THOUGHT
    (0-89453-331-2, Paper)
    (0-89435-360-6, Cloth)

Cover design: Lillian Brulc

We wish to acknowledge and thank Paulist Press for the limited use of translations of the texts of the Fathers of the Church in *Ancient Christian Writers*; Wm. B. Eerdmans Publishing Company for the limited use of translations of texts of the Fathers of the Church in *The Ante-Nicene Fathers*, eds. Alexander Roberts and James Donaldson, and *The Nicene and Post-Nicene Fathers*, ed. Philip Schaff; and the Catholic University of of America Press for the limited use of translations of the texts of the Fathers of the Church in *Fathers of the Church*.

Printed in the United States of America

*To
My
Parents*

CONTENTS

ABBREVIATIONS

ACW   Ancient Christian Writers

CCL   Corpus Christianorum, series latina (Turnhout)

CSEL Corpus scriptorum ecclesiasticorum latinorum
      (Vienna)

GCS   Die griechischen christlichen Schriftsteller der
      ersten Jahrhunderte (Berlin)

FOTC Fathers of the Church

PG   Migne, Patrologia Graeca

PL   Migne, Patrologia Latina

SC   Sources chrétiennes (Paris)

EDITOR'S INTRODUCTION

The *Message of the Fathers of the Church* is a companion series to The *Old Testament Message* and The *New Testament Message*. It was conceived and planned in the belief that Scripture and Tradition worked hand in hand in the formation of the thought, life and worship of the primitive Church. Such a series, it was felt, would be a most effective way of opening up what has become virtually a closed book to present-day readers, and might serve to stimulate a revival in interest in Patristic studies in step with the recent, gratifying resurgence in Scriptural studies.

The term "Fathers" is usually reserved for Christian writers marked by orthodoxy of doctrine, holiness of life, ecclesiastical approval and antiquity. "Antiquity" is generally understood to include writers down to Gregory the Great (+604) or Isidore of Seville (+636) in the West, and John Damascene (+749) in the East. In the present series, however, greater elasticity has been encouraged, and quotations from writers not noted for orthodoxy will sometimes be included in order to illustrate the evolution of the Message on particular doctrinal matters. Likewise, writers later than the mid-eighth century will sometimes be used to illustrate the continuity of tradition on matters like sacramental theology or liturgical practice.

An earnest attempt was made to select collaborators on a broad inter-disciplinary and inter-confessional basis, the chief consideration being to match scholars who could handle the Fathers in their original languages with subjects in which they had already demonstrated a special interest and competence. About the only editorial directive given to the selected contributors was that the Fathers, for the most part, should be allowed to speak for themselves and that they should speak in readable, reliable modern English. Volumes on individual themes were considered more suitable than volumes devoted to individual Fathers, each theme, hopefully, contributing an important segment to the total mosaic of the Early Church, one, holy, catholic and apostolic. Each volume has an introductory essay outlining the historical and theological development of the theme, with the body of the work mainly occupied with liberal citations from the Fathers in modern English translation and a minimum of linking commentary. Short lists of Suggested Further Readings are included; but dense, scholarly footnotes were actively discouraged on the pragmatic grounds that such scholarly shorthand has other outlets and tends to lose all but the most relentlessly esoteric reader in a semi-popular series.

At the outset of his *Against Heresies* Irenaeus of Lyons warns his readers "not to expect from me any display of rhetoric, which I have never learned, or any excellence of composition, which I have never practised, or any beauty or persuasiveness of style, to which I make no pretensions." Similarly, modest disclaimers can be found in many of the Greek and Latin Fathers and all too often, unfortunately, they have been taken at their word by an uninterested world. In fact, however, they were often highly educated products of the best rhetorical schools of their day in the Roman Empire, and what they have to say is often as much a lesson in literary and cultural, as well as in spiritual, edification.

St. Augustine, in *The City of God* (19.7), has interesting reflections on the need for a common language in an expanding world community; without a common language a man is more at home with his dog than with a foreigner as far as intercommunication goes, even in the Roman Empire, which imposes on the nations it conquers the yoke of both law and language with a resultant abundance of interpreters. It is hoped that in the present world of continuing language barriers the contributors to this series will prove opportune interpreters of the perennial Christian message.

Thomas Halton

PREFACE

Christianity is a religion based on an historical revelation and therefore by its very nature is immersed in the world in which it lives. From its very beginnings the authors of the New Testament have already reflected on the relation between the message of salvation which Christ proclaimed and the social and political environments surrounding the new religion. Their thoughts were later adopted, developed, and adapted to the new historical circumstances by those early thinkers we traditionally call the Fathers of the Church.

This book attempts to introduce the readers to the Father's social and political teachings in their own words. The Introduction will provide an overview of the involvement of the early Church in the society in the first six centuries and a synopsis of the Fathers' social doctrine, excluding the topics dealing with ethics, women, and war treated elsewhere in this series. The other chapters present the Fathers in chronological order, first Greek, then Latin, with short introductory notes on their main works and ideas. The titles of their works are given first, next a short headline summarizing the content of the extract, which is then given preceded by numbers indicating book, chapter, and verse where applicable.

A work of this nature obviously cannot lay any claim to originality. I gladly acknowledge my debt to many existing translations and studies. One work deserves special mention, R. Sierra Bravo's *Doctrina Social Y Economica de los Padres de la Iglesia* (Compi, Madrid 1967), which has been of invaluable help to me in making the textual selections.

I would like to express my thanks to Dr. Thomas Halton for having invited me to collaborate in the series and for his invaluable advice. My thanks are also owed to Mrs. Jeri Guadagnoli and Mrs. Carolyn Fouse who have expertly typed the manuscript.

Finally this work is respectfully dedicated to my parents, who have experienced in a most dramatic way the injustice of war and have courageously begun a new life all over again in the new world.

Peter C. Phan
University of Dallas
Irving, Texas

INTRODUCTION

I. A Social Doctrine of the Fathers?

There is no doubt that the rise and spread of the socialist movement has largely contributed, directly or indirectly, to the retrieval and sharpening of the social consciousness in Christianity in general and in the Roman Catholic Church in particular. Papal encyclicals (*Rerum Novarum, Quadragesimo Anno, Mater et Magistra, Pacem in Terris, Populorum Progressio, Octogesima Adveniens*, to name only the most important ones), Vatican II's *Gaudium et Spes*, theological currents (political theology, liberation theology, feminist theology, black theology, theology of revolution, etc.) are but some of the indications and fruits of this heightened sense of social responsibility.

It would be wrong, however, to claim that the social concern is the exclusive and original discovery of socialism or that the social doctrine of the Church is simply a belated attempt to respond to the challenges of modern social upheavals. On the contrary, it must be said that the social consciousness belongs to the very essence of Christianity since the salvation it proclaims affects not only the individual but also the whole human society, indeed, the whole universe itself, in its sociological, economic and political dimensions. The Fathers of the Church themselves have developed, some nineteen centuries before Karl Marx, many of the fundamental concepts of the social teaching of the Church, so much so that we can legitimately speak of a social doctrine of the Fathers. Indeed a careful study of the history of the early Church, as will be shown in the course of this general introduction and as the selected texts themselves demonstrate, will confirm the fact the Fathers not only were concerned about the social conditions of their contemporaries but also exhibited in their thought the essential requirements of a social doctrine: an ideal of justice and equality in the economic and social promotion of the oppressed and destitute classes; a critique of the exploitations and injustices perpetrated by the ruling and wealthy classes; and a proposal of concrete actions to remove this unjust situation.

The foregoing remarks should not, however, mislead one into thinking that the Fathers produced a comprehensive and autonomous system of social thought based upon their own philosophical understanding of man and society. Indeed they developed their thoughts on man and his social nature, examined the social institutions and practices of their times, and devised their social programmes in the light of the Scripture, and more specifically, the teachings of Jesus and apostolic Church, rather than in the light of ancient philosophy. This is of course not meant to deny the influence ancient philosophy, especially Platonism and Stoicism, has exercised on the Fathers in their elaboration of the social doctrine. They did appropriate these philosophies but only after a critical evaluation in the light of the Christian revelation.

In view of the fact that the Fathers primarily explicated the social teachings of the Holy Scripture and applied them to the changing situations of their times, in order to understand and appreciate their social doctrines, it is advisable to examine, however cursorily, both the social teachings of the Bible and the historical circumstances to which these teachings are applied and in the process developed and modified.

II. The Social Teachings of the Bible

Gerhard von Rad declares that there is no concept in the Old Testament as central and significant for all relationships of human life as justice or righteousness. Justice is the social principle that held the Hebrew social fabric together. It is the fidelity to the demands of a relationship as established by the Law—the web of relationships between king and people, judge and complainants, family and tribe and kinsfolk, the community and the resident alien, the whole humanity and God. Of course the Law also commands love. Yet, in point of fact, the sense of solidarity is for the most part limited to fellow members of religion and race, even though the prophets often urge the Hebrew people to go beyond these narrow limits.

In the New Testament love is the centripetal social principle. Justice, of course, is not rejected as a principle governing all social relationships but is transcended. Love is God's justice that surpasses man's justice. Human justice gives to each his due; love gives of oneself, one's very life. The law of charity removes all distinctions of race, class or sex; love is extended to all. It is not enough to love one's friends; one must do good to one's enemies (Mt 5:46-48). The new commandment obliges one, as well, to love the neighbor as Christ has loved him—to the point of giving one's life for him (1 Jn 3:16). It is both justice and love as taught by the Old Testament and fulfilled in the life of Jesus that become the principles shaping the early Church's understanding of particular issues of social justice and guiding its involvement in the surrounding society.

Whereas in the Old Testament religion includes politics and the authority that rules the state is regarded as being designated by God and therefore a sacral character is impressed upon government (theocracy), to which all subjects owe obedience and loyalty, in the New Testament Jesus explicitly recognizes a lay element in government: "Give to Caesar what belongs to Caesar, and to God what belongs to God" (Mt 12:17). He makes a distinction between the secular authority and that of God, although he does not separate them since the secular authority itself comes from God. If political authority, however, orders actions contrary to the law of God, God, rather than man, is to be obeyed (Acts 5:29). The opposition can reach the point of active persecution, and so there are two cities: the City of the Lamb (Jerusalem, the Church) as opposed to the City of the Beast (Rome, the Empire).

The family is considered by the Old Testament not only as a social but also as a religious unit. For the preservation of family life, adultery and other sexual sins are condemned. The personality and rights of children are protected (Dt 24:16). The sacrifice of the firstborn is rejected. Woman is of the same nature as man (Gn 1:27). Yet, in several respects Israelite society is androcratic. A husband may divorce his wife, but a wife may not divorce her husband. Adultery consists only in sexual intercourse between a married woman and a man other than her husband, not in illicit relations of a married man with a woman other than his wife. A woman is juridically subject to her father or husband or closest male relative; she cannot hold property in her own name, unless there is no male heir. Limited polygamy is permitted, at least in the patriarchal period. In the New Testament Jesus condemns divorce and adultery equally of the husband and the wife (Mk 10:9 and Mt 5:27-28). The marriage bond is declared to be "a great mystery" similar to the union between Christ and his Church (Eph 5:29-32).

Widows and orphans in the ancient patriarchal society were economically the most helpless since they did not have the aid of a male head of the family. The Old Testament displays a considerable concern not only for the widow and the orphan but also for the poor and the alien in the land (Ex 22:21-22; Dt 14:29; Jer 22:13, 15-16). Yahweh is said to be their defender and vindicator (Jer 22:3-4). The New Testament shows no less concern for them. Jesus himself associated with the poor and the sinner, denounced the scribes who devoured the houses of widows (Mk 12:40), bestowed a special favor on the widow of Nain by raising her only son from the dead (Lk 7:11-16). St. James proclaims: "Religion pure and undefiled before God the Father is this: to give aid to orphans and widows in their tribulation, and to keep oneself unspotted from this world" (Jas 1:27). Nor did the apostolic Church forget the poor and the needy: A part of the community's resources was set aside for them and special persons were appointed to take care of their needs (Acts 4:32-34; 6:1-6; 1 Cor 11:8-22).

Wealth and its use are the subject of many biblical teachings. Wealth itself is regarded by the Old Testament as God's blessing, but it must be used wisely. It must be shared with the poor (Dt 15:11) and detachment from it is strongly urged since it breeds anxiety, and may damage its possessor (Ec 5:10-20). Avarice is condemned. Ownership, particularly of farm land, is relative; it is more an occupancy than a possession (Lv 25:23). In the New Testament, in the story of the rich young man who rejected his invitation to follow him, Jesus made wealth an almost insuperable obstacle to salvation and urged his hearers to give it away (Mt 19:16-30). Almsgiving, both in the Old and New Testaments, is considered as one of the principal works of charity. In this context, loan may appropriately be mentioned. In the Old Testament there is stated the obligation to lend without interest (Ex 22:24); Israelites may exact interest from foreigners, but not from each other (Dt 23:20), although this was far more of an ideal than a real practice. In the New Testament Jesus presents the forgiveness of the bankrupt debtor as an example of generosity (Lk 7:41). Lending without expecting repayment is encouraged as an act of charity (Lk 6:35).

Work is viewed under two aspects in the Old Testament: it is both the destiny for which man is placed in the garden (Gn 2:15) and a curse for sin (Gn 3:17-19). In the Pauline writings work is accepted as a necessary part of human responsibility (Eph 4:29; 1 Th 4:11).

Slavery was an essential component of the social life and economy of the whole of antiquity, and to this Israel was no exception, although Hebrew laws demanded a more humane treatment of slaves, especially if they were Israelites. The New Testament does not attack the institution of slavery directly, but attacks the principle of inequality on which chattei slavery was based. There is no distinction between slave and free in Christ (1 Cor 12:13; Gal 3:28). The principles of Christian love and unity made it impossible for the Christian to regard another human being as a chattel, and this made slavery impracticable.

Such are the elements of biblical social doctrine in its barest outline—relationship between Church and State; family; aid to widows, orphans, and the poor; wealth; almsgiving; loan; work; and slavery—which the Fathers inherited and which it was up to their genius and inventiveness to develop and apply to the changing circumstances of their times.

III. The Social Involvement of Early Christianity

The age of the Fathers conventionally designates the first eight centuries of the Church in which Christianity, originally perceived as a Jewish sect, spread throughout the Roman world and eventually became the official religion of the Roman Empire. This time can be divided into two periods separated by what has often been called the "Constantinian turning-point." Before Constantine's "conversion" and his recognition of Christianity as the religion of the State, Christianity was an illicit, often cruelly persecuted religion, and consequently its involvement with the society was very curtailed, predominantly defensive, and mostly aimed at sheer survival. Its social concern in this period was mainly directed towards its own members. From the fourth century, after Constantine had made Christianity an integral part of public life, the Church faced a totally new situation, its concept of charity assumed a social dimension. Charitable institutions were organized, not only for the sake of the Christians but also for the non-Christians, under the sponsorship of the Church and even under papal patronage. We shall review briefly the history of the Church's social involvement in these two periods.

A. SOCIAL CONCERN IN PRE-CONSTANTINIAN CHRISTIANITY

Despite bloody persecutions by emperors and vicious attacks from pagan thinkers and despite internal heresies of Gnosticism, Marcionism, and Montanism, the post-apostolic Church, in the first three centuries, succeeded not only to survive but also to expand rapidly. This was due to its sense of community, which expressed itself in, among other things, the Christians' willingness to aid those in need and in its teachings on the social duties of the Christian.

Both from Christian and pagan sources, it is clear that the practical exercise of charity towards a needy brother in the faith, or towards a pagan afflicted with illness or misfortunes was an undeniable title of glory in the early church. Justin in his *Apologia* affirms: "We, who loved above all else the ways of acquiring riches and possessions, now hand over to a community fund what we possess and share it with every needy person" (*Apol.* 1.14). Tertullian observes: "Our care for the derelict and our active love have become our distinctive sign before the enemy... See, they say, how they love one another and how ready they are to die for each other." (*Apol.* 39).

This love took the concrete form of almsgiving, which was said to be a spiritual ransom, a penance for sin. Every Sunday, or whenever they wished, Tertullian informs us (*Apol.* 39), the believers brought their gifts during the celebration of the Eucharist and presented them to the bishop. These gifts, after being offered to the Lord, were distributed by the deacons to those present. A part of them was reserved for the needy who were not at the service and was later brought to their homes. It was the bishops who directed this work of assistance. In accord with the teaching of the Scripture, the primary beneficiaries of this aid were the widows and the orphans. But, in a period when Christians suffered imprisonment and forced labor for the sake of Christ, special concern and love were shown to these. It was a duty, especially of deacons, to visit and care for a prisoner and work for his liberation, and no one hesitated to bribe the jailors to that end (Eusebius, *Hist. eccl.* 6.61). Christian charity also reached the brethren condemned to forced labor in the mines. The community tried to keep in touch with them and obtain their liberty (Eusebius, *Hist. eccl.* 6.23). Some Christians even attempted to ransom their imprisoned brethren. Clement of Rome recalls: "We know that many among ourselves have given themselves up to chains in order to redeem others; many have surrendered themselves to slavery and provided food for others with the price they received for themselves." (*Ad Cor* 1.2). When in 253, Numidian brigands seized a number of Christians, the community of Carthage, under the leadership of Cyprian, collected a sum of money for ransom, declaring that they were ready to raise more if necessary. In 255 the Roman Christians contributed money to ransom some members of the Cappadocian community captured by the Goths (Basil, *Epist. 70 Ad Damasum*).

The same love and care were extended also to the sick, the dead, and the travelers. The community visited the sick, especially the incurable, and in times of plague and public disasters, fearlessly and generously assisted the victims and ministered to them. (Tertullian, *Ad Uxor.* 204; Eusebius, *Hist. eccl.* 7.22.9-10.) The faithful took great care to bury the dead and expenses for the burial of the poor were paid by the community (Tertullian, *Apol.* 39). Travelers were given hospitality (*Didache* 12; *Hermas* 8.10; Cyprian, *Epist.* 7 etc.). The Church of Rome was famous for its hospitality to strangers (Eusebius, *Hist. eccl.* 4.23.10). This concern was shown not only between individual Christians, but also between one Christian community and another. Dionysius, bishop of Corinth; Dionysius, bishop of Alexandria; Basil of Caesarea; and Eusebius have related how the Church of Rome used to take interest in the welfare of the other churches, and when they were in need, to send them monetary aid.

The Church of the first three centuries had also to deal with the question of slavery. Like the New Testament it did not reject slavery as a social system but tried to ameliorate the slaves' condition. Converted slaves were recognized as equal brothers and sisters with the rest of the faithful and were accorded equality of rights. Ecclesiastical offices, including that of bishop, were open to a slave. Slaves among the martyrs, both men and women, for example, Blandina and Felicity, were held in unqualified esteem. Degrading treatment of slaves by Christian masters was severely censured and, if need be, punished with ecclesiastical penalties. In some instances community funds were used to purchase the slaves' freedom, but those so released were not to regard their liberty as a right (Ignatius, *Ad Polyc.* 4.3).

Finally, the Church that was being persecuted by the pagan state had to sort out its relationship with this secular power. While Hippolytus saw the power of Satan behind the Roman *imperium*, the majority of Christian writers of the pre-Constantinian period entertained a positive attitude towards the pagan state. Clement of Alexandria affirmed the obligation of taxes and military service and recognized Roman law; if that State persecuted the Church, the hand of Providence was to be worshipped (*Paed.* 2, 14, 1; 3, 91, 3). The only limit to this recognition was set by the cult of the emperor and the idolatry encouraged by the State. This recognition was adopted by Origen (*In Rom. comm.* 9, 39). Tertullian, too, for all his bold defence of the freedom of the Christian conscience in the face of the Roman State, was profoundly convinced that it was under the authority of God. As the God of the Christians is also the God of the emperor, they pray for the emperor's well-being and in fact for the continuance of the Roman Government (*Apol.* 30; 32; 39).

B. THE CHURCH'S SOCIAL INVOLVEMENT FROM THE EDICT OF CONSTANTINE TO THE END OF THE PATRISTIC ERA

With Constantine's conversion and sole rule, Christianity became the official religion of the Empire. Many positive as well as negative possibilities presented themselves to the

Church. Freedom of worship and of preaching was guaranteed by law. New conditions were created for the development of liturgical celebrations through the possibility for reconstruction and the erection of new Christian places of worship which were generously funded by the State. The pastoral care of the faithful was facilitated through unrestricted catechetical instruction and sacramental services. The missionary task was also carried out unhampered. Opportunities offered themselves for Christian thinkers and writers to employ their talents to build up a body of theological literature and to undertake the enormous task of christianizing secular culture and public life. In general, one can say that previously the Church had lived consciously at a distance from the cultural world around it and had withdrawn from the pagan public life into its own moral and religious domain which was easier to preserve in complete isolation. Freedom now led it out of this secluded existence and forced it to assume its political and social obligations and even to elaborate a doctrine to justify and guide its social involvement.

The first and most urgent task for the Church was to determine its relationship to the State and vice versa. Fundamental to this relationship was the fact that the State's power and the Church agreed in principle on a close collaboration in the public sphere. Under Constantine, such a collaboration was to a large extent harmonious; no sharp conflicts had yet arisen between the Emperor and the bishops. The right of the Emperor to summon synods was in no way questioned, and his efforts to steer the course of the theological discussions through his ecclesiastical advisers were accepted as self-evident; the punishment of exile repeatedly decreed by him for heretics encountered no decisive resistance. On the other hand Eusebius of Caesarea undertook to elaborate a political theology in which the Emperor is regarded as God's vicar on earth called to promote the realization of God's plan of salvation, a sort of "universal bishop" whose full power over the Church has a quasi-priestly character.

Such a limitless power became a reality and a serious

problem under Constantius (337-361) whose inclination to exercise a strict control over the Church became apparent on the occasion of the Synod of Sardica (342) and reached its climax later at the Synod of Milan (355). Constantius's claim to be the *episcopus episcoporum* was resisted by Hilary of Poiters, Rhodanius of Toulouse, Hosius of Cordoba and Athanasius of Alexandria who was the first bishop of the fourth century to formulate the Church's claim to freedom vis-à-vis the State.

Under Valens (365-378) the Church in the eastern part of the Empire was again exposed for a time to the authoritarian interventions of secular power into the ecclesiastical affairs, especially in the Arian controversies. This time the Emperor was resisted by Basil. In connection with Romans 13:1-4, the Bishop of Caesarea was convinced that the earthly *Imperium* is always subordinate to God's law and therefore when the State is opposed to the divine law, the Christian is obliged to resist it.

But it was Ambrose, Bishop of Milan, who categorically defended the freedom of the Church in its own sphere against the intrusion of the State represented by Gratian (375-383), Valentinian II (383-392), and above all Theodosius the Great (379-395). For him "the Emperor is in the Church, not over the Church" (*Sermo c. Auxentium*, 36). Questionable as Ambrose's argumentation was in individual cases, his basic viewpoint, namely, the Church and the State stand in a positive relationship to each other, but the innermost sphere of the Church's life—faith, the moral order, ecclesiastical discipline—remains withdrawn from the State's competence, remained a norm in the Latin West for the relations between Church and State.

Far more varied and extensive was the Church's involvement in the social sphere. The reform of the Empire, begun by Diocletian and completed by Constantine, had long-range consequences for the Empire's social structure. The grandiose lifestyle of the court, the salaries of the officialdom, and the support of the army demanded huge revenues. Heavy taxes were levied, and the hardest hit were the small handcraft industries as well as the peasants and small tenants. There resulted a sharp opposition between the rich and the powerful on the one hand and the poor and the weak on the other. It was at this time that the Church, now granted the juridical right to own property, with the restoration of the wealth confiscated by Diocletian, and with the large fortunes given by converts, could extend substantially its charity and social concern to all.

As in the first three centuries, the Church did not see itself called to reform the unjust social and economic structures, which were viewed as consequences of sin and therefore were to be endured. It felt itself obliged, however, to improve the lot of those who were poor and exploited. This fundamental viewpoint is clear in the case of slavery. On the one hand the Church saw it as a necessary element of the contemporary economic order or as a form of property, and hence, as a whole, respected the enactments of civil law applying to slaves. It even took slaves into its service and possession when they came to it through legacies and, if necessary, defended its right to own them. On the other hand, more than any other institution of the time, the Church succeeded in ameliorating the lot of slaves. It regarded all its members—slave and master—as equal and treated them as such in the liturgy. In its preaching it urged the owners to treat their slaves with gentleness and to care for their religious welfare. (*Const. Apost.* 4, 6, 4; Chrysostom, *In ep. ad Eph. hom.* 22; Ambrose, *Ep.* 2, 31; Augustine, *De civ. Dei* 14, 14-15 etc.) It was due to the influence of the Church that from the fourth century the emancipation of slaves grew to a considerable extent. Sometimes the church purchased the freedom for the slaves with its own means. Perhaps it was due to this constant intervention of the Church for the voluntary emancipation of slaves that in 331 Constantine gave the Church the right to carry out the emancipation by a special act within the church building with all the legal consequences which were united to the civil law procedure (the *manumissio in ecclesia*). A further possibility of assisting slaves was offered to the Church when the ancient right of asylum was extended to Christian churches, and thus slaves who fled to a church were under its special protection.

Another group of people that received the Church's utmost care and concern was the poor and the needy. In the face of overwhelmingly unequal distribution of property and wealth, of the rich who wanted to dispose of their possessions unrestricted by any obligation towards the poor, of the luxurious lifestyle of the proprietors who placed no limits to their enjoyment of pleasure and wealth, of the extensive lack of a purposeful concern of the State for a legal basis which would have ameliorated the situation of the economically and socially weak, the Church, besides reflecting on the social function of property and appealing to the conscience of the faithful, to which we will come back later, sponsored and administered charitable institutions. This social welfare work was supported by the individual community with the local bishop bearing responsibility for it. The direct administration was entrusted to a deacon, who had deaconesses and widows at his disposal for specific services. Thus, in Caesarea of Cappadocia, St. Basil began to construct on the edge of the city a group of buildings destined to receive travellers, sick persons, and especially lepers, and staffed them with qualified personnel (Sozomen, *Hist. eccl.* 6.34). In Antioch also the community possessed a rather large hospital and a special hostel for strangers. The high estimation of hospitality by monasticism caused a guest house (*xenodocheion*) to appear in every larger ceno-bitic monastery. Another social work that distinguished monastic centers was the gathering and distribution of alms to the needy (the *diaconia*). Favored by the imperial government, the almshouses soon spread widely in Egypt, in Palestine, in the Greek East, and after the Justinian reconquest, in the Italian peninsula and even in Rome.

In the West such charitable works were not lacking. It is sufficient to name such bishops as Ambrose of Milan, Epiphanius of Pavia, Maximus of Turin, Paulinus of Nola, Martin of Tours, Nicetius of Lyons, and Sidonius Apollinarius. By this time the organized charity of the bishop has passed beyond the simple stage of a private duty performed primarily for the benefit of fellow-Christians to the stage of social welfare directed towards all.

Finally, in Rome, thanks to the solicitous vigilance of the popes, in particular, Leo the Great, Gelasius, Symmachus who founded three homes for the poor, and above all Gregory the Great, the practice of charity always held first place. The term "goods of the poor" was often used to indicate the patrimony of the Church. "We have no wealth of our own, but the care and administration of goods of the poor have been confided to us" (Gregory, *Registrum Epistolarum* 13.23).

IV. The Social Message of the Fathers

Concomitant with their social involvement the Fathers of the Church also elaborated a social doctrine. Their social teaching, as has been noted above, was fundamentally that of the Scripture, which they applied to and developed in the light of the new historical circumstances. In the last part of this Introduction we shall analyse the main tenets of this teaching, omitting aspects which are germane to it but which will be investigated in other works in this series: ethics, women, and war.

R. Sierra Bravo, in his monumental collection *Doctrina social y economica de los Padres de la Iglesia*, summarises the common points of the Fathers' social teaching as follows: 1. The social and economic relations are subjected to the norms of justice and charity. 2. The common good has primacy over the individual interest. 3. All human beings are essentially equal whatever their social conditions. 4. The social conditions are diverse and many and consequently human beings are accidentally unequal. 5. God wills that the inequalities, which are the necessary results of the natural diversities and of human freedom, be removed in the development of the social life. 6. God wills that all superiority, which causes inequality, should have a social function. 7. There is, therefore, the obligation of sharing with and placing in the service of others all individual superiority and personal gifts (p. 25). We will expound the patristic social teachings in three areas: politics, social relations, and economics.

A. THE POLITICAL ORDER

The Fathers discuss mainly the legitimacy of the State, its obligations, the duties of the subjects towards it, and the relationship between the Church and the State.

1. The Legitimacy of the State.

Borrowing from ancient political philosophy and the Scripture the Fathers justify the State with reasons both of the natural and supernatural order. Following Aristotle, and above all Cicero and Seneca, Lactantius considers the State as a natural structure in which man lives out his social nature, and not as a direct consequence of original sin. One can, however, also find in him the Epicurean idea that the State is a necessary means to put an end to violence and assure order since it disposes of force and exercises constraint against the wicked. Its necessity is therefore a consequence of original sin. Ambrose further develops these ideas. From the behavior of birds, bees, and fish, Ambrose concludes that man too needs not only a social organisation but also a state-controlled structure. Ambrose, however, distinguishes two forms of state-controlled organization separated by the Fall. At the beginning, all men had part in the honors and offices of the State, no one could exercise an arbitrary power over the other. After the Fall, ambition and desire to dominate produced an authoritarian regime in which power, acquired and preserved by force, is exercised by one individual and for his own interest. The State is not only a consequence of sin insofar it is necessary to fight evil, it is itself evil.

Following St. Paul (Romans 13:1-4), however, the Fathers also entertain a more positive view of authority: all authority comes from God and is willed by him. Hence

Ambrose affirms: "There can be no power that is intrinsically evil. Only the use of power is reprehensible." (*Expos. evang. sec. Lucam*, III, 29-31). Also following St. Paul (Rom 13:7), Ambrose develops the theory of the king's ministerial power: the king is God's minister if he makes a proper use of his power. (*Ibid.*) In the fourth century, Eusebius of Caesarea, in his *Panegyric on Constantine*, declares that the emperor is not only God's minister but also his earthly counterpart, providentially appointed to the sacred functions of ruling his people, protecting his Church, and promoting the salvation of souls. This exalted interpretation of kingship will serve as one of the foundations of Byzantine caesaro-papism.

Deserving a special mention is Augustine's political theology, which dominated all subsequent discussion of authority during the Middle Ages. Drawing both from pagan (especially Plato *via* Cicero) and biblical sources, Augustine puts forth the theory of the two cities. The *civitas terrena* is not identified with the State, nor is the *civitas Dei* with the Church. Both are ideal societies, the one according to the flesh, the other according to the spirit; both are partially realized in concrete historical structures. The Church is not only the society of the elect but comprises also the reprobated. The State is not always the city of the devil; Augustine does not condemn the State as such but its historical realizations vitiated by the passion to dominate by force, the corruption of magistrates, and the exploitation of the weak (*Civ. Dei*, 3, 14; 4, 3 and 7, etc.)

Augustine, like his contemporaries, justifies the State on two grounds: the social nature of man which makes it a natural institution (*Civ. Dei*, 18, 2; 19, 6, 12, 14, 19), and original sin which makes it a necessary evil (*Civ. Dei*, 19, 15). The State, willed by God, must exercise its power according to the divine will. By reason of its origin, its power can neither be arbitrary nor without limits. Its function is to assure order, peace, and unity (*Civ. Dei*, 19, 13, 17). Further the State must guarantee the material and economic as well as the moral and religious interests of its citizens.

2. The Obligations of the State.

A good ruler, according to Augustine, is one who governs with justice without forgetting that he is human; who uses his power to promote the divine cult; who fears, loves, and honors God; who is slow to vengeance and quick to forgive. The ruler is subject to the law. St. Ambrose, however, following Roman jurisprudence (*princeps legibus solutus*), is of the opinion that the ruler is not bound by human laws. Nevertheless he is bound by his conscience and hence must respect its own laws. (*Ep.* 21, 9)

3. The Duties of the Subjects.

The subjects are bound to obey the authority of the State. Such obedience is demanded by God (Augustine, *Sermo* 62, ch. 8, n. 13). It is due even to an unjust ruler, provided that his order is not sinful.

Christian Apologists were anxious to point out that their fellow Christians were faithful citizens, respectful of the laws and obedient to the authority. According to Ambrose (*Exp. Ev. sec. Luc.*, 4, 73) and Augustine (*Civ. Dei.*, 1, 35) Christians should be the best citizens. Discharging public offices is a form of obedience and service to the State. Paying taxes is a duty often insisted upon by the Fathers (Ambrose, *Ep. to Valentinian II*, 21, 33 and 35; Augustine, *Ep.* 96). The Christians must also submit themselves to secular justice. Ambrose affirms the legitimacy of the imperial judicial system, accepts torture and the death penalty. The Christians, finally, are bound to observe civil laws and respect the social order. Pope Gelasius insists many times on this duty (*Ep.* 14, 14; *Ep.* 22). Obedience to the State, however, is not without limits. God's law being superior to man's law, one ought not do anything contrary to the former under the pretext of obeying the latter. Thus resistance to an evil law or an unjust command is lawful. But it cannot take the form of insurrection. Both Ambrose and Augustine condemn recourse to violence: one should bear injustice, only God can chastise.

4. Church and State.

The patristic doctrine on the relationship between Church and State underwent an evolution from the fourth to the fifth century. Under Constantius who inordinately meddled with ecclesiastical affairs, the doctrine of non-intervention was taught by Hosius of Cordoba, Lucifer of Cagliari, Hilary of Poitiers, and above all Ambrose. Hosius's letter to Constantius is well-known: "Do not interfere in matters ecclesiastical, nor give us orders on such questions, but learn about them from us. For unto your hands God has put the kingdom; the affairs of the Church he has committed to us." (Athanasius, *Hist. Ar.*, 44). Ambrose proposes a more nuanced doctrine. He distinguishes between *religio* and *res publica*. Whereas the Emperor enjoys the highest power in the State, faith and discipline are the reserved domain of the episcopacy: "*Ad imperatorem palatia pertinere, ad sacerdotem ecclesiae.*" (*Ep.* 20, 19). In matters religious, the emperor must follow the instructions of the Church. As a Christian, he is in the Church and subject to the laws of God (*Contra Auxentium*, 36). The same doctrine is found in Gregory of Nazianzus (*Orat.* 17, 8) and John Chrysostom (*In Ep. 2 ad Corinth., Hom.* 15, c. 4-5). Furthermore, the Emperor must help the Church as well: Ambrose admits that the Emperor should convoke the council, assist the bishops to take part in it, ratify their decisions and see to it that these are carried out.

At the beginning of the fifth century, as the relation between Church and State improved and as the Empire, weakened in the West, had need of the Church, and the Church itself wanted more power and influence, a new *modus vivendi* beyond non-interference was seen as desirable and useful to both sides. This new situation helps us understand Augustine's doctrine of Church and State. More clearly than his predecessors he affirms the distinction of powers. The two powers, State and Church, are different in their nature (physical-moral), in their object (external life of the various peoples—spiritual life of the whole humanity), in their means (the sword-charity), in their aims (temporal-eternal) respectively. These differences justify the independence of each power in its sphere. Nevertheless, the religious society and the civil society are both made for man and his well-being. There is therefore between them, if not identity of purpose, at least concordance of tasks. This legitimates and requires their collaboration. The Church helps the State with its prayers, its moral teachings, its command to its faithful to be good citizens. The State, on the other hand, should grant the Church material assistance and privileges and guarantee it peace (*Ep.* 185, 28). This collaboration, of course, should not lead to theocracy.

The distinction and collaboration doctrine was later affirmed by Leo the Great, Celestinus I, Felix III, and above all Gelasius. The latter, in his famous letter to Emperor Anasthasius, wrote: "Two powers govern the world: the *auctoritas sacrata pontificum* and the *regalis potestas*" (*Ep.* 12, 2). Between them there must be an exchange of services. The Emperor is subject to the Church only insofar as he is a Christian and solely in matters religious. Gelasius does not pretend to have a *potestas directa in temporalibus*.

B. THE SOCIAL RELATIONS

1. Freedom and Slavery.

One of the most important social problems in the patristic era was, no doubt, slavery. It has been recounted above how the Church attempted to improve the conditions of slaves and how its efforts were in the long run successful in abolishing slavery as a social institution. It still remains to be examined how the Fathers viewed slavery as such.

The Fathers could not but affirm the basic equality and freedom of all human beings. The Gospel had already taught that all men and women are God's children and hence brothers and sisters to each other. Stoicism had proclaimed that slaves were no less human and that true slaves are those subjected to passions. On this point the Fathers' thought is unanimous: man is free by nature. (Ambrose, *Ep.* 37, 24; John Chrysostom, *Ep. ad Ephes. Homel.* 22, 6, 2; *Ep.*

I ad Corinth. Hom. 15; Gregory of Nyssa, *Hom. IV in Eccl.*,
Basil, *De Spiritu Sancto*, 20.)

Nevertheless the Fathers were too deeply imbued with the
spirit of their age to condemn such a universal practice as
slavery as contrary to human dignity. Slavery seemed to
them to be an economic necessity, a product of war and a
consequence of sin, one of the fundamental institutions of
the social order which the Church did not contemplate to
destroy. Indeed, the clergy and religious institutions themselves had slaves. Slavery was a form of private property
which the Church not only did not condemn but even
sought to justify. Slaves were commanded to obey their
masters "for the glory of God" (Basil, *De Spiritu Sancto*, 20;
Moralia, 75, 1). Whereas both Clement and Origen advocated treating slaves as equals, Tertullian and Jerome were
generally not too kindly disposed towards them. Tertullian
strangely compared demons to rebellious slaves (*Apol.*, 27,
7), and Jerome accused them of being money-grabbers and
of spreading scandal (*Ep.*, 38, 5; 54, 5; 107, 8). The Council
of Ganga in 340 decreed: "If anyone teaches a slave, under
pretext of piety, to despise his master, to forsake his service,
not to serve him with good will and all respect, let him be
anathema." (Canon 3)

In many of his letters, Pope Gelasius shows his great
anxiety in having the master's right of ownership respected,
even the Church's right to own slaves.

In examining the Fathers' teaching on slavery the modern
reader, while admiring their generous efforts to improve the
slaves' lot, can only wish that they had in conformity with
their profound conviction of man's fundamental equality
and freedom condemned slavery as an evil institution.

2. Work and Idleness

The early Christians were often accused of idleness. To
this charge, Tertullian replies by pointing out that Christians, like others, and with others, sail ships, serve in the
army, work in country and city (*Apol.*, 42, 1). Indeed,
following St. Paul, the Fathers encouraged not only slaves

but also free Christians to work. Clement of Rome writes: "The good workman receives the bread for his work with boldness, while the bad and careless one does not look his employer in the face" (*1 Clement*, 34:1). The Didache is much concerned with wandering Christians who ought to earn their keep: "If he wants to stay with you and is an artisan, let him work and eat." (*Didache*, 12:3). The *Didascalia apostolorum* shares the same view: "Be occupied in the things of the Lord or engaged upon your work, and never be idle." Again the author urges the Christians to "teach your children crafts that are agreeable and befitting religion, lest through idleness they give themselves to wantonness." All these injunctions are repeated in the fourth century *Apostolic Constitutions*, where one chapter is entitled "The Idle Believers Must Not Eat."

When a few adherents of the Messalian group claim to be following the words of Jesus: "Do not labor for the food which perishes," Epiphanius responds by urging that Christians should not be idle or sluggish or even eat at unseasonable times but should rather work with their own hands. (Cfr. *Haer.* LXXX 4, 1-5) Finally, work is seen not only as a means of procuring for oneself the basic necessities of life but also as a way to gain material goods with which to assist the needy and the poor. The true source of wealth is work (Ambrose, *De Cain et Abel*, 2, 2, 8); agricultural work and landed property are the preferred sources of gain (Ambrose, *De Off.*, III, 6, 38-41).

C. THE ECONOMIC ORDER

Under this last heading we will consider the patristic teaching on the nature of private ownership, the social function of wealth, and the question of interest and usury.

1. The Right of Ownership

Ambrose, among many other Fathers, following Cicero and Seneca, asserts the existence of a primitive state, prior to the Fall, in which private ownership was not known. God has originally created everything for the common use; everybody is to enjoy the goods of the earth. Private ownership introduces inequality of properties and conditions. In this sense it is a consequence of sin. (*De Off.*, 1, 28, 132; *De Nabutha*, 1, 2; *Expos. Evang. sec. Luc.* 7, 124; 247). In a famous sentence he declares: "*Natura ius commune generavit, usurpatio ius fecit privatum*" (*De Off.*, 1, 132). Even after the Fall, private ownership is only apparent. Man does not, strictly speaking, own anything. Everything has been created by God, everything belongs to him (Chrysostom, *In Ep. I ad Corinth. Hom.*, 10, 2). Properly speaking instead of property, one should speak of use and of administration of the goods given (Salvian, *Ad Ecclesiam*, 1, 5, 26).

From the contexts of their writings, it is clear that the Fathers do not condemn private ownership as such but the abuse of it. Basil, in his *Hom. 6 in illud Lucae "Destruam,"* 7, distinguished between the common destination of the goods created by God for the use of all and the right of property of which he, as well as the other Fathers, recognize the legitimacy. The Fathers, therefore, do not intend to advocate any form of communism of earthly goods. Clement of Alexandria, in his *Who is the Rich Man That is Saved?*, sees wealth as an instrument for producing fellowship and sharing. The right of private property thus depends upon the use made of it. There is a right of private property, but it is limited by the needs of our fellowmen, first Christians and then probably others. Origen, in his *Commentary on Matthew* criticises anyone who does not take the Gospel commandment literally and sell his possessions for the poor. He does not, however, put forth any theory about private property; rather he is appealing for voluntary poverty as a form of asceticism. Similarly at Carthage, Tertullian speaks of the usefulness of riches for philanthropy, and Cyprian, while emphasizing God's equal justice, does not question the legitimacy of private property. Lactantius, more explicitly than others, attacks the Platonic concept of communism as applied not only to wives but also to material possessions: "Private property contains the matter of both vices and virtues, but communal sharing holds nothing but license for vices"(*Div. Inst.*, 3, 22). He further states that perfect justice is the use of wealth not for personal enjoyment but for the advantage for the many (*Ibid.*, 6,12).

Only in the last decade of the fourth century, as the social and economic conditions of the Empire considerably worsened, do we find a more vigorous attack by some of the Fathers not so much on private property as on its excessive accumulation in the hands of the rich, and some of the Fathers very boldly discuss the abuse of private property. Basil of Caesarea, Gregory of Nazianzus, John Chrysostom, Ambrose of Milan, Augustine of Hippo, in their writings as in their homilies, denounce the love of money, the luxurious lifestyle of the rich, the lack of concern for the poor. But it is not possible to find in their writings any advocacy of compulsory communal sharing. Private property remains private.

2. The Social Function of Property

The Fathers, however, do not certainly defend private property as such. They simply take it for granted. Further, the early expectation of the reign of God keeps them from excessive love of worldly goods; so does the later development of asceticism and monasticism. Above all, imbued with the Gospel spirit of charity, they bring to the theory of private property a fundamentally new understanding.

Roman law views ownership as a human right without emphasizing its social obligations. On the contrary, the Fathers transform the sense of ownership, affirm the necessity of detachment from things, recall the identification of Christ with the poor, and finally require almsgiving as a form of sharing the earthly goods with others.

First of all, ownership is seen primarily not as possession but as stewardship. All creation is made available by God to all mankind and the rich are essentially its stewards. Those who have, therefore, should imitate God's beneficence and generosity in sharing their material goods with their neighbors (*The Epistle to Diognetus*, 10, 2; Cyprian, *On Works and Almsgiving*, 25). Ambrose writes: "God has ordered all things to be produced so that there should be food in common for all, and that the earth should be the common possession of all." (*De Off.* 1, 132) Although he recognizes the right of private property, Ambrose emphasises that almsgiving on the part of the avaricious is nothing but restitution of stolen goods, and giving to the poor is simply giving him what is his due: "You are not making a gift of your possessions to the poor person. You are handing over to him what is his" (*De Nabutha*, 12, 53). John Chrysostom clearly distinguishes between wealth which is God's gift and ruthless greed which makes ownership sinful: "Those I attack are not the rich as such, only those who misuse their wealth... Wealth is one thing, covetousness is another." (*Fall of Eutropius*, 2, 3). Augustine denounces the misuse of property: "*Male autem possidet, qui male utitur*" (*Ep.* 153, 6, 26). Thus, according to the Fathers, the things of the earth are created by God for the enjoyment of all; they should be used to meet the needs of all human beings, the poor as well as the rich, and their owners have the opportunity and the responsibility to imitate the goodness and liberality of God.

Material goods, though good and useful in themselves, are dangerous because they incite to sin and above all to the lack of charity. Hence conversion of the heart and detachment from things are necessary. Augustine urges that if one cannot renounce property totally, at least one should renounce the love of property (*Enarr. in Psalm.*, 131, 5). Clement of Alexandria, in his *Who is the Rich Man That is Saved?*, reminds the rich of their duty of being "poor in spirit," of freeing themselves from the addictive pursuit of wealth, and of converting their hearts to loving God and their neighbors. Origen considers greed as a form of idolatry. Cyprian interprets greed and avarice as forms of slavery. Addressing the rapacious rich, he writes: "The deep and profound darkness of avarice has blinded your carnal heart. You are the captive and slave of your money; you are tied by the chains and bonds of avarice, and you whom Christ has already freed are bound anew" (*On Works and Almsgiving*, 13).

Similarly for Chrysostom many wealthy men and women

are possessed by the evil passion of ruthless greed in much the same way as the demoniac of Gerasa was possessed by demons. The avaricious man is a slave of money, a Christian who worships mammon, not Christ. (*On Philippians: Homily* 6.5-6—

Christians, moreover, should aid the poor and the needy not simply because of justice but above all because Christ is identified with them. Cyprian, after raising ransom money for the release of Numidian Christians from their barbarian captors, says: "The captivity of our brethren must be reckoned as our captivity, and the grief of those who are endangered is to be esteemed as our grief... Christ is to be contemplated in our captive brethren..."(*Ep.* 59). Gregory of Nyssa reminds the rich that they must recognize Christ in the poor: "Do not despise these men in their abjection; do not think of them of no account. Reflect what they are and you will understand their dignity; they have often taken upon themselves the person of our Savior" (*Love of the Poor*). John Chrysostom draws similar conclusions from Matthew 25:31-46: "Because he is a poor man, feed him; because Christ is fed, feed him" (*On Matthew: Homily*, 48.9). Again: "Do you really wish to pay homage to Christ's body? Then do not neglect him when he is naked. At the same time that you honor him here with hangings made of silk, do not ignore him outside when he perishes from cold and nakedness"(*Ibid.*, 50, 4). Finally, for Augustine, there is a hidden but real identity between Christ and the Christian; hence the community must assist the needy: "For consider, brethren, the love of our head. He is in heaven, yet he suffers here, as long as his Church suffers here. Here Christ is hungry, here he is thirsty, is naked, is a stranger, is sick, is in prison. For whatever his body suffers here, he has said that he himself suffers." (*Sermon* 87.1-2).

The most practical way of demonstrating one's solidarity with the poor is almsgiving; thus it is not surprising that all the Fathers repeatedly insist on this duty of sharing one's goods with others. That the early Christians distinguished themselves by their charity is well testified by no other than Julian, the emperor who wanted to restore paganism: "No

Jew ever has to beg, and the impious Galileans support not only their own poor but ours as well" (*Ep.* 896). In *II Clement* (16:4) we are told that "almsgiving is as good as repentance from sin; fasting is better than prayer; almsgiving is better than either." In *I Clement* 37-38:2, we read: "Let the rich man supply the needs of the poor and let the poor man give thanks to God because he gave him someone to supply his lack." Hermas adds a charitable purpose to fasting: "On that day when you fast you shall taste nothing but bread and water, and you shall reckon the amount of the expense of the foods you would have eaten on that day you are going to observe, and you shall give it to a widow or an orphan or someone in need, and you shall fast that through your fasting he who receives may fill his soul and pray for you to the Lord." (*Hermas,* Sim. V 3, 7).

Clement of Alexandria in his *Who is the Rich Man That is Saved?* constantly points out the duty of the rich to give generous alms. Origen urges the clergy to be trustworthy and sensible administrators of the community's resources for the sake of the poor (*Commentary on Matthew,* 61). Tertullian describes the voluntary offerings of the Christians as "trust funds of piety" which were not spent "upon banquets or drinking-parties nor thankless eating-houses, but to feed the poor and bury them, for boys and girls who lack property and parents, and then for slaves grown old and shipwrecked mariners..." (*Apology,* 39.1, 5-7).

Cyprian has written a whole treatise on alms (*De opere et eleemosysis*), in which he argues that alms cancel the pollution caused by sin after baptism. In his work *On the Dress of Virgins,* 11 he advises the wealthy virgins: "Let the needy feel that you are rich. Lend your estate to God, give food to Christ." John Chrysostom develops almost a mania on the subject of alms. To the reluctant givers, he says: "You are not able to become propertyless? Give from your possessions. You cannot bear that burden? Divide your possessions with Christ. You do not want to surrender everything to him? Hand over even a half share, even a third" (*On Matthew: Homily* 45, 2). Elsewhere he points out that almsgiving covers and quenches sin, for acts of mercy counterbalance the weight of sin. It is the "matter of charity," for, without it, charity is a sham (*On Titus: Homily* 6, 2). Ambrose, in the West, is no less persistent on the duties of almsgiving and caring for the poor. One should care for orphans, make provision for their education, and provide dowries for orphan girls. One should be diligent in seeking out the poor who would otherwise remain hidden: those who are sick or in prison or who are simply too ashamed to beg. The Church, Ambrose maintains, has gold in its possession not for hoarding but to spend on those in need. Even sacred vessels should be sold to ransom captives. (See *De Off.*, 2)

3. Interest and Usury

Although the Fathers do not condemn commerce as such, they denounce its dangers and greedy merchants (Ambrose, *De Off.*, I, 49, 242; II, 6, 25). What offends the Fathers is the profit that merchants derive from their activities. They sell at a higher price what they have not bought or produced. Bankers make more money than what they have put in. Money not being productive by itself, this profit seems to be an unjust collection on the client.

This profit is all the more condemnable when it is gotten by raising prices of goods in time of scarcity (Ambrose, *De Off.*, III, 9, 41) and when someone's properties are bought at a lower price because of his bankruptcy (Ambrose, *De Off.*, III, 9, 41; 9, 57; 10, 66).

Although Roman law allows interest (*usurae*) and fixes a legal rate, and despite the fact that Deuteronomy 23:20-21 allows lending with interest to aliens, the Fathers, especially the Cappadocians, unanimously condemn the taking of interest on the ground that it is unjust (Lactantius, *De Inst. divina*, 6, 18; *Epist.* 64; Hilary of Poitiers, *Tract. in Ps.*, 14, 15; Augustine, *Enarr. in Ps.*, 128, 6; *De Bapt.*, 4, 9). Only Ambrose makes an exception in the case of lending to an enemy: "Interest is a sort of war where one strikes one's enemy without using the sword" (*De Tobia*, 14, 51).

V. Contemporary Relevance of Patristic Social Thought

In conclusion one may raise the question whether the patristic social doctrine elaborated some fifteen hundred years ago still possesses any validity in our present rapidly changing times. A detailed answer to this question is obviously impracticable in these pages; we shall limit ourselves to a few essential remarks regarding both methodology and content.

1. As far as content is concerned, there are obviously certain aspects on which the Fathers' teachings are, in our contemporary experience, no longer acceptable either by excess or by default. Their negative attitude towards commerce and interest-taking seems obsolete since both of these activities are the normal facts of our present economic life. Already the oft-repeated condemnations of interest-taking by councils and popes in the fourth and fifth centuries are signs that the patristic teaching was not universally effective. On the other hand, the Fathers' position on slavery as a social institution appears too weak in view of our affirmation of the basic human rights and the actual abolition of slavery as a social institution.

On other points, however, the social teaching of the Fathers should continue to shape the social teaching of the Church today. Among these are the affirmation of the basic equality of all human beings; the doctrine of the right of private ownership; the principle that the material goods are destined by God for the use of all human beings to satisfy their basic needs; the insistence on the necessity of conversion of heart and detachment from earthly possessions; the inculcation of the duty of almsgiving not only out of charity but also of justice; the doctrine of the identity of Christ with the poor. These elements are the perennial heritage that the Church should cherish and preserve in presenting its message of solidarity and hope to the world of today.

2. No less important and relevant is the method with which the Fathers interpreted the social message of the Scripture to the people of their age. Challenged by the social and economic conditions, first as a persecuted minority in a

hostile environment, then as a privileged religion in a converted Empire, the Fathers attempted with varying success on the one hand to be faithful to the message of the Scripture and on the other to interpret it and make it applicable to their times. Many of their writings on social and economic issues are but commentaries and homilies on the Scripture. But they did not simply repeat verbatim the words of the Scripture; there were not a few issues on which the Scripture has said nothing or precious little, and for which there were consequently no ready-made solutions. Their fidelity to God's word was not a mechanical repetition of formulas but a creative and dynamic reinterpretation of the scriptural message in the experience of new situations and a critical judgment of these in the light of the Scripture. An example will make this clear. From a few scattered scriptural statements on the relationship between the Christians and the temporal power, the Fathers developed first a theory of non-interference in the first three centuries when the Church and the State were at a hostile distance, then a theory of distinction of powers and collaboration from the fourth century onwards when the two societies recognized their proper autonomy and mutual need.

Of course the Church of today is encountering many problems which the Fathers did not and could not envisage: strikes and unions, the arms race and nuclear warfare, organ transplants and genetic engineering, just to mention a few, and for which there are not cut and dried answers from the Scripture. The Church must, however, do now what the Fathers then did, namely carry out "the responsibility of reading the signs of the time and of interpreting them in the light of the Gospel"(*Gaudium et Spes*, no. 4). In this process it will recover, not only the traditions but also the Tradition by which the Good News of salvation is made effective in a world that is socially and economically more complex than ever.

1

EARLY CHRISTIAN FATHERS

Part One: The Apostolic Fathers

The Didache

The complete title of this anonymous work is *The Lord's Instruction to the Gentiles through the Twelve Apostles*. Discovered in 1875, it was probably composed between 70 and 90, though some critics would place the date of its composition in 120 or 150. It contains, besides moral precepts, liturgical instructions and disciplinary regulations. Its social teachings can be summarised as follows.

It praises hospitality, strongly urges almsgiving and sharing of goods, recommends kind treatment of slaves. It also stresses the necessity of hard work and condemns idleness; work is seen as a means to earn the wherewithal to help others. The famous statement "Call nothing your own" does not intend to deny private ownership but to emphasize most strongly the duty of sharing the goods of the earth.

[Give to all]

1, 5.[1] Give to everybody who begs from you, without looking for any repayment, for the Father wants that we should share his gracious bounty to all men. A giver who gives freely, as the commandment bids him, is blessed, for he is guiltless. But woe to the receiver! If he receives because he is in need, he is guiltless. But if he is not in need, he will be required to show why he received and for what purpose. He will be thrown into prison and his action will be investigated, and he will not get out until he has paid the last penny.

6. Indeed, there is a further saying that pertains to this: "Let your alms grow damp with sweat in your hand, until you know who it is you are giving them to."

[Work and Sharing]

4, 5.[2] Do not be one who reaches out to take, but shuts his hands when it comes to giving. 6. If your labor has brought you earnings, make an offering as a ransom for your sins. 7. Give without hesitation and without grumbling, and you will discover who He is that will requite you with generosity. 8. Never turn away the needy; share all your possessions with your brother, and call nothing your own. If you and he share what is immortal in common, how much more should you share what is mortal!

[Slaves]

4, 10. Do not be harsh when giving orders to male or female slaves, since they trust in the same God as yours; otherwise they may cease to fear Him who is over you both. He has not come to call men according to their station but those whom the Spirit has made ready. 11. And you, slaves, obey your masters with respectfulness and fear, as if they represented God.

[1]Text: SC 248.144.
[2]Text: SC 248.160.

[Hospitality and Work]
12, 2.[3] If the newcomer is only passing through, assist him as much as you can. But he must not stay with you more than two days, or, if necessary, three. 3. If he wants to settle down among you, and if he is a skilled worker, he must work for his living. 4. If, however, he knows no trade, use your judgment to make sure that he does not live in idleness on the pretext he is a Christian. 5. If he refuses to do this, he is only trying to exploit Christ. You must be on your guard against such people.

Clement of Rome

Towards the end of the first century (c. 96) in the Corinthian Church some arrogant and hot-headed Christians had rebelled against the presbyters and driven them out of office. Clement, the third successor to Peter in Rome, wrote them a letter, now known as the *First Letter to the Corinthians*, in which he reminded the rebels of the duty of submission to the authority established by God himself. Besides its most important teachings on ecclesiastical jurisdiction, apostolic succession, the primary role of the Church of Rome, the bodily resurrection and liturgy, Clement's letter is of great interest to us with its emphasis on social order and structure, on the necessity of mutual solidarity, and on the duty of praying for the governing authority.

[Social Order and Cooperation for the Common Good]
37, 1.[4] So now, my brothers, let us campaign resolutely under his irreproachable directions. 2. Think of the men who serve our generals in the field, and the discipline, readiness, and obedience with which they carry out their orders. 3. Not everyone of them is a general, colonel, captain, sergeant, and so on. But each at his own rank executes

[3]Text: SC 248.188.
[4]Text: SC 167.160.

the orders of the emperor and of the generals. 4. The great cannot exist without the small; nor the small without the great. Every organism is composed of different elements; and this ensures the common good. 5. Take the body as an instance. The head cannot function without the feet. Nor, likewise, can the feet function without the head. Even the smallest of our physical members are indispensable and valuable to the whole body; yet all of them work together and are united in a single obedience to preserve the whole body intact.

[Social Solidarity]
38, 1. In Christ Jesus, then, we must preserve this corporate body of ours in its entirety. Each must be subject to his neighbor, according to his special gifts. 2. The strong are not to ignore the weak, and the weak should respect the strong. The rich must provide for the poor, and the poor should thank God for giving him someone to meet his needs.

[Prayer for the Poor]
59, 4.[5] We beseech you, O Lord, be our Helper and Protector. Rescue the afflicted, pity the lowly, raise up the fallen, assist the needy, heal the sick, bring back those of your people who stray, feed the hungry, release our captives, support the weak, comfort the faint-hearted. Let all the nations realize that you are the only God, that Jesus Christ is your Child, and that we are your people and the sheep of your pasture.

[Prayer for the Governing Authority]
61, 1. It is you, O Lord, who gave them imperial power through your majestic and ineffable might, so that we, acknowledging the glory and honor you have bestowed upon them, should submit ourselves to them. Grant them, Lord, health, peace, harmony, and stability, that they may exercise without offence the power you have accorded them. 2. For it is you, Lord, the heavenly and eternal King, who

[5]Text: SC 167.196.

give the sons of men glory and honor and authority over the dwellers upon earth. Deign to direct their plans in accord with what is good and pleasing to you, so that they may administer the authority you have given them, with peace, considerateness, and reverence, and so deserve your mercy. 3. We praise you, who alone can grant to us these and still better things, through the High Priest and Guardian of our souls, Jesus Christ. Through him be the glory and the majesty now and for all generations and forevermore. Amen.

Ignatius of Antioch

Ignatius of Antioch, on his way to martyrdom in Rome (c. 107), wrote seven letters, six to different churches and one to Polycarp. Although he was intensely preoccupied with the unity of the Church gathered around the hierarchy in the Eucharist, with the suppression of heresies, and with his imminent death, he found time to care for the needy and the slaves.

[Widows and Slaves]
The Letter to Polycarp 4, 1.[6] Take care that widows are not neglected. Next to the Lord, you must be their protector... 3. Do not treat slaves, whether men or women, in an overbearing manner. On the other hand, they must not grow insolent. It should be their aim to be better slaves, for the glory of God, so that they may obtain from God a better freedom. Moreover they should not be overanxious to gain their freedom at the Church's expense, for then they only become slaves of selfish passion.

The Letter to Diognetus

This so-called *Letter to Diognetus* written by an unknown Christian to an otherwise unknown inquirer,

[6]Text: SC 10.174.

probably in the years 190 and 200, is really an apology for Christianity. Chapters 1-10 were probably written by Quadratus in Asia Minor; chapters 11 and 12 presumably by Hippolytus. Most interesting for our purpose are the letter's description of the position of the Christian in the world, its condemnation of economic exploitation, and its insistence on the need to imitate God's liberality in providing for the needy.

[The Christians and the World]

5, 1.[7] Christians are not different from the rest of mankind by nationality, or language, or customs. 2. They do not live in cities of their own; they do not speak any special language; they do not practice an eccentric manner of life. 3. The doctrine they profess has not been discovered by the ingenuity or cleverness of inquisitive minds, nor do they propose a merely human teaching, as some people do. 4. They pass their lives in whatever city—Greek or barbarian—as each man's lot has been cast, and follow the customs of the country in clothing, diet, and other habits. Nevertheless they give proof of the remarkable and even surprising organization of their own commonwealth. 5. For instance, they live in their own countries, but only as aliens. They take their full part as citizens, but they also endure everything as foreigners. Every foreign country is for them a motherland, and any motherland is a foreign land. 6. Like other men, they marry and beget children, but they do not expose their children. 7. They share their board with each other, but not their marriage bed. 8. By destiny they live in the flesh, but they do not live according to the flesh. 9. They spend their lives on earth, but their citizenship is in heaven. 10. They obey the prescribed laws, but in their private lives they go beyond what the laws require. 11. They show love to all men, and yet all men persecute them. 12. They are unknown, and still they are condemned; they are put to death, and yet they are brought to life. 13. They are poor, yet

[7]Text: SC 33[2].62.

they make many rich; they lack all things, yet they enjoy complete abundance.

[The Role of the Christians in the World]
6, 1.[8] To put it briefly, what the soul is to the body, that the Christians are to the world. 2. As the soul is diffused through every part of the body, so are Christians through all the cities of the world. 3. As the soul dwells in the body, but does not form part of it, so Christians dwell in the world, but do not belong to it. 4. The soul, which is invisible, is kept under guard in the visible body; in the same way, Christians are recognized in the world, but their religion itself remains hidden from the eye. 5. The flesh hates the soul and treats it as an enemy, even without provocation because it is prevented from enjoying its pleasure; so too the world hates Christians without provocation, because they are opposed to its pleasures. 6. The soul loves the flesh and all its members, despite their hatred for it; and Christians, too, love those who hate them. 7. The soul, shut up inside the body, nevertheless holds the body together; while Christians are confined within the world as in a dungeon, it is they who hold the world together. 8. The soul, which is immortal, must dwell in a mortal receptacle; and Christians, as they are settled for a while among corruptible things, look for incorruptibility in the heavens. 9. The soul, when faring badly as to food and drink, grows better; so too Christians, when subjected to ill-treatment, increase the more in numbers. 10. Such is the high post of duty in which God has placed them, and they must not try to evade it.

[True Happiness]
10, 5.[9] To be happy does not, indeed, consist in dominating one's neighbors, or in wanting to have more than one's weaker brethren, or in possessing riches and ordering one's inferiors about. No one can become an imitation of God like

[8]Text: SC 33².64.
[9]Text: SC 33².76.

that, for such things are wholly alien to his majesty. 6. But if a man takes his neighbor's burden on himself, and is ready to supply another's need from his abundance; if, by sharing the blessings he has received from God with those who are in want, he himself becomes a god to those who receive his bounty—such a man indeed is an imitator of God. 7. Then, while you walk on earth, you will see that there is a God who rules in heaven; then you will begin to discourse on the mysteries of God; and you will love and admire those who are being punished for their refusal to deny God.

The Shepherd of Hermas

The Shepherd of Hermas purports to have been written in consequence of a series of visions. It is basically an ascetico-moral treatise of apocalyptic nature. It contains five 'visions,' twelve 'mandates' and ten 'similitudes.' Its social teaching is quite extensive and significant. The author recognizes the existence of two social classes, the rich and the poor, and uses the image of the vine and its branches to emphasize their mutual dependence. He suggests that one should not desire for more than what is sufficient and that riches are made to be shared to all. He admits that the rich can be saved, provided that they practice penance and almsgiving.

[Sharing of Goods to the Needy]
Third Vision, 17;(9), 2.[10] Now, then, listen to me: Live in peace with one another, care for one another, help one another. Do not enjoy God's creatures excessively and all by yourselves, but give a share also to those who are in need. 3. For some people, from the abundance of things to eat, bring on disease to their bodies and weaken them, while others, having nothing to eat, are weakened in their bodies from lack of sufficient food and suffer ill health. 4. So this failure to share is harmful to you who have and do not share to

[10]Text: SC 53².122.

those who have not. 5. Keep in mind the judgment to come. You rich, seek out those who are hungry so long as the tower is not yet completed, for, after the completion of the tower, you will be wishing to do good and will not have the opportunity. 6. Now then, you who pride yourselves on your riches, take care lest the poor groan at any time, and their cry will reach the Lord, and you and your goods be shut out from the door of the tower.

[Give to All from the Fruits of Your Labor]
Second Mandate, 2, 4.[11] Clothe yourself with holiness, in which there is no evil, which gives no offence, and in which everything is smooth and cheerful. Do good, and from the fruit of your labors, which is God's gift to you, give to all those in need without distinction, not debating to whom you will and to whom you will not give. Give to all, since it is God's will that we give to all from his bounties. 5. Those who have received will give an account to God why they received and for what purpose. For, those who receive because they are in need will not be judged, but those who receive under false pretenses will be punished. 6. Under these circumstances, the giver is innocent, since he only performed the service that the Lord had commanded him to perform, with simplicity and without distinguishing to whom to give and to whom not to give. This service, then, performed with simplicity, becomes acceptable in God's eyes. Therefore, the man who thus serves with simplicity will live unto God.

[A Christian is a Foreigner in This World. With His Riches He Should Acquire Riches before God by Sharing His Wealth with Others]
First Similitude, 1, 6.[12] Be careful therefore, while you live in a foreign land, not to acquire anything more than an adequate sufficiency. Be ready, so that, when the ruler of this city wishes to expel you for opposing his law, you may come out of his city and enter your own, and there observe your

[11]Text: SC 53².146.
[12]Text: SC 53².212.

own law with joy and without detriment to anyone. 7. Be on your guard, then, you who serve the Lord and hold him to your heart. Remember God's commandments and the promises he made, and do his works. Trust that he will fulfill his promises if you keep his commandments. 8. Instead of fields, then, buy souls that suffer tribulation, according to your ability. Look after widows and orphans and do not neglect them. Spend your wealth and all your possessions you have received from the Lord on this kind of fields and houses. 9. It is for this purpose that the Master has made you wealthy, to perform this ministry for him. It is far better to buy such lands and possessions and houses, for you will find them when you settle in your own city. 10. Such is your luxury, good and holy, free from sadness and fear, full of joy. Do not live then in the luxury of the pagans; it is of no use to you, servants of God.

[The Rich and the Poor Help Each Other]
Second Similitude, 5.[13] . . . "The rich man has great wealth, but, so far as the Lord is concerned, he is poor, because, distracted as he is by his wealth, he can offer only a very limited praise and prayer to God; and when he does, his praise and prayer is brief and weak and has no power to come before God. So, when a rich man goes to a poor man and gives him what he needs, he can be confident that what he does for the poor man can obtain a reward from God (for the poor man is rich in his prayer and in his praise, and his prayer has great power with God). With this faith, then, the rich man does not hesitate to supply the poor man with everything. 6. On the other hand, the poor man who has been assisted by the rich intercedes for him and gives thanks to God for his benefactor. And the latter is more committed to help the poor man, so as not to let him wanting in anything during his life, because he knows that the poor man's prayer is acceptable and rich in God's eyes. 7. Both fulfill their duties in this way: The poor man offers his

[13]Text: SC 53².216.

prayers—these are his riches—and gives back to the Lord the gift of prayers that he has received. In the same way the rich man unhesitatingly gives to the poor the riches he has received from the Lord. This is a great and acceptable deed in the sight of God because the rich man knows how to administer his riches correctly and distributes to the poor God's gifts and rightly accomplishes the Lord's ministry. 8. From men's point of view the elm seems not to bear fruit. But, they do not know or reflect that in case of a drought the elms hold water and supplies it to the vine. Thus the vine, lacking no water, yields double the amount of fruit, both for itself and for the elm. In the same way, the poor, offering prayers to the Lord for the rich, round out their riches, whereas the rich, by supplying the needs of the poor, make up for the shortcomings of their souls. 9. Both in this way become associates in the just work. By doing this, then, you will not be abandoned by the Lord; rather will your names be inscribed in the books of the living. 10. Blessed are those who possess such riches and understand that riches are from the Lord. Those who understand this will be able to do some good deed."

[The Social Function of Fasting]
Fifth Similitude, 56(3), 6.[14] This is the way to keep the fast you intend to observe: Before anything else, abstain from every wicked work and every evil desire, and purify your heart of all the vanities of this world. If you do this, your fast will be perfect. 7. Act as follows: After having done what is prescribed, on the day of your fast do not taste anything except bread and water. Add up the total expense for the food you would have eaten on the day you intended to keep a fast and give it to a widow, an orphan, or someone in need. In this way you will humble yourself, so that the beneficiary of your humility may satiate his soul and pray to the Lord for you. 8. If you perform your fast in the way I have just commanded, your sacrifice will be acceptable in the sight of

[14]Text: SC 53^2.230.

God and this fast will be noted in your favor; a service so performed is beautiful, joyous, and acceptable in God's eyes.

[All Should Be without Material Difficulties]
Tenth Similitude, 114; (4), 2.[15] Tell all who can perform charitable acts not to cease doing them, since doing good works is useful to them. Now I say that every man should be relieved in his difficulties. For a person who is in need and suffers inconveniences in his daily life is in torment and anguish. 3. Whoever delivers a needy man from his necessities draws great joy for himself. For the man who is harrassed by this kind of misfortune suffers the same torture and affliction as the man in prison. Indeed, many who are incapable of enduring these calamities take their own lives. Therefore, whoever knows the misfortune of such a person, and does not release him, commits a serious sin and is guilty of that man's blood. 4. So, all you who have received riches from the Lord, perform good deeds, lest, while you are delaying, the building of the tower be finished. For your sakes, the construction of the tower has been interrupted. So, if you do not hurry to do good, the tower will be completed and you will find yourselves excluded from it.

Part Two: The Apologists

Justin Martyr

The second century witnessed the birth of a new genre of Christian literature, the apologetical writings. The

[15]Text: SC 53².362.

name of Apologists is given to those who on the one hand sought to prove the innocence of the Christians in order to obtain toleration from the hostile civil authority, especially the Emperor, and on the other hand endeavored to prove the value and truth of their religion, especially to pagan thinkers.

Foremost among these is Justin, who, born in Palestine between the years 100-110, converted to Christianity about the year 130 and suffered martyrdom in Rome in 165. His main works include two *Apologies* and the *Dialogue with Trypho.* Our selections will show how Justin considers the relation of the Christians towards civil authority and towards secular culture; the sharing of goods in the early Christian community; and the law of love towards all human beings.

FIRST APOLOGY

[The Sharing of Goods in the Early Christian Community]
14.[16] ... Those who once delighted in fornication now embrace chastity alone; those who made use of magic arts have dedicated themselves to the good and unbegotten God; we who once took most pleasure in accumulating wealth and property now bring what we have into a common fund and share with everyone in need; we who hated and killed one another and would not associate with men of different tribes because of their different customs, now, since the coming of Christ, live familiarly with them and pray for our enemies and try to persuade those who hate us unjustly to live in accordance with the good precepts of Christ, so that they may share with us the same joyful hope of a reward from God the Ruler of all.

[Submission to and Prayer for the Emperor]
17. More than any others we endeavor to pay the taxes and assessments to those appointed by you, as we have been taught by him (Jesus Christ). For once in his time some

[16]Text: PG 6.348,353.

came to him and asked if one ought to pay taxes to Caesar. And he answered: "Tell me, whose image is on the coin?" They said: "Caesar's." And he replied: "Then give to Caesar what is Caesar's and to God what is God's." So we worship God alone, but in other matters we gladly serve you, acknowledging you as emperors and rulers of men, and praying that with your imperial power you may be found to possess also sound judgment.

[Assistance to the Needy among Christians]

67.[17] And those who are prosperous, and who so wish, contribute, each one as much as he chooses to. The collection is deposited with the president (of the eucharistic liturgy). Who will take care of orphans and widows, those who are in want on account of sickness or any other cause, those who are in prison, and the strangers sojourning among us, in a word, he is the guardian of all who are in need.

SECOND APOLOGY

[The Christians' Attitude towards Secular Culture]

13.[18] For myself, when I learned the wicked disguise which the evil spirits had cast over the divine teaching of Christians in order to turn away others, I laughed at this disguise and at the opinions of the crowd; and I confess that I prayed and strove with all my strength to be found a Christian, not because the teachings of Plato are contrary to those of Christ, but because they are not in all respects similar to them, as neither are the doctrines of the others, Stoics, poets, and historians. For each spoke correctly, seeing that which was related to Christianity through a share in the seminal divine reason (Word). But those who have uttered contrary opinions seem not to have had the invisible knowledge and the heavenly wisdom. Whatever has been said rightly by any men in any place belongs to us Christians.

[17]Text: PG 6.429.
[18]Text: PG 6.465.

For, next to God, we worship and love the reason (Word) which is from the unbegotten and ineffable God, since for our sakes he has been made man, so that, being made partaker of our sufferings, he may also bring us healing. For all the authors were able to see the truth darkly, through the implanted seed of reason (Word) dwelling in them.

DIALOGUE WITH TRYPHO

[The Law of Love towards All Men]
93.[19] For God sets before every race of mankind what is always and universally just as well as all righteousness. And every race knows that adultery, fornication, and homicide, and such like, are sinful. Though they all commit such acts, they do not escape the knowledge that they act wrongly whenever they do so, with the exception of those who are possessed with an unclean spirit and corrupted by bad education, wicked customs, and perverse laws, and who have lost, or rather quenched and destroyed, their natural ideas. The proof for this is that such persons are unwilling to endure the same things which they inflict upon others, and reproach others with hostile consciences for the acts they themselves perpetrated. Hence I think our Lord and Savior Jesus Christ spoke well when he summed up all righteousness and piety in two commandments which are: "You shall love the Lord your God with all your heart and with all your strength, and your neighbor as yourself." (Mt 22:37). For the man who loves God with all his heart, and with all his strength, filled with a religious sentiment, will reverence no other god. And since God wills it, he will also reverence that Angel who is beloved by the same Lord and God. And the man who loves his neighbor as himself will wish for him the same good things that he wishes for himself, and no man will wish evil things for himself. Accordingly, he who loves his neighbor will pray and work that his neighbor may enjoy the same benefits as himself.

[19]Text: PG 6.697.

Irenaeus of Lyons

Irenaeus, without doubt the most important theologian of the second century, was born in Asia Minor between the years 140 and 160, and later became bishop of Lyons. In his five books *Against the Heresies*, or *The Refutation and Overthrow of Knowledge Falsely So-Called*, Irenaeus discusses many issues of great significance for contemporary Christian theology: Tradition, the Rule of Faith, the authority of the Church of Rome, the doctrine of "recapitulation," and eschatology. His voluminous writings do not however evince deep interest in social problems.

Our selections will illustrate Irenaeus's understanding of Christ's command of love, of the origin of human authority, and of private property. With regard to the last topic, in his answer to the Marcionites, who charge that the Old Testament God was an unjust god because he ordered the Hebrews to take the property belonging to the Egyptians, Irenaeus affirms the legitimacy of the acquiring of goods, of ownership and of profit in commerce. Nevertheless he seems to see a certain injustice in all of this and that property is justified only if the material goods are shared with others.

THE REFUTATION AND OVERTHROW OF THE KNOWLEDGE FALSELY SO-CALLED

[The Duty of Giving and Sharing Goods]
Book IV, 13, 3.[20] For this reason, instead of that commandment, "You shall not commit adultery," the Lord forbade even concupiscence; and instead of the commandment, "You shall not kill," he prohibited anger; and instead of the law enjoining the giving of tithes, he commanded us to share all our possessions with the poor, and to love not only our neighbors, but even our enemies; not only to give and grant

[20]Text: PG 7.1008.

liberally but also to offer a gratuitous gift to those who take away our goods. For "to him that takes away your coat," he says, "give him your cloak also; and from him who takes away your goods, do not ask them back; do to others what you would have them do to you." In this way, we may not grieve as those who are unwilling to be defrauded, but may rejoice as those who have given willingly, and as conferring a favor upon our neighbors rather than yielding to necessity.

[The Right of Acquiring Goods]
Book IV, 30, 1.[21] Those (the Marcionites), again, who cavil and find fault because the people, on the eve of their departure, by God's order, took vessels of all kinds and clothings from the Egyptians and escaped with them, and used them later to build the tabernacle in the desert, show their ignorance of the righteous dealings of God and of his dispositions... For in some cases there follows us a small, and in others a large amount of property, which we have acquired from the riches of iniquity. For from what source do we get the houses we live in, the garments in which we are clothed, the vessels which we use, and everything else we dispose of in our everyday life, unless it be from those things which, when we were gentiles, we acquired by avarice, or received them from our pagan parents, relatives, or friends who acquired them unjustly?

But even now, when we are in the faith, we do acquire such things. For who is there that sells and does not wish to make a profit from the buyer? Or who purchases anything and does not wish to obtain good value from the seller? Or who is there that carries on a trade and does not do it in order to earn a livelihood thereby? And the believers who are in the royal palaces, do they not derive the utensils they employ from the property which belongs to Caesar? And to the poor and needy, does not each Christian give according to his ability? The Egyptians were debtors to the Hebrew people, not only with respect to property, but also to their

21Text: PG 7.1064.

very lives, because of the generosity of patriarch Joseph in former times; but in what way are the pagans debtors to us, from whom we receive both gain and profit? Whatever they acquire with labor, we make use of without labor, although we are in the faith.

2. ... In what way, then, did the Hebrews act unjustly, if out of many things they took a few, they who might have possessed much property had they not served them, who might have marched forth wealthy, while, in fact, by receiving only a very insignificant recompense for their heavy servitude, they went away poor? In the same manner, should anyone be accused of having acted improperly if a free man, he is forcibly carried away by another, made to serve him for many years and thus increase his possessions, and when ultimately he obtains some support, he thinks he can appropriate some small portion of his master's property and march off, having obtained only a little as the payment of his own great labors and out of vast possessions which have been acquired?

3. ... For, because God knew that we would make a good use of our substance, which we should possess by receiving it from another, he says, "Let the man with two coats give to him who has none. The man who has food should do the same." And, "For I was hungry and you gave me food; I was thirsty and you gave me drink; I was naked and you clothed me." And, "In giving alms you are not to let your left hand know what your right hand is doing." And we are proved to be righteous by whatever else we do well, redeeming, as it were, our property from strange hands... For whatever we acquired from injustice when we were pagans, we are proved just, when we have become believers, by applying it to the Lord's advantage.

[The Origin and Function of Authority]
Book V, 24, 2.[22] Since man, by separating himself from God, became so ferocious that he even looked upon his brother as

---

[22]Text: PG 7.1187.

his enemy and committed without fear any kind of riotous act, murder, and avarice, God instilled in him the fear of man since he does not have the fear of God. Thus subjected to the authority of men, and kept under restraint by their laws, he will be able to attain some degree of justice and exercise mutual forbearance through dread of the sword suspended fully in his view... And for this reason too, magistrates themselves, having laws as a clothing of justice whenever they act in a just and legitimate manner, shall not be called in question for their conduct, nor be liable to punishment. But whatever acts of injustice they commit, iniquitously, impiously, illegally, and tyrannically, these shall be cause for their death. God's just judgment comes equally upon all, and will never fail. Earthly power, therefore, has been appointed by God for the benefit of all peoples, and not by the devil, who never rests and never wants to see them live in peace, so that under the fear of human rule, men may not eat each other up like fishes, but that, by means of established laws, they may reduce the excess of wickedness among the nations. From this point of view, those who levy tribute from us are "God's ministers, serving for this very purpose."

2

THE THIRD CENTURY FATHERS

Part One: The Alexandrian School

Clement of Alexandria

Clement of Alexandria, born at Athens about the year
150, became a Christian and a disciple of Pantaenus, and
later succeeded his master as head of the school of cate-
chumens. His main works include *The Exhortation to the
Greeks, The Tutor, The Stromata,* and in social matters
his homily on Mk 10:17-31 *Who is the Rich Man that is
Saved?* With Clement began a new patristic period.
Before the third century the writings were mostly apolo-
getic and anti-heretical, engaged in defense and attack.
As Christianity penetrated the ancient world, the need
was felt for a comprehensive, orderly and more sophisti-
cated elaboration of the Christian faith. One of the most
famous centers of theological learning was the catechetical school of Alexandria. The cultural environment in
which it developed shaped its predominant interest in the
metaphysical investigation of the doctrine of faith, its
predilection for Platonic philosophy, and the allegorical
interpretation of the Sacred Scripture.

In social doctrine, Clement's most relevant work is, of course, *Who is the Rich Man that is Saved?* Clement had in mind his well-to-do audience whose luxurious lifestyle he had already described in great detail in his *The Tutor* and who found difficulties in a literal interpretation of Mk 10:17-31, especially Jesus' commandment, "Go and sell what you have and give it to the poor" (Mk 10:21). In interpreting this scriptural passage Clement discusses two important issues, the right of private property and the purpose of wealth.

As regards the first question, against the gnostic Carpocrates and his son Epiphanes who advocated a community of goods, and even of women, Clement's answer is peremptory: "The Lord, therefore, did not forbid us to be rich but to be rich unjustly and insatiably" (*Stromata*, 3, 6) and "The Lord did not command that he (the rich young man) throw away the property that belongs to him and renounce his wealth" (*Who is the Rich Man that is Saved?*, 11). Clement also develops the notion that riches are "useful instruments": "These things are called 'possessions' because they are possessed, and 'wealth' (χρηματα) because they are useful (χρηδιμα) and provided by God for the use (χρηδις) of men" (*Who is the Rich Man that is Saved?*, 14).

If possessing wealth is not evil in itself and does not exclude one from salvation, wealth can be dangerous, according to Clement, if one's heart is not free from an inordinate attachment to it and if it is not used for the benefit of all. For Clement, sharing one's goods with others is not simply a duty of charity but also of social justice, since God has created everything for the use of all. "Therefore, everything is common, and the rich should not grasp a greater share... God has given us the power to use our possessions, I admit, but only to the extent that is necessary: He wishes them to be in common. It is absurd that one man lives in luxury while so many others suffer in poverty" (*The Tutor*, 2, 12).

THE EXHORTATION TO THE GREEKS

[Detachment from Wealth and the True Rich Man]
12.[1] ... Let us seek, then, what is good; let us become God-loving men, and obtain the greatest of all things that cannot be destroyed, namely, God and life. Our helper is the Word; let us put confidence in him. Let us never crave for silver and gold, and glory, but only for the Word of truth himself. For we will not be pleasing to God if we value least those things which are worth most, and hold in the highest esteem the manifest enormities and the utter impiety of folly, ignorance, thoughtlessness, and idolatry...

It is time, then, for us to say that the pious Christian alone is rich, wise, and noble, and thus call and believe him to be God's image and likeness, since he has been made righteous, holy, and wise by Jesus Christ and through him like God.

THE TUTOR

[Avoid Luxurious Living and Learn to Share]
2, 3.38.[2] ... I maintain, then, that food and clothing and dishes, and, in a word, all the items of the house, ought to be, as a general rule, in keeping with a Christian way of life and in conformity with what is serviceable and suitable to one's person, age, profession, and occasion. Since we are the servants of the one God, we ought to see to it that our possessions and furniture manifest the one beautiful way of life. Each one of us, in unquestioning faith and in his or her individual way of life, should openly perform the duties that naturally derive from, and are in harmony with, this one mentality. Now what we acquire without difficulty and use with ease, we praise willingly, preserve easily, and share readily. However, things that are useful are better, and inexpensive things are without doubt better than costly ones. Generally speaking, riches that are not under complete control are the citadel of evil. Those casting their eyes

[1]Text: SC 2.191.
[2]Text: SC 108.82.

covetously on them will never enter the kingdom of heaven, because they allow themselves to be contaminated by the things of this world and are living proudly in luxury. Those concerned for their salvation should take this as their first principle, that, although the whole creation is ours to use, it is made for the sake of self-sufficiency, which anyone can obtain with a few things. Those who take delight in what they have hoarded up in their storehouses are foolish in their greed. "He that has earned wages," Scripture reminds us, "puts them into bags with holes." Such is the man who gathers and stores up his harvest, for by not sharing his wealth with anyone he becomes poorer.

It is farcical and downright ridiculous for men to bring out urinals of silver and chamber-pots of transparent alabaster as if they were introducing their advisors, and for rich women in their silliness to have gold receptacles for excrements made, as though being wealthy they were unable to relieve themselves except in a grandiose style. I wish that for the rest of their lives they considered gold worthy only of dung. But, the truth is that love of money is proved to be the stronghold of evil, or, in the Apostle's words, "the root of all evils." "Some in their covetousness for riches have strayed from the faith and so given their souls any number of fatal wounds" (1 Tim 6:10). True wealth is poverty of desires, and the true nobility is not that founded on riches, but that which comes from a contempt for them. Boasting of one's possessions is utterly disgraceful. For it is wrong to be much concerned about what anyone who likes may buy from the market. Past wisdom cannot be bought with any earthly coin or in any market; it is acquired in heaven, at a good price: the incorruptible Word, the gold of kings.

[Be Content with What is Sufficient and Share Goods with Others]
2, 12.120³ God himself has created human beings for communion or sharing with one another, by sharing himself first of all, and by sending his Word to all men alike, and by

³Text: SC 108.228.

making all things common. Therefore, everything is common, and the rich should not grasp a greater share. The expression, then, "I own something, and have more than enough; why shouldn't I enjoy it?" is neither worthy of man nor proper to the sharing of goods. It is more conformable to charity to say: "I have something; why shouldn't I share it with those in need?" Whoever says so fulfills the command: "You shall love your neighbor as yourself" and is perfect. This is true luxury, the lavishness that stores up treasure; spending money on foolish desires is to be reckoned as waste, not expenditure.

God has given us the power to use our possessions, I admit, but only to the extent that is necessary: He wishes them to be in common. It is absurd that one man lives in luxury, while so many others suffer in poverty. How much more glorious it is to serve many than to live in luxury. How much more reasonable to spend money on human beings than on stones and gold! How much more useful to have friends as our ornamentation than lifeless decorations! Can possessing lands ever give more benefit to anyone than practicing kindness? The only question left to answer, then, is this: For whom do precious things exist if everyone is going to choose what is less costly? Human beings, I should say, provided that we use them without attachment and distinction. And if it should be impossible for all to practice self-restraint, then at least in our use of the necessities let us confine ourselves to those things that are more easily obtainable and not seek after the exotic articles...

[How to Share Our Riches]
3, 6.34[4] Riches should be possessed in a becoming manner, shared generously, not mechanically and ostentatiously. We should take care not to turn the love of the beautiful into the love of self lest someone say to us: "His horse, or land, or servant, or gold plate is worth fifteen talents, but he himself costs only three cents." First of all, take ornaments away from a woman, and servants from a master, and you will

[4]Text: SC 158.76.

discover that the master is no different from the slaves he has bought neither in bearing, nor in look, nor in voice. In fact, he is very similar to his slaves in all these things. He differs from his slaves in one respect only, namely, he is weaker, and, because of his upbringing, more susceptible to sickness.

At any rate, we should reiterate on every occasion that most enlightening of all maxims, that is, the good man, in his temperance and righteousness, 'stores up treasure in heaven.' Whoever sells his earthly possessions and distributes them to the poor will find the imperishable treasure where there is neither moth nor robber. Such a man is truly blessed, even if he is small and weak and insignificant, and is rich indeed with the greatest of all riches. On the other hand, if a man becomes wealthier than Midas and Cinyra, but is unjust and haughty, like the man who was luxuriously clothed in purple and fine linen, yet despised Lazarus, he is miserable, lives in wretchedness, and will never find true life. Wealth, in fact, seems to me like a snake; it will twist around the hand and bite unless one knows how to grasp it properly, dangling it without danger by the point of the tail. In the same way, wealth, wriggling either in an experienced or inexperienced grasp, tends to cling to the hand and bite unless a person rises above it and uses it with discretion, so as to crush the beast by the charm of the Word and escape unharmed.

However, in my opinion, only he who possesses things of higher value and only he is truly wealthy, though he may not be recognized as such. Now it is not gems, nor silver, nor clothes, nor beauty of body that are of high value, but virtue, which is the Word translated into deeds under the guidance of Christ the Tutor...

[The Rich Man is the One Who Gives]
3, 6.35[5] If distinctions be made, let it be granted that the rich man is the one who has many possessions, loaded with gold

---

[5]Text: SC 158.78.

like a dirty purse; but that the righteous man alone is the honest one, for honesty is the quality that preserves order and proper balance between managing and giving. "Some distribute their own goods," it is written, "and become richer." (Prov 11:24) Of such men, Scripture says: "He has distributed; he has given to the poor; his justice remains forever" (Ps 111:9). Therefore, it is not he who possesses and keeps his wealth who is wealthy, but he who gives; it is giving, not receiving that makes a man happy. Generosity is the fruit of the soul, true wealth resides in the heart.

Good things should be considered the property only of good men. But Christians are good; a fool or a libertine can neither perceive nor truly possess the good. Therefore Christians alone possess good things. But nothing brings greater wealth than good things, so Christians alone are wealthy. Holiness is true wealth, and the Word is more valuable than all treasure; these are not increased by cattle or fields but are given by God. They cannot be taken away for the soul alone is such a man's treasure. It is the best possession to its owner, making man truly blessed. If a man abstains from desiring things that are beyond his reach but possesses by asking from God the things he desires in a holy way, is not that man abundantly wealthy, and indeed possessed of all things, since he has God as his everlasting treasure?

THE STROMATA

[Property and Social Order]

3, 6.[6] ... But the righteousness of Carpocrates and his followers who advocate a perverse form of sharing can be dissolved in the following way. Indeed, said the Lord: "Give to anyone who asks," to which he added: "And if anyone wants to borrow, do not turn away." This is the form of sharing that he taught, not the one that is incestuous and lascivious. Now, how can anyone ask and receive if there is

[6]Text: GCS 52.221.

no one who has anything to give and lend? What did the Lord mean when he said: "For I was hungry and you gave me food; I was thirsty and you gave me drink; I was a stranger and you made me welcome; naked and you clothed me." He further adds: "I tell you solemnly, insofar as you did this to one of the least of these brothers of mine, you did it to me." Had not the Old Testament promulgated the same laws: "Whoever gives to beggars, lends to God." And: "Do not refuse a kindness to anyone who begs it." And again: "Whoever does not lend his money for interest will be given credit..."

Does not the Scripture make it clear that just as the world is made up of contraries, hot and cold, wet and dry, so there are those who give and those who receive? The same thing was affirmed by the Lord when he said: "If you wish to be perfect, go and sell what you own and give the money to the poor." Thus he reproached the man who boasted of "having observed all these commandments since youth" and did not fulfill the other commandment: "Love your neighbor as yourself." When the Lord raised this commandment to perfection he taught us the duty to share and communicate with love.

The Lord, therefore, does not forbid us to be rich but to be rich unjustly and insatiably. "Possessions that are accumulated unjustly will dwindle away." "One is extravagant, yet his riches grow, another excessively mean, but only grows the poorer." Of the former, it is written: "Quick to be generous, he gives to the poor, his justice will remain forever." Those who "sow and collect much" are those who by sharing and distributing the earthly goods acquire the heavenly and eternal ones. On the other hand, those who do not give anything to anyone are those who vainly gather their treasures on earth "where moths and woodworms destroy them." Of them it is written: "The wage earner gets his wages only to put them in a purse riddled with holes."

WHO IS THE RICH MAN THAT IS SAVED?

[The Need to Understand the Lord's Saying, Mt 19:24]
2.[7] Perhaps the reason why the rich man's salvation appears more difficult than that of the poor man is not one but many. For some, merely hearing the Lord's saying: "It is easier for a camel to go through the eye of a needle than for a rich man to enter the kingdom of heaven," and without giving much thought to it, give up all hope of attaining eternal life, surrender themselves totally to the world, cling to the present life as if it were the only thing left to them, and so move father away from the path to the life to come, no longer inquiring either whom the Lord and Master calls rich, or how that which is impossible to man becomes possible to God. Others correctly and adequately understand this saying, but attach slight importance to the works which lead to salvation and therefore do not make the necessary preparation for attaining to the objects of their hope...

[Salvation is Possible for the Rich, but not without Effort]
3. Those then who love the truth and their brethren, and who neither rudely attack those rich who have been called to the faith nor cringe to them for their selfish ends, must first with good reasons relieve them of their groundless despair, providing them with satisfactory explanations of the Lord's sayings and showing them that they are not quite cut off from inheriting the kingdom of heaven if they obey the commandments. Next they should be shown that their fear is without cause and that the Lord will gladly receive them, provided they are willing. They should further be taught how and by what deeds and dispositions they can win the object of their hope, insofar as it is neither out of their reach nor can be attained without effort. But, as is the case with athletes—to compare things small and perishing with things great and immortal—let the man endowed with earthly wealth consider that this depends on himself...

[7]Text: LCL, ed. Butterworth, 272.

[The Meaning of the Story of the Rich Young Man in Mt 19:26-22]
11. What was it that turned him (the rich young man) to flight and made him abandon his teacher, and reject his entreaty, his hope, his life, and his past achievement?—"sell your possessions." But what does this mean? It is not, as some hastily interpret it, a command that he should throw away what he possesses and renounce his wealth. What he is told to banish from his soul are his notions about wealth, his attachment to it, his excessive desire for it, his morbid excitement over it, and his anxieties—those thorns of existence which choke the seed of true life.

There is nothing great or enviable about having no money, unless it is for the purpose of gaining true life. Otherwise it must be said that people with nothing at all, the destitutes who beg for daily bread in abject poverty by the roadside, even though they are 'ignorant' of God and 'of God's righteousness,' would be the most blessed of men, the dearest to God, the sole possessors of eternal life, merely in virtue of their complete lack of any ways or means of livelihood and of their want of the smallest necessities. Again, there is nothing new in renouncing one's riches and giving them in charity to the poor or to one's fatherland. Many did this before the Savior's coming, some to have leisure for the pursuit of dead wisdom, others to gain empty fame and vainglory—men like Anaxagoras, Democritus and Crates.

[Christ Asks Us to Renounce Our Passions]
12. Why then does he give this command which failed to bring salvation to men of old as if it were something new, divine, and uniquely life-giving? If there is something extraordinary that the new creation, the Son of God, reveals and teaches, then it cannot be the outward action that he is commanding; others have done that. It must be something else that is being indicated through it—something greater, more divine and more perfect. It is the stripping off of the passions from the soul itself and from its disposition; all that is alien must be uprooted and expelled from the mind. This

is the appropriate lesson for the believer to learn, and the worthy doctrine for the Savior to teach.

Men of old gave up their possessions and abandoned them entirely in their contempt for external things, but they exacerbated, I believe, the passions of their soul. They became arrogant, boastful, vain, and contemptuous of other men, as if they had done something superhuman. How then could the Savior have given to those destined to eternal life what would turn out to be injurious and harmful advice in respect of the life that he promises? Moreover, it is possible for a man to get rid of the burden of wealth and none the less to lust and hanker for it. He has renounced the use of it and then, finding himself both needing and longing for what he has given up, he suffers doubly both from the absence of support and the presence of regret. For when someone lacks the necessities of life he cannot but be broken in spirit; he will have no time for better things since he will make every effort to procure what he needs however and whenever he can.

[The Right of Property and the Common Use]
13. How much more beneficial is the opposite condition, in which one not only possesses enough so as not to have to worry about possessions oneself, but also is able to give assistance to others as one ought. For if no one had anything, what opportunity would there be left for sharing one's good? Would not this precept prove to be in open and direct opposition to many other excellent teachings of the Lord? "Make friends for yourselves by means of the mammon of unrighteousness, so that when it fails, they may receive you into the eternal habitations." "Acquire treasures in heaven, where neither moths nor rust destroys, nor thieves break in." How could one give food to the hungry, and drink to the thirsty, clothe the naked, and shelter the homeless (and those who fail to do so are threatened with fire and outer darkness), if no one has any of those things himself? The Lord himself was a guest of Zacchaeus and Matthew, the rich tax collectors, and never told them to give up their wealth. Rather, after ordering the just and forbidding the

unjust use of it, he says: "Today salvation has come to this house, for he too is a son of Abraham." Thus he praises the use of property, although he does add the injunction to share it by giving drink to the thirsty, and bread to the hungry, taking in the homeless and clothing the naked. If on the one hand it is impossible to supply those needs except with wealth and on the other we are also commanded to give up wealth, then what the Lord would be doing is telling us to give and not to give the very same things, to feed and not to feed, to take in and to shut out, to share and not to share? And that is utterly absurd!

[Wealth is a Useful Instrument for Doing Charity]
14. We must not then throw away the wealth which is also beneficial to our neighbors. These things are called 'possessions' because they are possessed, and 'wealth' because they are useful and provided by God for the use of men. They lie at our disposal like materials or like instruments which can be well used by those who know how. An instrument, if you use it skillfully, will produce a skillful effect. If you lack the skill, it will be affected by your lack of skill, but it is itself free from blame.

Wealth is an instrument of this kind. If you are able to make a right use of it, then it will serve justice. If it is wrongly used, then it will serve injustice. For its nature is to serve, not to rule. That which is in itself incapable of good or evil is blameless, and must not be blamed; that which is capable of using it well or ill by reason of its free choices is to be held responsible. And this is the human mind, which possesses both independent judgment and the power of free choice in the disposal of what has been given it. So what is to be destroyed is not one's possessions but the passions of the soul, which hinder the right use of one's property. By thus becoming virtuous and good, a man will be able to make good use of his riches. The renunciation, then, and selling of all possessions, is to be understood in reference to the passions of the soul.

[Passions and the Right Use of Riches]
15. I could put the matter as follows. Some things are internal to the soul, and others external. The latter, if the soul uses them well, appear to be good; if badly, then bad. So when the Lord commands us to do away with our property, is he forbidding those things after the removal of which our passions still remain? Or is he rather forbidding those after the removal of which even our outward possessions become beneficial? The one who renounces his worldly wealth can still be rich in passions, even when his material possessions are gone. For his disposition produces its own effects, strangling and stifling his reason, inflaming in him its inborn lusts. Thus it is of no advantage to him to be poor in material things, while being rich in passions. The things he has rejected are not things that need to be rejected, but things neither good nor bad. He has deprived himself of things that could be of service to him, and at the same time, by his want of outward things, has set on fire the fuel of evil within him. We must therefore renounce those possessions that are harmful, not those that are capable of being service-able to us if we know how to use them rightly. What is managed with prudence, moderation, and piety is profitable; what is harmful must be cast away. Things external, however, do us no harm. Thus the Lord allows us the use of external things. What he bids us to reject is not the means of livelihood, but the things that make bad use of them. And these, as we have seen, are the infirmities and passions of the soul.

[The Poor in Spirit]
16. A wealth of these passions is deadly to all, whereas their removal brings salvation. This is the wealth of which the soul must be purified, that is, impoverished and stripped bare. Only then can one hear the Savior's call, "Come and follow me." For to the pure heart he himself now becomes the way. But the grace of God cannot penetrate into the impure heart. That soul is unclean which is rich in lusts and is in the throes of many worldly affections.

Imagine a man who holds his possessions, his gold, silver and houses, as the gifts of God; who serves the God who gave them by using them for the welfare of mankind; who knows that he possesses them more for the sake of his brethren than his own; who is superior to and not a slave of his possessions; who does not go about with his possessions in his heart or let himself be enclosed within them; who is always engaged in some good and holy work; and who, should he be deprived of them, is able to bear their removal as cheerfully as their abundance. Such a man is the one whom the Lord calls 'blessed' and 'poor in spirit.' He is worthy to inherit the kingdom of heaven; he is not the rich man who cannot obtain life.

[Harmful Attachment of Possessions]
17. Imagine, on the contrary, the man who has money in his soul, who carries in his heart not the Spirit of God but gold or land; who is constantly accumulating his possessions and always on the lookout for more; whose eyes are fixed downward; who is trapped in the snares of the world; who is earth and to earth will return. How can such a man set his desires or thoughts on the kingdom of heaven, who carries about with him not a heart, but an estate or a mine? Will he not be found among those things on which he has fixed his choice? "For where a man's heart is, there will his treasure also be."

Origen

A successor to Clement at the Alexandrian catechetical school, Origen (185-253) is doubtless one of the greatest and most original thinkers of the Ancient Church. His writings are voluminous, and these are mainly exegetical, apologetical, dogmatic, and ascetical in character. Very few of his works explicitly deal with social issues. Basically his position is in accord with the traditional teaching: he recognizes the legitimacy of property and insists on the duty of sharing it with others as well as the responsibility that ownership entails. Particularly noteworthy is his distinction of things into good, bad, and indifferent; to the third category belong riches, which Clement has already considered as instrument. Interesting also are Origen's ideas on the natural law and the political order, his understanding of man as a creature full of wants so that he can use his intelligence to satisfy them.

AGAINST CELSUS

[Man's Intelligence and Needs and the Origin of the Arts] 4, 76.[8] ... He (Celsus) does not see that from a desire that human understanding should be exercised everywhere, in order that it might not remain inactive and ignorant of the arts, God made man a creature full of wants. These very wants will compel him to discover the arts, some for food, others for shelter and protection. Moreover, it was better that those who would not seek for the divine things and study philosophy should be in distress so that they might use their intellect to discover the arts rather than by being in prosperity they should entirely neglect their intellect. To provide for the necessities of life, in fact, was the origin of the art of agriculture and of the cultivation of vineyards, the arts of gardening, carpentry, and blacksmith, which made the tools for the arts which supply food to mankind. Need of shelter and protection introduced the art of weaving after that of wool—carding and spinning, and that of building, and in this way the mind also advanced to architecture. Lack of the necessities of life has also caused things, which are produced in other places, to be transported to those who do not have them by the arts of sailing and navigation.

For these reasons one should admire Providence for having made the rational creature differently from irrational animals, full of needs for his own benefit. The irrational animals have their food ready for them because they have nothing to urge them to practise arts; they also have natural

[8]Text: SC 136.374.

protection, for they are covered with hair or feathers or scales or a shell.

[Divine Law and Natural Law]

5.40.[9] ... Celsus then goes on to say this of the different laws: "Pindar seems to me to have been right when he said that law is king of all." Let us discuss this statement too. What law, sir, do you say is king of all? If you refer to the laws by which particular cities are governed, then the affirmation is patently false, for all men are not ruled by the same laws. You ought to have said that "laws are kings of all," for in every nation some law is the king of all its citizens. But if you understand law in the proper sense, this is by nature king of all, even if, as there are robbers who violate the laws, there are those who deny them and, like robbers, live lives of violence and injustice. We, Christians, then, recognize the law is by nature king of all when it is the same as the law of God; we try to live in accordance with it, thereby renouncing the laws that are no laws.

COMMENTARY ON MATTHEW

[Salvation of the Rich is not Impossible, but Difficult]

15.20.[10] As soon as the other (the rich young man) departed, Jesus said to his disciples: "I assure you, only with difficulty will a rich man enter into the kingdom of God." It is important to note the precise meaning of the Savior's words as they were written. He did not say that a rich man will not enter the kingdom of heaven; had he said so, he would have excluded the rich from the kingdom of heaven. What he said is that "only with difficulty will a rich man enter into the kingdom of God." He made it clear therefore that the rich man's salvation is difficult, not that it is impossible. That this is true can be seen from the context itself, since only with difficulty can the rich resist their passions and sinful inclinations and not allow themselves to be dominated by

[9]Text: SC 147.120.
[10]Text: PG 13.1509.

them. Moreover, if the rich man is understood in a figurative sense, it is fitting to ask why he will enter the kingdom of heaven only with difficulty. Further, the difficulty of entering, as it should be understood, is explained in the comparison: "It is easier for a camel to pass through a needle's eye than for a rich man to enter the kingdom of God."

The rich man, then, is compared with a camel, not only by reason of the impurity of the animal, as the Law teaches, but also of its total tortuosity. On the other hand the kingdom of heaven is likened to the eye of a needle to indicate how extremely narrow and tight the entrance into the kingdom of heaven is for the rich man. The Lord, then, declares that it is impossible for the camel to enter the eye of a needle; but since all things are possible with God, he makes such an entry possible either by trimming the fat of evil with his ineffable power or by widening the narrow entry.

And the proof that the Lord took the example of the eye of the needle and the camel in order to declare that it is difficult, but not impossible, for the rich man to enter the kingdom of heaven, lies in the fact that the disciples asked: "Then who can be saved"? And he answered: "For man it is impossible, but for God all things are possible." It is quite possible for a camel to pass through the eye of a needle, but it is not possible for a man. In the same way, it is possible for a rich man to enter the kingdom of God. In which ways and manners God makes it possible, only he knows, and his Christ, and those to whom it pleases him to reveal.

HOMILY ON LEVITICUS

[Seven Ways of Obtaining Forgiveness of Sins]
Homily 2, 4.[11] ... You have heard how many sacrifices there were in the Law to expiate sins, listen now to find out how many ways there are to have sins forgiven in the Gospel. The first way for the remission of sins is through baptism. The second, through the suffering of martyrdom. The third, through almsgiving, as the Savior says: "If you give

[11]Text: PG 12.417.

alms then all things will be clean for you." The fourth way, when we forgive sins to our brethren... The fifth way to obtain forgiveness of sins is by repenting of the sinful error of one's life... The sixth way is through the abundance of charity... There is, finally, the seventh way of remission of sins, though hard and laborious, by means of penance, when the sinner bathes his couch with tears, which serve as his food day and night, and when he is not ashamed to submit himself to the judgment of the priest of the Lord and ask for medicine, as it is written: "I said: I confess my sins to the Lord, and you took away the guilt of my sin."

Part Two: The African Writers

Tertullian

Although the Church of Africa had a relatively late beginning, it has provided Latin Christianity with the most original thinker of the ante-Nicene period, Tertullian; one bishop martyr, Cyprian; and two lay theologians, Arnobius and Lactantius.

Tertullian (155-220), combines a profound knowledge of philosophy, law, Greek and Latin letters with inexhaustible vigor, burning rhetoric, and biting satire. Converted to Christianity in about 195, he left Rome to return to Carthage, his native city, became a catechist, and according to Jerome, a priest. His rigorism led him to sympathise with Montanism, and c. 207 officially joined the sect. Later he founded his own party, the Tertullianists.

His voluminous writings are usually divided into four groups: apologetical, in defence of Christianity; controversial, against the heresies; moral, explaining Christian ethics and virtues; and sacramental discipline.

Though his doctrines on the trinity, christology, ecclesiology, and sacraments have earned him the title of founder of theology in the West, Tertullian offers only an occasional teaching on social issues. He admits the legitimacy of private property, though his statement that "all things are common among us except our wives" (*Apology*, 39) may suggest that he is advocating a form of communism of goods. From the context, however, it is clear that what is meant is not communism as such but common sharing of goods. Noteworthy also are his ideas about the relationship of Christianity to culture and to the civil authority.

THE APOLOGY

[The Christian Attitude to the Emperor]
29.[12] ... This, then, is the ground on which we are accused of treason against the imperial majesty, namely, that we do not make him subject to his possessions; that we do not perform a mockery by offering a service for his safety, when we do not believe that his safety rests in hands soldered with lead. But you are, to be sure, impious in seeking it where it is not, in asking it from those who have not to give, passing by him in whose power it lies. Moreover, you persecute those who know where to seek it, who, because they know, are also able to obtain it.

30. For we offer prayer for the safety of the Emperor to God the eternal, God the true, God the living, whose favor, beyond all others, the Emperor himself should desire...

31. But, you say, we merely flatter the Emperor, and feign the prayers we utter, to evade persecution... Examine God's words, our sacred books, which we do not conceal,

[12]Text: CCL 1.140.

and which many accidents put into the hands of those who do not belong to our group. Learn from them that a large abundance of benevolence is enjoined upon us, even so far as to pray God for our enemies and to entreat blessings for our persecutors. . .

32. There is another and greater need for us to pray for the Emperor, and indeed, for the whole stability of the empire, and for the interests of Rome in general. For we know that a great upheaval impending over the whole earth, in fact, the very end of all things, threatening terrible woes, is only delayed by the respite granted to the Roman empire. We have no desire then to be overtaken by these dire events; and in praying that their coming may be delayed, we are working for the survival of Rome. . . In the Emperor we reverence the judgment of God, who has set him over all the nations. . .

[The Social Involvement of Early Christians]
39.[13] After having refuted the calumnies against the Christians, I will now proceed to show their good works. We form a single body, united together by a common faith, a common discipline, and by the bond of a common hope. We meet together as an assembly to offer up prayer to God as with a united front. We wrestle with God by means of our supplications. This violence pleases God. We pray, too, for the Emperor, his officers and for all in authority, for the welfare of the world, for the reign of peace, for the delay of the final condemnation. We gather to read the sacred books, in which we find the warnings that we deem necessary for every practical case. At any rate, with the sacred words we nourish our faith, we enkindle our hope, we strengthen our confidence. With God's precepts we improve our discipline and confirm our virtues. In this assembly, too, exhortations are given, rebukes and sacred censures are administered. . .

Men of proven character preside over us, obtaining that honor not by money, but by proof of their virtue and ability.

[13]Text: CCL 1.150.

There is no buying and selling of any sort in the things of God. Though we have a treasure-chest, it is not made up of purchase-money as if religion could be obtained at a price. Once a month, each member, if he wishes, puts in a small donation, but only if he so desires and to the extent he is capable. There is no compulsion, everything is voluntary. These gifts are, as it were, piety's deposit fund. They are not withdrawn to be spent on feasts, and drinking, and on eating-houses, but to support and bury poor people, to help needy boys and girls, orphans, and shut-in old folks. They are also used to assist those who have suffered shipwreck, who are condemned to the mines, deported to the islands, or incarcerated, for being faithful to God's cause...

Since we form but one mind and one heart, we do not hesitate to share our earthly goods with one another. All things are common among us except our wives. We do not practice community in only one respect as it is practiced by others, who not only take possession of their friends' wives, but most tolerantly also accommodate their friends with theirs, following the example, I believe, of those wise men of ancient times, the Greek Socrates and the Roman Cato, who shared with their friends the wives they had married...

THE PRESCRIPTION OF HERETICS

[Christianity and Secular Culture]

7.[14] These are the 'doctrines' of men and 'of demons' produced for itching ears of the spirit of this world's wisdom: this the Lord called 'foolishness' and 'chose the foolish things of the world' to confound even philosophy itself. For it is this philosophy which is the subject-matter of this world's wisdom, that rash interpreter of the nature and plan of God. Indeed, heresies themselves are instigated by philosophy... From all these (heresies), when the Apostle would restrain us, he expressly names *philosophy* as that which he would have us to be on guard against. Writing to the Colossians, he says: "See that no one beguile you through philos-

[14]Text: CCL 1.192.

ophy and vain deceit, after the tradition of men, and contrary to the wisdom of the Holy Spirit." He had been at Athens, and had in his contacts become acquainted with that human wisdom which pretends to know the truth, but which only corrupts it, and is itself divided into manifold heresies, by the variety of its mutually destructive sects. What is there in common between Athens and Jerusalem? What between the Academy and the Church? What between heretics and Christians?... Away with all the projects for a 'Stoic,' a 'Platonic,' or a 'dialectic' Christianity! After Jesus Christ we desire no subtle theories, no acute disquisitions after the Gospel! With our faith, we desire no further belief.

ON PATIENCE

[Contempt for Wealth and Patience in Losing It]
7.2.[15] If someone is disturbed by the loss of property, then in many places of the holy Scriptures he is admonished to despise the world. One can meet no better exhortation to be indifferent to money than the example of Jesus Christ who did not own any worldly goods. He always defended the poor and condemned the rich. Thus he has set disdain for wealth ahead of the endurance of losses, pointing out through his rejection of riches that one should make no account of the loss of them. Hence, we should not seek wealth, since our Lord did not seek it; and if we happen to lose the whole of it, we ought to bear the loss with equanimity. The Spirit of the Lord, through the mouth of the Apostle, has said: "The love of money is the root of all evil."

The love of money does not consist only in the desire for another person's property. Even what seems to be our own belongs to another, for nothing is our own, since all things belong to God to whom, we, too, belong. Therefore, if we feel impatient when we suffer some loss, we show that we entertain a love for money, since we grieve for the loss of what is not our own. We are seeking what belongs to

[15]Text: CCL 1.306.

another when we are unwilling to bear the loss of what belongs to another. The man who is upset and unable to bear his loss, sins against God himself by preferring the things of earth to those of heaven. For, the soul which he has received from the Lord is consumed with care for the things of this world...

It is for pagans to be unable to bear all loss, since they would set worldly goods before their own lives. And they do this when, in their love for wealth, they engage in lucrative but dangerous commerce on sea; when, to get rich they take up causes in the forum which have no chance to be won; when, lastly, they hire themselves out for the games and military service, or when, in desolate regions, they commit robbery regardless of the wild beasts. On the contrary, since we are different from them, we should not give up our life for money but money for our life, either by voluntary charity or by the patient endurance of loss.

Cyprian of Carthage

Cyprian (c. 200-258), bishop of Carthage and martyr, distinguished himself by his social concern and his charitable activities, especially during the plague that devastated his city. By no means a systematic thinker, and certainly less original and speculative than Origen and Tertullian, Cyprian did not produce a complete presentation of Christian doctrine, though his teachings on the unity of the Church, the position of the bishop of Rome, baptism, penance, and eucharist are quite influential.

On social matters, his "On Works and Almsgiving" is certainly one of the most important writings. It is the first work that discusses and develops systematically the doctrine of almsgiving. For Cyprian almsgiving is not simply an act of charity but a serious obligation of justice deriving from the duty of sharing the goods that God has destined for the common use. It is also a means of purification and a means of obtaining forgiveness of sins.

ON WORKS AND ALMSGIVING

[Almsgiving and Forgiveness of Sins]

1.[16] Many and great, dear brethren, are the divine blessings by which the abundant and infinite mercy of God the Father and of Christ has worked and is always working for our salvation, because the Father has sent his Son to preserve us and give us life in order that he might restore us, and because the Son wished to be sent and to be called the son of man so that he might make us the sons of God. He humbled himself so that he might raise up the people who before were prostrate; he was wounded that he might cure our wounds; he served that he might bring those who served to freedom. He suffered death that he might hold forth immortality to mortals. These are the many and great gifts of divine mercy. Further, what providence and what great mercy that is, that by a plan of salvation, we are provided with a more abundant care so that we may be preserved after we have been redeemed! For when the Lord had come and healed the wounds which Adam had borne, and had cured the old poisons of the serpent, he commanded the man who had been made whole to sin no more, lest something worse should befall him. We were restricted and shut within a narrow space by the commandment of innocence. Nor would the infirmity of human frailty have any resource to do anything unless the divine mercy, coming once more in aid, should open some way to obtain salvation by pointing out the works of justice and mercy, so that by almsgiving we may wash away whatever pollutions we later contract.

2. The Holy Spirit speaks in the Scripture, saying: "By alms and by faith sins are cleansed." Surely not those sins that had been committed before, for they have been purged by the blood and sanctification of Christ. In another place, he says again: "As water extinguished fire, so almsgiving and good works quench sin." Here also it is shown and proved that just as with the font of saving water the fire of hell is

---

[16]Text: CCL 111A.55.

extinguished, so by almsgiving and good works the flame of sin is put out. And because the forgiveness of sin is once granted in baptism, God's mercy is again bestowed upon us if we constantly act in accordance with the spirit of baptism. This is also taught by the Lord in the gospel. For when it was remarked that his disciples were eating without first having washed their hands, he replied saying: "He who made the inside made the outside as well. Truly give alms, and behold all things are clean to you." Thus, he taught and showed that not the hands but the heart ought to be washed and the uncleanness within rather than without ought to be taken away, and that he who cleanses what is within has cleansed also what is without, and that he whose mind has been made clean is also clean in his skin and body. Further advising and showing how we can be purified and cleansed, he added that alms must be given. The merciful One advises that mercy be shown, and because he seeks to save those whom he redeemed at a great price, he teaches that those who have been polluted after the grace of baptism can be cleansed again.

[The Scripture and the Duty of Almsgiving]
7.[17] Thus in the Gospel, the Lord, the Teacher of our life and Master of eternal salvation, who bestows life on those who believe in him and provides for them forever, among his divine commands and heavenly precepts, orders and prescribes nothing more frequently than that we continue in almsgiving and not cling avariciously to our earthly possessions but rather store up heavenly treasures. "Sell your possessions," he says, "and give alms." Again: "Do not lay up for yourselves treasures on earth, where rust and moth consume, and where theives break in and steal, but lay up for yourselves treasures in heaven where neither rust nor moth consumes and where thieves do not break in. For where your treasure is, there also will be your heart." And when he wished to show the man who had been made perfect

[17]Text: CCL III A.59.

and complete by the observance of the law, he said: "If you wish to be perfect, go, sell all that you have, and give to the poor, and you will have treasure in heaven, and come follow me"...

[Against the Fear of Giving Alms]
9.[18] Should you be afraid and fear lest, if you begin to act very generously, your patrimony would thereby be exhausted and you would be reduced to poverty, be of good cheer and rest assured: That which is spent in the service of Christ and transformed into a heavenly work, can never be exhausted. I do not promise you on my own authority, but I vouch for it on the faith of holy Scriptures and on the authority of God's promise. The Holy Spirit speaks through Solomon and says: "He that gives to the poor shall never be in want, but he that turns away his eyes shall be in great want." It is said therefore that the merciful and those who do good can never be in want, rather the sparing and barren will come to want. Likewise the blessed apostle Paul, full of the grace of the Lord's inspiration, says: "He who provides seed for the sower, also will give bread to eat and will multiply your seed and will increase the growth of the fruits of your justice, so that in all things you may be enriched." And again: "The administration of this service not only will supply what the saints lack but will overflow in much gratitude to God." This is so because, while the action of thanks is directed to God by the prayer of the poor for our almsgiving and good works, the wealth of him who does good is increased by the retribution of God...

[The Example of the Poor Widow for the Rich to Imitate]
15.[19] But from you (the rich who do not give) the Church cannot expect to receive much, for your eyes, obscured by darkness and covered with the shadows of night, do not see the needy and the poor. You, wealthy and powerful, do you suppose you can celebrate the Lord's Feast worthily, you

[18]Text: CCL 111A.60.
[19]Text: CCL 111A.64.

who do not at all consider the offering, who come to the Lord's Feast without a sacrifice, who take part in the sacrifice offered by the poor? Behold in the Gospel the widow mindful of the heavenly precepts, doing good in the very midst of the pressures and hardships of poverty, casting two mites which were her only possessions into the treasury. When the Lord noticed and saw her, judging her work not for its quantity but for its intention, and considering not how much but from how much she had given, said: "Truly I assure you, this poor widow has put in more than all the rest. They make contribution out of their surplus, but she out of her want has given all that she had to live on." A greatly blessed and glorious woman, who even before the day of Judgment merited to be praised by the voice of the Judge. Let the rich man be ashamed of his lack of generosity and unbelief. A widow, and a poor one at that, is found to be rich in good works. If all collections are destined to be distributed to orphans and widows, she gives who deserves to receive, so that we may know what punishment awaits the rich man without good works, since in this example, not even the poor are exempt from doing good works. And that we may understand that these works are given to God and whoever does these deserves well of God, Christ calls them 'gifts of God' and points out that the widow has placed two mites among the gifts of God so that it is made abundantly clear that whoever pities the poor lends to God.

[The Number of Children is No Excuse for Not Giving Alms]
18.[20] Now you may argue that you have many children in the family and the number of children does not allow you to perform good works. My reply is that by this very fact you ought all the more to do good works, since you are the father of many pledges. You have more people for whom you should pray to the Lord, more people whose sins must be forgiven, more people whose consciences must be cleansed, more people whose souls must be freed. Just as in the

[20]Text: CCL 111A.66.

material life the greater the number of your children, the greater is the expense for their nourishment and sustenance, so too in the spiritual life and heavenly life, the greater the number of your children, the greater is the number of good works. . . . If then you truly love your children, if you want to show them fully your fatherly and tender love, you should do more good works so that you may commend your children to God by your good works.

[The Right Way to Provide for the Future of Your Children] 19. Do not look for someone as father for your children who is temporary and weak but find someone who is the eternal and strong Father of your spiritual children. Assign to him your wealth which you are keeping for your heirs, let him be your children's guardian, their caretaker, their protector with his divine majesty against all worldly harms. When your patrimony is entrusted to God, the state does not seize it, the tax-collector does not assail it, and an unjust suit will not destroy it. The inheritance is placed in safety, which is kept under God's care. This is to provide for the future of your dear children; this is to provide for your future heirs with fatherly love. . . . So you would not be a father but a transgressor and a betrayer, if you do not look out faithfully for the welfare of your children and attend to their salvation with religious and true love. Why are you eager for earthly rather than heavenly patrimony? Why do you prefer to entrust your children to the devil rather than to Christ? You would commit a double crime: first, because you do not make the help of God the Father available to your children and second, because you teach your children to love riches more than Christ.

[The Sharing of Goods among the First Christians] 25.[21] Let us consider, dear brethren, what the community of the believers did under the Apostles, when at the beginning the mind flourished with greater virtues, when the faith of believers was warm with a fervor of a faith still new. Then

[21]Text: CCL 111A.71.

they sold their homes and estates, and gladly and generously offered the proceeds to the Apostles to be distributed among the poor, by selling and distributing their earthly patrimony, transferring their property to where they might receive the fruits of an eternal possession, preparing homes where they may live forever. . .

This is truly to become a child of God by spiritual birth; this is to imitate God's justice by the heavenly law. For whatever belongs to God, is for the common use of all, nor is anyone excluded from his benefits and gifts, nor is the human race prevented from equally enjoying God's goodness and generosity. Thus, the day illuminates for all equally, the sun shines, the rain moistens, the wind blows; for those who sleep there is but one sleep, the stars and the moon shine for all. Whoever owns property and follows this example of equity, sharing his returns and fruits to his brethren and showing himself fair and just with his gratuitous bounties, is an imitator of God.

ON THE LORD'S PRAYER

[Poverty and Perfection]
20.[22] St. Paul here (1 Tm 6:7-10) teaches that we should not only despise riches but also fear them, that in them lies the root of all evils which allure and deceive the human mind with false appearances. So the Lord rebukes the foolish rich man who thinks of his earthly wealth and boasts of his overflowing harvest, saying: "You fool! This very night your life shall be required of you. To whom will all this piled-up wealth of yours go?" The fool was rejoicing in his possessions in the very night when he was about to die; he whose life was slipping away thought of the abundance of his food.

On the contrary, the Lord teaches that he becomes perfect and complete who by selling all his possessions and distributing them to the poor lays up for himself a treasure in heaven. Only those can follow and imitate him in the glory of his passion, he says, who, free and unencumbered, are not

[22]Text: CCL 111A.102.

entangled in the snares of personal possessions and, having dispatched first their possessions to God, are dedicated in the service of the Lord.

[Prayers are Worthy only if Accompanied by
Almsgiving and Fasting]
32. Moreover, let those who pray not come to God with fruitless and destitute prayers. Prayer with no good works is not effective. For, as every tree that does not bear fruit is cut down and thrown into the fire, so words without fruits cannot give God's favor since they are not fruitful in works. And so divine Scripture instructs us with these words: "Prayer is good with fasting and alms." For he who on the day of judgment will reward good works and almsgiving, today also listens favorably to prayers which come with good deeds...

33. Quickly do those prayers ascend to God, which the merits of our works impose upon God... For when one has pity on the poor, one lends to God; and he who gives to the needy, gives to God himself; in a sense he offers to God spiritual sacrifices of pleasing odor.

Lactantius

Lactantius (250-after 317), the pupil of Arnobius, is often called "the Christian Cicero" on account of the elegance of his style. His main work, *The Divine Institutes*, attempts to demonstrate the falsehood of pagan religion and thought, and to set forth the true doctrine and worship. Though his theology is generally neither profound nor original, Lactantius is the first patristic author to develop, in social matters, a relatively complete, organic and coherent doctrine, based upon the dignity of the human person and on man's social consciousness, which he calls humanity or mercy.

The dignity of the human person lies in the fact that he is God's image for whom God creates the whole universe and whom he places at the head of all creatures, because he alone is able to admire his works (cf. *The Divine Institutes*, 7, 4). A consequence of this dignity is the duty of humanity or social living. Whereas for Aristotle men must live together because they are weak and cannot survive by themselves, for Lactantius, man's sociability is something intrinsic to man's nature itself; we must live together because of our humanity. Another consequence of man's dignity is his fundamental equality. Of course such equality does not deny the existence of social classes or material differences. The evil does not lie in the existence of social classes or material inequalities but in the lack of social spirit or consciousness among men. Lastly, Lactantius energetically rejects the form of communism proposed by Plato and defends the right of private ownership.

THE DIVINE INSTITUTES

[Plato's Communism and the Right of Private Ownership] 3.21.[23] ... Under the teaching of Socrates, therefore, Plato could not doubt that the strength of justice consists in equity if, indeed, all are born in an equal condition. "Therefore," he said, "let them have nothing private or personal, but, that all may be equal which the system of justice desires, let them possess all things in common" (*Republic* 416D). This can be accepted as long as money is involved, although, I was able to show in many ways how this itself is impossible and unjust. Still, let us grant that it is feasible, for all will be wise men and despise money. Where, then, did that idea of community lead him? "Marriages also ought to be common," (*Ibid*, 457C) he said, meaning that many men, as though dogs, might possess the same woman. And, I suppose, among them he might win the prize who has overcome with his strength, or, if they are patient, as philosophers, they may wait for their turn as if they were going to a

[23]Text: CSEL 19.248; cf. FOTC 49.223.

whore-house. Marvelous equity in Plato! But where is the virtue of chastity? where conjugal fidelity? If you remove these, all justice disappears...

22. Clearly, therefore, that form of community of wives is nothing but a monstrous mixture of lust and adultery, for the complete uprooting of which virtue is especially necessary. Plato did not find the concord that he sought, because he did not know whence it comes. For justice cannot be found in things external, nor does it lie in the body, but in the heart of man. He who wishes to make men equal, then, ought to suppress, not marriage or possessions, but arrogance, pride, boastfulness, so that those who are powerful and noble may know that they are the equals of even the most beggarly. For when insolence and injustice are removed from wealth, it will make no difference whether some are rich and others are poor, since their spirits will be equal, and nothing but their religion of God can realize this equality...

Private property contained the origin of both vices and virtues, but communal sharing holds nothing but licence for vices. Nothing else can be said of the men who have many wives than that they are lustful and wanton. Likewise, the women who are possessed by many, are, to be sure, not adulteresses, since there is not certain marriage, but surely they are prostitutes and whores.

[Community of Goods in the Golden Age]
5, 5.[24] ... [In the golden age] Who would have to worry about his own protection, as long as justice was present and flourishing, since no one would make any encroachments; or who would contrive to ruin another, since no one would covet anything? Satisfied with little, they preferred to live religiously, as Cicero narrates in a poem (*Aratus*, fragment 21), which is in accord with our religion. "It was not right even to mark off or divide the fields with a measure; they

---

[24]Text: CSEL 19.414; cf. FOTC 49.339.

possess everything in common" (Vergil, *Georgics* 1.126-127). In fact, God has given the land for the common use of all men, so that all may enjoy the goods its produces in common, and not in order that someone with grasping and raging greed may claim everything for himself, while another may be deprived of the things the earth produces for all.

It is necessary that this saying of the poet should not be understood to mean that there was absolutely no private ownership at that time. Rather, we should interpret it as a poetic expression to indicate that the first men were so generous that they did not exclude others from profits gained for themselves, nor did they in solitude brood upon hidden wealth, but they freely allowed the poor to share the fruits of their own work.

[The Two Sources of Justice: Piety and Equity]
5, 14.[25] ... Although justice embraces all the virtues at the same time, there are two, the most important of all, which cannot be removed or separated from it: piety and equity. For faith, temperance, equity, innocence, integrity, and other virtues similar to these can be found in those who do not know justice, either by nature or by education of parents. The old Romans who used to glory in justice, gloried certainly in these virtues which, as I said, are derived from justice and can be separated from it. But piety and equity are its veins, as it were. In these two sources all justice rests: its head and origin is the first, in the second all its strength and reason.

Piety is nothing other than knowledge of God, as Trismegistus has defined it very accurately. If piety is to know God and if this is the highest kind of knowledge that can be cultivated, then he certainly does not know justice who does not hold to the religion of God...

The other part of justice is equity. By equity I do not refer to the virtue of good judgment, which is itself praiseworthy in a just man, but I mean that of deeming oneself equal to

[25]Text: CSEL 19.445; cf. FOTC 49.363.

others, which Cicero calls 'equability' (*Rep.* 1.27.43). God who creates and gives life to all men wants them to be equal. He put us all into the same condition of life; he made us capable of wisdom; he promised immortality to all; he excluded no one from the heavenly benefits. . . With him, no one is master, no one is slave. For if he is the same father to all, we are all free by equal right. No one is poor with God except him who is in need of justice; no one rich, but him who has done the works of mercy with largesse; no one perfect, except him who has fulfilled all the laws. . .

[Foundation and Origin of Social Life]
6, 10.[26] I have spoken about what is owed to God. Now I will tell what ought to be given to man, although what is given to man is given to God, for man is the image of God. The first work of justice is to be discharged with respect to God; the second, with respect to man. The first is called religion; the second is named mercy or humanity. The latter is a proper virtue of those who are just and serve God, because it alone is the foundation of common life. God, who has not given intelligence to the other animals, made them safe from danger and attacks by natural protection, whereas, because he made man uncovered and weak, he gave him intelligence so as to teach him wisdom. Moreover, he gave him the love for piety so that man might kindly regard his fellowman, and love him, and cherish him, and protect him from all dangers. Humanity, therefore, is the greatest bond that unites men together and whoever violates it must be regarded as impious and parricidal. . .

Therefore, men who harm other men, men who spoil, torture, kill, exterminate others against human kindness and every right, should be considered as ferocious beasts. Because of this bond of brotherhood, God teaches us always to do good, never evil. He himself tells us what to do good means: to aid the lowly and the unfortunate, to give food to the needy. Because God is merciful, he wishes that men

[26]Text: CSEL 19.514; cf. FOTC 49.417.

should live in society and that we should see in each human being our own nature. We do not deserve to be set free in dangers if we do not help others; we do not deserve aid if we refuse it to others.

[Humanity and Compassion]

6, 11.[27] We must always practice humanity if we want to be truly men and not only in name. What is practicing the virtue of humanity if not to love a man because he is a man, because he has the same nature as mine? Discord, then, and hatred are not in accord with the nature of man. Hence, Cicero's saying is so true: "A man who follows his nature is not able to harm another man" (*On Duties*, 3.5.25). If to harm a man is against nature then to do good to him is in accord with human nature. Who does not do this deprives himself of the name of man, since it is the duty of humaneness to come to the aid of man in need and danger.

[Perfect Justice and the Works of Mercy]

6, 12.[28] This is that perfect justice of which the philosophers speak which sustains the human society, this is the greatest and most authentic fruit of riches: not to use wealth for one's own personal enjoyment but for the benefit of many; not for one's own present profit, but for justice, which alone endures forever. It is necessary, therefore, to hold that we should do charity without looking for material profit. On the contrary we should expect reward from God alone, since if we look for it from men, then our action would not be an exercise of the virtue of humanity, but a transaction for profit, and it cannot be meritorious because it is not done for another but for oneself.

This does not mean, however, that the one who does good to another without expecting anything from him, will receive no benefit, since he will be rewarded by God. God himself teaches us that, if ever we prepare a banquet, we

[27]Text: CSEL 19.519; cf. FOTC 49.420.
[28]Text: CSEL 19.524; cf. FOTC 49.425.

should invite to the dinner those who cannot invite and repay us in return, so that every act of our life may be inspired by mercy. However, no one should think that he is forbidden to entertain his friends or to show charity to his relatives; rather he should know which acts are true works of justice. Thus it is fitting for us to consort with our relatives and associates, provided that we distinguish those acts that pertain to our relationships with our associates from those that concern God's command and justice...

The redemption of captives is a great and outstanding work of justice... It is a proper work for the just, then, to care for the poor and to redeem captives, since those who do this are called serious and great even among the unjust...

It is no less great a work of justice to protect destitute children and widows and to defend those needing help which the divine law so prescribes to all, since all the best judges think it pertains to their office to favor them with natural humaneness and to strive to be of help to them...

To take up also the work of caring for and cherishing the sick who have no one to assist them is a most noble work of humaneness. Whoever does this brings a living offering to God, and what he has given another in time, he will receive from God in eternity.

The last and greatest work of piety is the burial of strangers and the poor, a work which even those teachers of virtues and justice did not mention. They, measuring all duties by utility, were not able to see that... We, however, do not say what a wise man ought to bear, but what he ought to do. And so we do not ask whether the whole matter of burying is useful or not; but even if it is useless, as they think, still it must be done, even for this reason alone, namely, among men it seems good and humane to do it. The intention is questioned and the proposition is weighed. We will not, therefore, allow the image and workmanship of God to lie as prey for beasts and birds, but we shall return it to the earth, from where it sprang...

6, 13.[29] ... The first step of justice is to refrain from doing evil; the second, from speaking evil; and the third, from thinking evil. Whoever has ascended the first step is just in a sufficient or moderate degree; whoever makes the second is already perfectly virtuous, since he fails in neither deeds nor words; but whoever reaches the third seems, in truth, to have attained a likeness to God. For it is almost beyond human nature not even to admit into one's thoughts what is evil in act or wicked in speech. And so even just men who are able to refrain themselves from every unjust work are sometimes overcome by this very frailty, so that they speak evil in anger, or in the sight of desirable things covet them in silent thoughts.

[Lending without Taking Interest]
6, 18.[30] ... If someone lends money, he should not exact interest, so that he may not lose the merit of assisting a person in need and may not take something not his own. He should be content with receiving back what is his and even should be willing to lose some of it in order to do good. For him to receive back more than what he has given is unjust. Whoever does this is getting rich on the expense of the want of another. The just man, on the contrary, will never pass over a chance of doing a work of mercy and will not let himself be tarnished by a complaint of this sort. He will part with his money in such a way that without suffering any loss he will have what he lends counted as a good work...

[Man's Intelligence and His Dominion over the Universe]
7, 4.[31] ... To the other animals who lack intelligence God gave cover and natural protection. To man, however, in compensation for all these gifts, God gave reason, which is a much more noble gift. So he made man bare and unarmed, so that his intelligence may serve him as arms and clothing. This protection and covering he placed not on the outside,

[29]Text: CSEL 19.533; cf. FOTC 49.431.
[30]Text: CSEL 19.547; cf. FOTC 49.444.
[31]Text: CSEL 19.595; cf. FOTC 49.482.

but within; not in his body, but in his heart. Unless there were evils from which he must be protected and which he must distinguish from the good and the useful, wisdom would not be necessary for him...

Great and admirable are the reason and the power of man for whom God created the universe and all things contained therein and on whom he conferred so much honor that he placed him in charge of all, because he alone could admire his works... The Most High God has constituted all things, then, not on account of himself, since he lacks nothing, but on account of man who might use them fitly.

3

THE GOLDEN AGE OF GREEK PATRISTIC LITERATURE

The fourth and fifth centuries are often described as the golden age of patristic literature. With the conversion of Constantine, Christianity became a tolerated, and then preferred religion, and finally under Theodosius I the religion of the state. The Christian writers then were freed to devote their talents not simply to defend the Church against pagan attacks but also to develop a theological science. Critical but wholesale assimilation of secular learning and education and unrestricted appropriation of traditional literary forms took place. Most of the Fathers combined excellent theological training with Hellenistic culture, with brilliant eloquence and a mastery of style learnt in the ancient schools and academies.

The following two chapters will deal with the Greek Fathers. The present chapter will present the political writings concerning the relations between Church and State and the social writings of the Cappadocian Fathers. The scope and importance of John Chrysostom's social teaching require a separate treatment in chapter four.

Part One: Church and State

Eusebius of Caesarea

Eusebius (c. 260-c. 340), Bishop of Caesarea, is often called 'The Father of Church History.' A man of immense erudition, but of questionable orthodoxy, especially in the Arian controversy, Eusebius was an indefatigable worker and displayed in his writings an amazing breadth of learning and an astonishing variety of interests: Scripture, pagan and Christian history, ancient literature, philosophy, geography, technical chronology, exegesis, philology and paleography. But undoubtedly his chief claim to fame lies in his historical writings, in particular the *Ecclesiastical History*, the *Life of Constantine*, and the *Oration in Praise of Constantine*.

Eusebius was the first Father to discuss at length the relations between Church and State. His theory on the relationship between these two societies was greatly influenced by his unbounded admiration for Constantine. He advanced the view that as the Empire was becoming Christian the two societies were merging into a single Christian society with the emperor as its head. He thus laid the foundations for what has been called caesaropapism in practice, if not in theory. Despite the opposition of Athanasius and other Eastern Fathers to Eusebius's concept of the merging of the two societies, and above all, to the supremacy of the emperor in the field of religion, this concept received constant imperial support and elaboration until it culminated under Justinian the Great, who regarded himself as 'priest-emperor.'

THE LIFE OF CONSTANTINE

[Constantine as Bishop]

4, 24.[1] Hence it was not without reason that once, on the occasion of his entertaining a group of bishops, he let fall the expression, "that he himself too was a bishop," addressing them in my hearing in the following words: "You are bishops whose jurisdiction is within the Church; I also am a bishop, ordained by God to oversee those outside the Church." And indeed his measures corresponded with his words, for he watched over all his subjects with an episcopal care, and exhorted them as far as in him lay to follow a godly life.

ORATION ON THE TRICENNALIA OF CONSTANTINE

[The Word of God and the Christian Emperor]

2, 1-5.[2] The only begotten Word of God reigns, from ages which had no beginning, to infinite and endless ages, the partner of his Father's kingdom. And our emperor, ever beloved by him, who receives his imperial authority from above, and is strong in the power of his sacred title, has controlled the empire of the world for a long period of years. Again, that Preserver of the universe orders the whole heaven and earth, and the celestial kingdom, in accord with his Father's will. In the same way our emperor whom he loves, by bringing those whom he rules on earth to the only begotten and saving Word, renders them fit subjects for his kingdom. And as he who is the common Savior of mankind, by his invisible and divine power as a good shepherd, drives far away from his flock, like ferocious beasts, those apostate spirits which once flew through the air above this earth and fastened on the souls of men, so this friend of his, graced by his heavenly favor with victory over all his enemies, subdues and chastens the open adversaries of the truth in accordance with the usages of war.

[1]Text: GCS Eusebius 1.128.
[2]Text: PG 20.1325.

He who is the pre-existent Word, the Savior of all things, imparts to his followers the seeds of true wisdom and salvation, making them at the same time truly wise, and assisting them to understand the kingdom of their Father. Our emperor, his friend, acting as interpreter to the Word of God, aims at recalling the whole human race to the knowledge of God, proclaiming clearly in the ears of all, and declaring with powerful voice the laws of truth and godliness to all who dwell on the earth. Once more, the universal Savior opens the heavenly gates of his Father's kingdom to those who are journeying towards it from this world. Our emperor, imitating his divine example, having purged his earthly dominion from every stain of impious error, invites each holy and pious worshipper into his imperial mansions, earnestly desiring to save with all its crew that mighty vessel of which he is the appointed pilot.

[The Excellence of Monarchy]
3, 5-7.[3] Finally, invested as he is with a semblance of heavenly sovereignty, he directs his gaze upwards, and organizes his earthly government according to the pattern of that divine original, feeling strength in its conformity to the monarchy of God. And this conformity is granted by the universal Sovereign to man alone of the creatures of this earth: for he only is the author of sovereign power, who decrees that all should be subject to the rule of one. And surely monarchy far transcends every other constitution or form of government, for that democratic equality of power, which is its opposite, may rather be described as anarchy and disorder. Hence there is one God, and not two, or three, or more; for to assert a plurality of gods is plainly to deny the being of God at all. There is one King; and his Word and royal Law are one: a Law not expressed in syllables and words, not written or engraved on tablets, and therefore subject to the ravages of time, but the living and self-subsisting Word, who himself is God, and who administers

[3]Text: PG 20.1329.

his Father's kingdom on behalf of all who are under him and subject to his power.

[The Virtues of the Christian Emperor]
5, 1-4.[4] And in this hope (i.e. of the heavenly kingdom) our divinely-favored emperor partakes even in this present life, gifted as he is by God with native virtues, and having received into his soul the outflowings of his favor. His reason he derives from the universal Reason (i.e. the Word): he is wise by communion with wisdom; good by participation in the good; just by sharing in justice; prudent by fellowship with prudence; and courageous by sharing in the heavenly power. And truly may he deserve the title of emperor, who has formed his soul to royal virtues, according to the standard of that heavenly kingdom...

Let our emperor, then, on the testimony of truth itself, be declared alone worthy of the title; who is dear to the Supreme Sovereign himself; who alone is free, nay, who is truly Lord: above the thirst for wealth, superior to sexual desire; victorious even over natural pleasures, controlling, not controlled by, anger and passion. He is indeed an emperor, and bears a title corresponding to his deeds; a victor in truth, who has gained the victory over those passions which overmaster the rest of men: whose character is formed after the divine model of the Supreme Sovereign, and whose mind reflects, as in a mirror, the radiance of his virtues.

Hence our emperor is perfect in prudence, in goodness, in justice, in courage, in piety, in devotion to God. He alone is truly a philosopher since he knows himself, and is fully aware that an abundance of blessings is showered on him from a source quite external to himself, even from heaven itself. Declaring the august title of supreme authority by the splendor of his vesture, he alone worthily wears that imperial purple which so well becomes him.

[4]Text: PG 20.1333.

THE ORATION IN PRAISE OF
THE EMPEROR CONSTANTINE

[One Empire, One Church, One Authority]
16.[5] ... Of old the nations of the earth, the entire human race, were variously distributed into provincial, national, and local governments, subject to kingdoms and principalities of many kinds. The consequences of this variety were war and strife, depopulation and captivity... The origin of these may justly be ascribed to the delusion of polytheistic error. But when that instrument of our redemption, the thrice holy body of Christ was raised...the force of these evil spirits was at once destroyed. The manifold forms of government, the tyrannies and republics, the siege of cities, and devastation of countries caused thereby, were now no more, and one God was proclaimed to all mankind. At the same time one universal power, the Roman empire, arose and flourished, while the enduring and implacable hatred of nation against nation was not removed... Our Savior's mighty power destroyed at once the many governments and the many gods of the demons and proclaimed to all men, both Greek and barbarian, to the extremities of the earth, the sole sovereignty of God himself. Meantime the Roman empire, the cause of multiplied governments being thus removed, achieved an easy conquest of those which yet remained; its object being to unite all nations in one symphonic whole; an object in great measure already secured, and destined to be still more perfectly attained, even to the final conquest of the ends of the habitable world... The falsehood of demon superstition was convicted; the inveterate strife and mutual hatred of the nations was removed; at the same time One God, and the knowledge of that God were proclaimed to all: one universal empire prevailed. The whole human race, subdued by the controlling power of peace and concord, received one another as brethren, and responded to the feelings of their kindred nature. Hence, as children of one God and Father, and owning true religion as

[5]Text: PG 20.1421.

their common mother, they saluted and welcomed each other with words of peace. Thus the whole world appeared like one well-ordered and united family; each one might journey unhindered as far as and wherever he pleased; men might securely travel from West to East, and from East to West, as to their own native country. In short the ancient oracle and predictions of the prophets were fulfilled, "And they shall beat their swords into plough-shares, and their spears into sickles; and nation shall not take up sword against nation, neither shall they learn war any more."

Hosius of Cordova

Hosius (256-357), Bishop of Cordova, has earned the name of *The Athanasius of the West*, since all his life, by word and deed, he was one of the chief defenders of the Council of Nicaea in the West. In 354 or 355, when almost a hundred years old, he wrote a temperate but courageous letter to Constantius to protest against the latter's interference in the affairs of the Church, defending Arianism and condemning Athanasius.

THE HISTORY OF THE ARIANS (by Athanasius)

[Separation of the Two Powers]
44.[6] ... Cease, I implore you, from these activities. Remember that you are but mortal; and fear the day of judgment and keep yourself pure with that day in view. Do not interfere in matters ecclesiastical, nor give us orders on such questions, but learn about them from us. For into your hands God has put the kingdom; the affairs of his Church he has committed to us. If any man stole the empire from you, he would be resisting the ordinance of God; in the same way you on your part should be afraid lest, in taking upon yourself the government of the Church, you incur the guilt of a grave offence. "Render unto Caesar the things that are

---

[6]Text: PG 25.745.

Caesar's and unto God the things that are God's." We are not permitted to exercise an earthly rule; and you, Sire, you are not authorized to burn incense..."

Part Two: The Cappadocian Fathers

Basil the Great

One of the three Cappadocians, Basil (330-379) earned the title of 'the Great' on account of his outstanding qualifications as an ecclesiastical statesman and organizer, as a great exponent of Christian doctrine, as the Father of oriental monasticism, as reformer of liturgy, and as an effective social activist.

Basil's social teaching is particularly interesting since it deals directly with the social character of man and the nature of private property and riches. Basil repeats in many places that man is a political and social animal, not a solitary and ferocious beast, incapable of satisfying his needs by himself. The ground of man's sociability for Basil is his nature itself, not simply because man cannot survive by himself but because there is innate in him an inclination to live together with and love his fellowmen. In his *Long Rules*, to the question whether it is better for the monks to live alone in isolation or in community, he answers that the cenobitic life is to be preferred to the hermitic life. The reasons are: in solitary life what is at hand to us becomes useless and what is lacking cannot be provided; solitary life leads to egoism and self-seeking; in solitary life there is no opportunity for mutual correction;

and finally in common life there are better opportunities for sharing and doing good works.

More than any other Father so far, Basil emphasises the social purpose of riches, the limitations and the social function of the right of private ownership, the duty of sharing one's possessions. He also sharply criticises the rich for their lack of social consciousness, condemns lending with interest, and insists on sharing as an obligation of social justice. For him, riches are essentially to be communicated: "As a great river flows by a thousand channels through fertile country, so let your wealth run through many conduits to the homes of the poor. Wells that are drawn from flow the better; left unused, they go foul. So money kept standing still is worthless; moving and changing hands, it helps the community and brings increase." (Homily on "I will pull down my barns," 5). As to the right of private ownership, Basil considers it not as something absolute and exclusive but as stewardship of one's material goods for the benefit of all: "Remember yourself—who you are, what you are steward of, from whom you had it, why you have been favored above most. You have been made the minister of a gracious God, steward for your fellow-servants" (*Ibid*, 2).

THE HEXAMERON

[The Greed of the Rich]
Homily 7, 3.[7] The food of fish differs according to their species. Some feed on mud; others eat seaweed; others content themselves with the plants that grow in water. But the greater part devour each other, and the smaller are food for the larger. And if by chance a fish that has eaten another smaller than itself is itself eaten by another larger, both are swallowed up in the belly of the last. And do we men act otherwise when we oppress our inferiors? What difference is

[7]Text: SC 26.402; cf.FOTC 46.109.

there between the last fish and the man who, urged by devouring greed, swallows the weak into the belly of his insatiable avarice? One person took possession of what belongs to the poor, you caught him and made him a part of your wealth. You have shown yourself more unjust than the unjust, and more miserly than the miser. Take care that you do not end up like the fish, by hook, by snare, or by net. Surely we too, when we have done the deeds of the wicked, shall not escape punishment at the last.

HOMILIES ON THE PSALMS

[Sharing Our Possessions with Others]
Psalm 14, Homily 1, 6.[8] "Give to the man who begs from you; do not turn your back on the man who borrows from you" (Mt 5:42). This saying of our Lord invites us to adopt the spirit of sharing, mutual love, and what is proper to our nature. Man, indeed, is a political and social animal. Now, in social relations and in common life, a certain disposition to share one's goods is necessary in order to assist the needy. "Give to those who beg from you." Our Lord asks that for charity's sake we should be ready to give to those who ask; moreover, for the sake of reason, we should discern the needs of each one who asks.

From the Acts of the Apostles we learn how this was carried out by those who accomplish wisely the purposes of religion. "Nor was there anyone needy among them, for all who owned property or houses sold them and donated the proceeds; they used to lay them at the feet of the Apostles to be distributed to everyone according to his need" (Acts 4:34-35). There are, then, many who, going beyond the use of what is necessary, turn poverty into an occasion for profit and a source for disgraceful pleasures; hence those who have charge of the poor must form a common treasury and with wise administration, distribute it to each one according to his needs.

[8]Text: PG 29.261.

HOMILY AGAINST LENDING WITH INTEREST
(ON PSALM XV)

[The Inhumanity and Injustice of Taking Interest]
1.[9] ... The prophet, describing the perfect man who has suffered through life, recounted, among the many exploits worthy of a man, the fact that he had never lent his money for interest. In many passages of the Scripture, lending with interest is condemned as sinful. Thus Ezekiel places taking interest among the major evils (Ez 22:12) and the Law clearly forbids it: "You shall not demand interest from your brother and your neighbor" (Dt 23:20). Elsewhere it is said: "Deceit upon deceit, usury upon usury" (Jer 9:5). And of the city that prospers on a multitude of sins, it is said in the psalm: "Usury and fraud never depart from its streets" (Ps 55:12). And the prophet, pointing out something as the mark or seal of human perfection, says: "He never lent his money for interest." Indeed, it is extremely inhuman that one has to beg for the most basic necessities to support his life while another is not satisfied with the capital he has, but excogitates ways of increasing his opulence at the expense of the poor in distress.

[Sharing and Lending without Interest]
5. Rich men, listen to the advice that, in view of your inhumanity, we give to the poor: Bear any suffering rather than the calamities that will come from usury. But if you obey the Lord, you will not need such an advice. Now, what does the Lord advise? "Lend to those from whom there is no hope of repayment" (Lk 6:34). But, you say, how can it be called "lending" if there is no hope of repayment? Try to understand the meaning of the Lord's saying and you will admire the goodness of that law. When you give to the poor for the love of God, the same thing is both gift and loan. Gift, first, because there is no hope of receiving anything in return; loan, secondly, because the Lord will reward you abundantly through the poor and because for such a trifle

[9]Text: PG 29.265.

that you give to them, you will receive huge sums in return.

Thus "whoever gives alms to the poor lends to God" (Prov 19:17). Would you not hold the Lord of the universe as your debtor who is obliged to repay? Would you accept the warranty of a rich man in the city who receives the payment of others and not that of God who will pay abundantly through the poor? Give your surplus money, burden it not with interest, and both you and your debtor will fare well. You will keep your money secure; the other who receives it, will derive benefit from its use. But if you look for interest, be satisfied with those given by the Lord. He will pay, through the poor, the due interest. From the one who is the true lover of men, it is good that you expect payment worthy of his love.

If you take from the poor, you commit the worst crime of inhumanity: you derive profit from miseries, you gain money from tears, you oppress the needy, you starve the hungry. You have no mercy whatever, you do not realize the bond you have with those who suffer. And yet you call acts of humanity the profits you receive. "Woe to those who call evil good, and good evil, who change darkness into light, and light into darkness, and change bitter into sweet, and sweet into bitter" (Is 5:20) and those who give the name of philanthropy to the hatred of man.

HOMILY ON "I WILL PULL DOWN MY BARNS"

[Temptation of the Rich through Prosperity]

1.[10] There are two kinds of temptations. There are afflictions which try the hearts of men like gold in the furnace, testing their metal by patience. But sometimes—and this is true of many—the very prosperities of life become a temptation. When things go ill, it is hard not to be depressed; when they go too well, it is not less hard not to be puffed up with insolent pride. The first kind of temptation we see in Job, that great and invincible champion; the devil's violence bore

[10]Text: PG 31.261.

down on him like a torrent, but he met it all with unshaken heart and firm purpose; the fiercer and closer his adversary's grip, the greater his triumph proved over his temptations.

Then there is temptation through prosperity, and among examples here is the rich man of our text. He had wealth already; he hoped for more. God in his mercy did not doom him outright for his thanklessness; rather he added riches to riches, to make the man tire perhaps of plenty and to move his soul to generosity and the common sharing. The Gospel says: "The land of a certain rich man brought forth crops in plenty, and he thought within himself: What can I do? I will pull down my barns and build greater ones." Why was the land left to bring forth in plenty if the man was to put it to no good use? So that God's forbearance should be the more evident. Even to men such as this his goodness is imparted; "he sends his rain on the just and on the unjust, and makes his sun to rise on the evil and on the good" (Mt 5:45). But this goodness of God brings greater punishment on the wicked. He sent his showers on the soil, though covetous hands tilled it; he gave his sun to warm the seed and multiply crops with fruitfulness. From God, then, there came these things—a fit soil, temperate weather, abundant seed, oxen to work with, and all that farming thrives on. And on the man's side what was there? Surliness, uncharitableness, selfishness; these were his answer to his benefactor. He never thought that others were men as much as he; he held it no duty of his to distribute his surplus to those in want; he did not heed the commandment: "Refrain not from doing good to the needy" (Prov 3:27) or "Let not alms and faithfulness forsake thee" (Prov 3:3); or "Break thy bread for the hungry" (Is 58:7).

[Greed and Worries of the Avarious Rich Man]

And all the prophets and all the teachers cried, and they were not heard; his barns groaned with the press of stored harvests, but the miser's heart was not satisfied. He added continually new to old, swelled his plenty with yearly increase, and came at length to the hopeless pass where greed forbade him to let the old be brought out, yet he had no room to store the new. Thus his schemes are vain, his cares desperate. "What can I do?" Poor creature, what distress he is in—miserable in his prosperity, pitiable for his present wealth, more pitiable for the looked-for increase! The land that should bring him revenue bears lamentations instead; in place of rich harvest, it heaps up troubles and cares and utter hopelessness. He complains as the poor do. Will not the destitute, the beggar, utter the selfsame words? "What can I do? Where can I find food and clothing?" These are the rich man's words too. He is broken-spirited, eaten away with care. What heartens others distresses the miser. It does not cheer him to have his granaries filled within; his heart is wrung by the overflow of wealth; he fears it may reach the folk outside and help to relieve the destitute.

[The Rich Man is a Steward of God's Goods]
2. Surely what ails his soul is much what ails the glutton, who would burst with cramming rather than give the poor any of his leftovers. Man, remember who gives you these goods. And remember yourself—who you are, what you are steward of, from whom you had it, why you have been favored above most. You have been made the minister of a gracious God, steward for your fellow-servants. Do not suppose that all these things were provided for your belly. The wealth you handle belongs to others; think of it accordingly. Not for long will it delight you; soon it will slip from you and be gone, and you will be asked to give strict account of it. Yet you keep it all locked away behind doors and sealed up; and then the thought of it keeps you awake at nights; you take counsel about it inwardly, and your counsellor is yourself—a fool. "What can I do?" How easy it would have been to say: "I will fill the souls of the hungry; I will open my barns; I will invite all the poor. I will be like Joseph in his charitable summons; I will speak generous words—"All you who have need of loaves, come to me; each shall have his fill from God's bounty, which flows for all." But that is not your way; no; you grudge men satisfaction;

you contrive evil schemes within your soul; you are not concerned how to distribute to each according to his needs but how to get everything yourself and keep everyone from using it.

Thus the rich man discoursed on food with his soul, and beside him were those who required his soul. Thus he pictured his enjoyment for many a year to come; and that same night he was snatched away. He was permitted to weigh the whole matter, permitted to make his resolve express, that he might receive a sentence that fitted his resolve.

[The Social Function of Riches]
3. My hearer, see that it goes not so with you. These things have been written that we may not act in such ways ourselves. Imitate the earth; bring forth fruit as it does; shall your human status be inferior to a lifeless thing? The earth brings forth fruits not for its own pleasure but for your service; you can reap for yourself the fruit of all generosity because the rewards of good works return to those who offer them. If you give to the hungry, the gift becomes your own and comes back to you with increase. As the wheat falling on the ground turns to gain for the man who lets it fall, so the grain bestowed on the hungry brings you profit a hundredfold hereafter. Make the end of husbandry the beginning of heavenly sowing. "Sow for yourselves unto justice," the Scripture says (Hos 10:12). Why then be anxious, why torture yourself, why strive to shut in your riches with bricks and mortar? "A good name is better than great riches" (Prov 22:1). And if you admire riches for the honor they bring, consider which is more glorious—to be called the father of children innumerable, or to have gold pieces innumerable in your purse. Your money you must leave behind you, whether you will or not, but the glory of good works you will bear with you to the Master, when a whole people, standing about you before their judge and yours, call you their foster-father and benefactor and all the names won by charity...

[The Tragedy of a Poor Man Who Has to Sell His Son]
4. The bright gleam of gold delights you; you are heedless of all the lamentation of the needy that rises loud in your wake. How can I bring home to you what the poor man's sufferings are? He casts his eyes round the house, sees that he has no gold and never will have; his clothes and furniture are what the poor's always are—worth a few pence all together. What then? What is left? He looks at his sons, and thinks he may stave off death by selling them in the market-place. Watch the battle between starvation and fatherhood. The one threatens him with the most pitiful of deaths, the other holds him back and bids him die with his children; again and again he starts forward, again and again he checks himself; but the stress of pitiless want is on him, and succumbs at last. And what are his thoughts! 'Which shall I sell first? Which will please the corn-merchant best? Shall I take the eldest? He has rights I dare not violate. The youngest then? I pity his youth, still innocent of misery. This one is his parents' living image; this other is ripe for schooling. What hopelessness! What am I to do? Can I turn against any of them? Can I become a brute beast? Can I forget nature? If I cling to them all, I shall see them all wasting away with hunger. If I sacrifice one, with what face can I look at the others? They will suspect me of treachery at once. How can I stay in a house which I myself have orphaned? How can I sit down to my table when these are the means of filling it?'

The poor man goes off in tears to sell his darling son; but you—you are cold to his misery, you feel no touch of nature. He, poor wretch, is starving; and you keep him in suspense, you beat about the bush, drawing out his agony. To keep alive, he offers his own flesh and blood; and you, whose very hand should be palsied at receiving the price of such wretchedness, you haggle about the bargain, you try to give less than you get, and in every way you can make the poor creature's burden worse. Tears do not move you, groans do not soften your heart, you are unrelenting and pitiless. Everything is gold to your eyes and fancy; gold is your dream at night and your waking care. As a raving madman does not see things themselves but imagines things in his diseased fancy, so your greed-possessed soul sees gold and silver everywhere. Sight of gold is dearer to you than sight of the sun. Your prayer is that everything may be changed to gold, and your schemes are set on bringing it about...

[The Rich Man Who Does Not Share His Possessions with Others Commits Injustice]
7. "I am wronging no one," you say, "I hold fast to my own, that is all." Your own! You gave it you to bring into life with you? You are like a man who takes a seat in a theatre and then keeps out newcomers, claiming as his own what is there for the use of everyone. Such are the rich; they seize what belongs to all and claim the right of possession to monopolise it; if everyone took for himself enough to meet his own wants and gave up the rest to those who needed it, there would be no rich and no poor. Did you not come naked out of the womb, and will you not go back naked to earth again? Whence came the riches you have now? If you say from nowhere, you deny God, you ignore the Creator, you are ungrateful to the Giver. But if you acknowledge they came from God, tell us the reason for your receiving them. Is God unjust when he distributes the necessaries of life unequally? Why are you rich and another poor? Surely it is that you may win the reward of charitableness and faithful steward-ship, and he the noble prizes of patience? And yet you store up everything in the pockets of insatiable covetousness and think you wrong no one when you are defrauding so many. Who is the covetous man? One for whom plenty is not enough! Who is the defrauder? One who takes away what belongs to everyone. And are not you covetous, are not you a defrauder, when you keep for private use what you were given for distribution? When someone strips a man of his clothes we call him a thief. And one who might clothe the naked and does not—should not he be given the same name? The bread in your board belongs to the hungry: the cloak in your wardrobe belongs to the naked, the shoes you let rot belong to the barefoot; the money in your vaults belongs to the destitute. All you might help and do not—to all these you are doing wrong.

HOMILY DELIVERED IN TIMES OF
FAMINE AND DROUGHT

[Social Injustices Are the Causes of the Disasters
God Sent Us]
2.[11] . . . We know that the Lord sends us all these plagues
because we have separated ourselves from him and because
we have been negligent in his service, not in order to exterminate us but to correct us. The Lord acts like our good
parents, concerned about the welfare of their children; they
become angry against their children and punish them, not
because they desire to do them harm, but because they want
to correct their youthful carelessness and to draw them
away from their sinful ways and back to the path of
virtue...

What then, is the cause of such disorder and confusion?
What is the reason for the new things, in these days? Let us
investigate this, since we are endowed with reason; let us
reason, since we are rational beings. Is it because there is no
one to govern the universe? Is it because God, the best of
artists, has neglected his administration? Is it because he has
lost all power and authority?...

No, the reason why we are not governed in the usual way
is clear and self-evident: We receive, but give to nobody; we
praise charity, but do not practise it to the needy. Slaves we
were, and we have been made free, and yet we do not have
sympathy for those who, like ourselves, are slaves of the
Lord. When we are hungry, we eat, and yet we close our eyes
to those who are needy. We have God as our unfailing
provider and dispenser, and yet we have shown ourselves
niggardly and close-fisted towards the poor. Our ewes have
produced numerous sucklings, and yet the poor are more
numerous than our ewes. Our barns and granaries are too
tight for what we store in them, and yet we ourselves do not
have compassion for those who suffer from tight circumstances. For all these things we are threatened with a just

---

[11]Text: PG 31.308.

sentence. If God does not open his hands for us, it is because we have cast out brotherly love...

[Lack of Sharing is Comparable to Murder]
7. The pain of starvation, from which the hungry die, is a horrible suffering. Of all human calamities, famine is the principal one, and the most miserable of deaths is, no doubt that by starvation. In other kinds of death, either the sword puts a quick end to life, or the roaring fire burns out the sap of life in some instances, or the teeth of beasts, mangling the vital limbs, would not prolong the tortureT. Hunger, however, is a slow torture which prolongs the pain; it is an infirmity well established and hidden in its place, a death always present and never coming to an end. It dries up the natural liquids, diminishes the body heat, contracts the size, and little by little drains off the strength. The flesh clings to the bones like a cobweb. The skin has no color... The belly is hollow, contracted, formless, without weight, without the natural stretching of the viscera, joined to the bones of the back. Now, what punishment should not be inflicted upon the one who passes by such a body? What cruelty can surpass that? How can we not count him among the fiercest of fierce beasts and consider him as a sacrilegious person and a murderer? The person who can cure such an infirmity and because of avarice refuses his medicine, can with reason be condemned as a murderer.

THE LONG RULES

[Man is a Social Animal]
Answer to the Third Question:[12] ... Who does not know that man is a political and social animal, neither savage nor a lover of loneliness? Nothing, indeed, is so comparable with our nature as living in society and in dependence upon one another and as loving our own kind. Now, our Lord himself gave us the seeds of these qualities and expected

[12]Text: PG 31.917.

them to yield fruits in due time, for he said: "A new commandment I give to you: that you love one another (Jn 13:34).

[The Advantages of Common Life Over Solitary Life]
Answer to the Seventh Question: I am of the opinion that life in a community of a number of people in the same place is more advantageous in several respects. My reasons are, first, that none of us is self-sufficient as regards bodily necessities but need one another to provide them. The foot, to cite an example, possesses one kind of power and lacks another, and without the cooperation of the other members of the body it finds itself incapable of carrying on its activities independently for any length of time, nor does it have any means to supply what is lacking. Similarly, in the solitary life, what is at hand becomes useless to us and what is wanting cannot be provided, since God the Creator decreed that we should require the help of one another...

Again, apart from this consideration, the doctrine of charity of Christ does not permit one to be concerned solely with one's own private interest. "Charity," says the Apostle, "seeks not her own" (1 Cor 13:5). But a life passed in solitude is concerned only with the private fulfillment of individual needs... Furthermore, a person living in solitary retirement will not readily discern his own defects, since he has no one to admonish and correct him with mildness and compassion. In fact, admonition even from an enemy often produces in a prudent man a desire for amendment...

Moreover, the majority of the commandments are easily observed by several persons living together, but not so in the case of one living alone. For, while he is obeying one commandment, he is prevented from obeying another. For example, when he is visiting the sick, he cannot show hospitality to the stranger and, in giving and sharing the necessities, especially when these ministrations are prolonged, he is prevented from giving zealous attention to other tasks. As a result, the greatest commandment and the one especially conducive to salvation is not observed, since the hungry are not fed nor the naked clothed.

THE SHORT RULES

[Private Property and Its Use]

Question 92:[13] How can you be certain that the Lord commands us to sell all our possessions? For what reason should we do so? Is it because the goods are in themselves condemnable or is it because they cause distractions to the soul?

Answer: To this question it may be answered first that if the goods were bad in themselves, then they could have in no way been created by God. "Everything God created is good; nothing is to be rejected" (1 Tm 4:4). Secondly, the Lord's command does not teach that we have to reject and flee the goods as though they are bad, but that we should administer them. And the one who is condemned is condemned not because he possesses things, but because he makes a bad use of what he possesses. Thus a detached attitude towards and a respect for the earthly goods and a wise administration of them according to the command of the Lord are of great help in obtaining many things. First, to purify us of our sins...and secondly, to gain the kingdom of heaven and possess an inexhaustible treasure...

LETTER 97:[14] TO THE SENATE OF TYANA

[The Necessity of Fellowship]

... I know perfectly well that I stand more in need of the help of each of the brethren than one hand does of the other. Indeed, from our bodily constitution, the Lord has taught us the necessity of fellowship. When I look to these my limbs and see that no one of them is self-sufficient, how can I reckon myself competent to discharge the duties of life? One foot could not walk securely without the support of the other; one eyes could not see well, were it not for the alliance of the other and for its being able to look at objects in conjunction with it. Hearing is more exact when sound is

---

[13]Text: PG 31.1145.
[14]Text: PG 32.493.

received through both channels, and the grasp is made firmer by the fellowship of the fingers. In a word, of all that is done by nature and by the will, I see nothing done without the concord of fellow forces. Even prayer, when it is not a united one, loses its natural strength and the Lord has told us that he will be in the midst where two or three call on him in concord...

Gregory of Nazianzus

A close friend of Basil, Gregory of Nazianzus (c. 330-390), was called "the Christian Demosthenes" because of the power of his eloquence. Ordained a priest by his father, and consecrated a bishop of Sasima by Basil, Gregory later became the bishop of Constantinople. Not a prolific writer, Gregory left us only a collection of orations, poems, and letters. In his prose as well as in his verse, he always remains the greatest Christian rhetorician of the fourth century.

Gregory's work most relevant to our topic is his fourteenth discourse "On the Love for the Poor" which he probably delivered at Caesarea in 373. Like Basil, Gregory considers private ownership as administration, insists on the strict obligation of sharing, and criticises the rich for their lack of social conscience. For Gregory, compassion or humanity is a duty derived from the fact that we share a common human nature.

ON THE LOVE FOR THE POOR (XIV)

[The Principal Part of Charity is Love for the Poor]
5.[15] ... Now, if following Paul and Christ himself, we have to maintain that charity is the first and greatest of all commandments, the sum of all the laws and prophets (Mt

[15]Text: PG 35.864.

22:26), I suggest that the main part of charity is the love for the poor and mercy and compassion for our fellow brethren. There is no better sacrifice that can be offered to God than mercy, as kindness and truth go before him (Ps 89:15) and as he himself asks that mercy be offered rather than condemnation. And God, who measures justly and puts mercy in the balance, will with kindness repay kindness.

[Compassion Towards All the Afflicted,
Including the Lepers]
6. We must, then, open the doors to all the poor and all those who are victims of disasters, whatever the causes may be, since we have been told to rejoice with those who rejoice and to weep with those who weep (Rom 12:12). And since we are human beings, we must pay our debt of goodness to our fellow human beings, whatever the cause of their plight: orphanhood, exile, cruelty of the master, rashness of those who govern, inhumanity of tax-collectors, brutality of blood-thirsty bandits, greediness of thieves, confiscation or shipwreck. All are equally miserable and look up to our hands in the same way as we look up to those of God whenever we stand in need of something.

Among them those who suffer unmerited calamities are more miserable than those who are already accustomed to misfortunes. Nevertheless we should have a special pity for those who are attacked by the abominable disease which eats away their flesh, bones and marrow, the disease with which the Scripture threatens some sinners (Is 10:18). They are betrayed by their own ailing, abject, and faithless bodies. This is the body to which I came to be joined, how, I know not, in which I am the image of God, and in which I return to dust. If it is healthy, it makes war against me; and if I make war against it, it gets sick. I love it as my companion and yet hate is as an enemy; I flee from it as from a prison and yet respect it as a coheir; I am bent on destroying it and yet it is my collaboration with which I make the most beautiful things, a collaborator who knows why it has been created and by means of actions has to ascend to God...

[Compassion, Law of Nature and of Christ]
15. What shall we do, then, we who have inherited a great
and new name, taken from the name of Christ himself; we
who are a holy nation, a royal priesthood, a people chosen
and set apart (1 Pt 2:9), doing good and salutary works (Tit
2:14); we, who are the disciples of the meek and merciful
Christ who carried upon himself our infirmities (Is 53:4),
who humbled himself to the point of assuming our human
condition and made himself poor to clothe himself with our
flesh and dwell in this earthly tent, who for our sake suffered
pains and weakness, so that we might be enriched by his
divinity? Now, we, who have such an example of mercy and
compassion before our eyes, what do we think and what
shall we do with these unfortunate people? Are we going to
look down upon them, pass them by, abandon them as
dead, as abominable, as the most dangerous snakes and
beasts? No way, my brethren! We who are the flock of
Christ will not be allowed to do so by the Good Shepherd,
who looks for those who have gone astray, goes in search of
those who are lost and strengthens the weak. Much less will
we be allowed by our human nature, which promulgates
compassion as law and teaches us to have mercy and kindness for those who are weak.

[Social Conscience and Sharing]
19. What is it, my brethren and friends? Why are we sick in
the soul as well, which is a sickness much more serious than
that of the body? You know well that the bodily sickness is
involuntary, whereas spiritual sickness comes to us because
we look for it; the one ends with the present life, the other
accompanies us as we leave this world; the one deserves
compassion, the other, hatred, at least on the part of those
who are intelligent. Why do not we assist nature while we
still have time? Why do not we, who are flesh, suffer the
humiliation of the flesh? How can we enjoy pleasures
amidst the calamities of our brethren? May God preserve
me from being rich while they are indigent, from enjoying
robust health if I do not try to cure their diseases, from
eating good food, clothing myself well and resting in my

home if I do not share with them a piece of my bread and give them, in the measure of my abilities, part of my clothes and if I do not welcome them into my home...

[The Origin of Wealth, Poverty, and Avarice]
25. Let us observe the supreme and first law of God, who rains on the just and the unjust and makes the sun rise on all equally (Mt 4:45). He spread out the earth for all the animals, with its fountains, rivers and forests; he gave air to winged animals, water to aquatic creatures, and to all the basic elements of life, not dominated by any power, not restricted by any law, not separated by any boundaries. No, all these necessities of life he has put at the disposal of all and abundantly, so that no one would lack anything. In this way he honors by equality of the gift the equality of nature and at the same time manifests the abundance of his goodness. But no sooner do men bury gold, or silver, or luxurious and unnecessary clothes, or glittering stones or any other thing for its style, than there are signs of war and mutiny and tyranny, and instantly eyebrows are raised with contempt and they deny mercy to the unfortunate people, even though they are their kinsmen. Nor do they try to help the needy, not even with their superfluity.

They should at least consider that poverty and wealth, freedom (as we call it) and slavery and other similar names were introduced quite late into the history of mankind, as a sort of common diseases following the iniquity and its inventions. But, in the beginning, as the Gospel says, it was not so (Mt 19:8). He who created man at the beginning made him free and endowed him with freedom of choice, subjected only to his law, and made him rich in the delights of Paradise. The same things he desired for and the same grace he gave to the rest of mankind because they descend from the first and only man. Freedom and wealth were the only law; true poverty and slavery are its transgression.

26. But after life was infected by envy, contentiousness, and the astute tyranny of the serpent, men were more and more enticed by the bait of pleasure and the more powerful ones

rose against the weaker; what was the same family broke away and split itself into a variety of groups; avarice suppressed what nobility there was in nature, making law an aid of power. You, however, look at the primitive equality, not at the later distinction, not at the law of the powerful, but at the law of the Creator. Help, as much as you can, nature; honor the primitive freedom; respect yourself; cover the dishonor of your family; assist those who are sick and aid those who are needy.

You, who are strong, help those who are weak; you, who are rich, assist those who are poor. You, who have not stumbled, raise up those who have fallen and are afflicted; you, who are full of spirit, comfort those who are discouraged; you, who enjoy prosperity, aid those who suffer adversities. Give thanks to God that you are among those who can do favors and not among those who need to receive them; that you need not look up to the hands of others and that others to yours. Do not be rich only in your wealth but also in your piety; not only in your gold but also in your virtue, or, better still, only in the latter...

[Duty of Compassion and Sharing]
39. I am encouraged by the richness of Christ as well, who exhorts us to care for the poor and the decision of Peter and Paul, who, when they divided the fields of their preaching of the Gospel, both dedicated themselves to the poor (Gal 2:10), and the fact that the Lord defined and established perfection to the rich young man as giving everything one has to the poor. Do you think that kindness towards your neighbor is not something necessary, but free; not law but exhortation? I would wish and think that it were so, were I not frightened by the possibility of being numbered among the goats on the left hand of the Sovereign Judge who will hurl his condemnations; and this not because they have robbed or committed sacrileges or adulteries, nor because they have done something forbidden; nothing of the sort attracts condemnation on them, but their having failed to care for Christ himself in the person of the poor.

40. In conclusion, servants of Christ, brothers and coheirs of mine, if you want to give me any credit, while there is still time, let us visit Christ, let us take care of Christ, let us feed Christ, let us welcome Christ, let us honor Christ, not only by inviting him to our table, as some have done (Lk 7:36), not only with ointments, like Mary (Jn 12:3), not only with burial, like Joseph of Arimathea, not only those things necessary for the burial, like Nicodemus who loved Christ only half-heartedly; not with gold, frankincense and myrrh, like the Magi had done before all these things happened. No, the Lord of the universe asks for mercy rather than sacrifice (Mt 9:13), large entrails of compassion rather than thousands of lambs. Offer them to him, then, through the poor and those who are spread throughout the earth, so that, when we leave this world, we will be welcomed by them into the eternal dwelling with the same Christ, our Lord, to whom be glory forever and ever. Amen.

Gregory of Nyssa

Younger brother of Basil, Gregory (c. 335-394) was bishop of Nyssa. Of the three Cappadocians, he is the most gifted speculative theologian and mystic. He is also the most versatile and successful author. His writings include dogmatic treatises, exegetical works, ascetical tracts, and many discourses and letters.

Fundamental to Gregory of Nyssa's theology is his anthropology. Man, for him, is what the Scripture says he is: the image and likeness of God, and consequently enjoys the highest dignity among the earthly creatures over which he has received from God dominion and power. This dignity is the foundation for the respect that is owed to human beings in social life. Gregory radically condemns slavery as opposed to the freedom and dignity of man.

As regards the right of ownership, Gregory insists most strongly that man enjoys by nature the power to dispose of irrational creatures and hence, to possess the temporal goods. Such a right is a natural one and cannot be taken away against man's will. Gregory, however, does not advocate an exclusive and absolute right of ownership since it is limited by God's supreme power and by the others' right of ownership as well. This means that property has an essentially social function. Finally, the social inequalities, which for Gregory are the unavoidable consequences of man's egoism and lack of social conscience, exist as opportunities for us to share our possessions with one another.

HOMILY ON ECCLESIASTES

[Slavery and the Dignity of Man]
Fourth Homily.[16] ... "I have bought male and female slaves." Tell me, how much is your life worth? What have you found among the creatures that is as valuable as your human nature? How many cents did you pay for reason? How many pence did you think God's image is worth? How many coins were you charged for the creature that God has made? "Let us make," God said "man in our image and likeness" (Jn 1:26). Now, tell me, who is the one who buys, who is the one who sells the one who is God's image, who must rule over the whole earth, who has received from God the dominion over all that exists on earth as heritage? Such a power belongs to God alone, and may I say, not even to God. "God never takes back his gifts or revokes his choice," says the Apostle (Rm 11:29). Let no one think, therefore, that God wants to reduce us back to slavery, when, as we were voluntarily slaves to sin, he has called us anew to freedom.

ON THE BEATITUDES

[Mercy and the Social Order]
Fifth Homily.[17] ... Now what is mercy, and in regard to what is it practised? And how is he blessed to whom is

[16]Text: PG 44.665.
[17]Text: PG 44.1252.

returned what he gives? For he says: "Blessed are the merciful, for they shall obtain mercy." The obvious meaning of these words invites men to mutual charity and compassion, which are demanded by the capricious inequality of the circumstances of life. For not all live in the same conditions, neither as regards reputation, nor physical constitution, nor other assets. Life is in many ways often divided into opposites, since it may be spent as slave or as master, in riches or poverty, in fame or dishonor, in bodily infirmity or in good health—in all such things there is division.

Therefore the creature in need should be made equal to the one who has a larger share, and that which is lacking should be filled by what has abundance. This is the law mercy gives men in regard to the needy... Mercy is a voluntary sorrow that joins itself to the suffering of others... Mercy is the loving disposition towards those who suffer distress. For as unkindness and cruelty have their origin in hate, so mercy springs from love, without which it could not exist... Mercy is intensified charity. Hence a man of such dispositions of soul is truly blessed, since he has reached the summit of virtue...

[The Advantages of Mercy]

Let no one think that this virtue is concerned solely with material things; else it could be attained only by someone who has the necessary means for doing good. No; it seems to me more adequate to place such a virtue in the choice of the will. For if a man only wills the good, but is prevented from accomplishing it by lack of means, he is not inferior, as regards his state of soul, to the person who shows his intentions by works. Therefore we need not explain in detail how much we gain for our life if we understand the meaning of the Beatitude in this way. Even to those who are uneducated the advantages this counsel brings to our life should be quite obvious. If, indeed, such attitude of mind to our inferiors were innate in all of us, there would no longer be either superfluity or want. Life would no longer be lived in diametrically opposite ways; man would no longer be distressed by want or humiliated by slavery, nor would dishonor sadden him. For all things would be common to all, and man's life as a citizen would be marked by complete equality before the law, since the person who was responsible for the government would of his own free will be on a level with the rest.

[Mercy as the Pledge of Charity]

If such a state of affairs existed, no cause would be left for enmity. Envy would be futile, hate would disappear, remembrance of injuries would be banished along with lies, fraud, and war, all of which are bred by covetousness... And with the departure of evils there would enter instead the whole array of good things, peace and justice with all their train of virtues... Therefore mercy is the parent of kindness, the pledge of charity, the bond of all loving disposition...

LOVE OF THE POOR[18]

[Fasting and Sharing]

... There is a kind of fasting which is not bodily, a spiritual self-discipline which affects the soul; this is abstinence from evil, and it was as a means to this that our abstinence from food was prescribed. Therefore I say to you: Fast from evil-doing, discipline yourselves from covetousness, abstain from unjust profits, starve the greed of mammon, keep in your houses no snatched and stolen treasure. For what use is it to touch no meat and to wound your brother by evil-doing? What advantage is it to forgo what is your own and to seize unjustly what is the poor's? What piety is it to drink water and thirst for blood, weaving treachery in the wickedness of your heart? Judas himself fasted with the eleven, but since he did not curb his love for money, his fasting availed him nothing to salvation...

If we bear ourselves no better than this, Isaiah will say to us: "Why do you fast for strife and contention, and strike the

18Text: PG 46.453.

hungry with your fists?" (Is 58:4). Let Isaiah too set forth the actions of a pure and sincere fast: Loosen every bond of injustice, undo the knots of covenants made by force. Break your bread to the hungry; bring the poor and homeless into your house. When you see the naked, cover him; and despise not your own flesh" (Is 56:6-7). These days have brought us naked and homeless men in plenty; a host of captives is at everyone's door; strangers and fugitives are not lacking, and on every side their begging and stretched-out hands are there to see. Their house is the open air; their lodgings are the arcades, the streets, the deserted corners of the markets; they lurk in holes like owls and birds of the night. Their clothing is tattered rags; their means of subsistence, the feeling of the compassionate. Their food is anything thrown by the passers-by; their drink, the springs they share with the beasts... They live a wild and vagabond life, not by habit but because need and misfortune have brought them to it.

You who are fasting, these are the men I bid you help. Be generous to these, your distressed brothers. Give to the hungry what you deny to your own appetite... Clasp the afflicted man as if he were gold. Take the sufferer to your arms as if he were your own health, the welfare of your wife and children and servants and all your house. A poor man that is sick is doubly in want. Those without means who are in good health can pass from door to door; they can go in search of the well-to-do; they can sit at the cross-roads and cry out to all comers. But men shackled by illness, men cooped up in some narrow lodging-place or corner like Daniel in the den, these wait for you—the religious man, the friend of the poor—to be another Habacuc to them...

But you will say: "I am poor as well." Granted; suppose you are. Nevertheless, give what you can; God asks for nothing above your powers. You can give a loaf yourself, another will give a cup of wine, another clothing; thus one man's hardship will be relieved by your combined aid. It was not from one benefactor but from the whole people that Moses took what was needed for the tabernacle; one who was rich in gold brought that, another silver; a poor man brought skins, and one still poorer the hair of goats. Con-

sider too how the widow's mite was more than the offerings
of the rich; she gave everything that she had; they cast in but
little of what was theirs.

[Do Not Despise the Poor]
   Do not despise these men in their abjection, do not think
them of no account. Reflect what they are and you will
understand their dignity; they have taken upon them the
person of our Savior. For he, the compassionate, has lent
them his own person wherewith to shame the unmerciful
and the haters of the poor—as men lift up images of the
emperor against those who would do them violence, putting
their despisers to shame by the likeness of the prince. The
poor are the treasurers of the good things that we look for,
the keepers of the gates of the kingdom, opening them to the
merciful and shutting them on the harsh and uncharitable.
They are the strongest of accusers, the best of defenders—
not that they accuse or defend in words, but that the Lord
beholds what is done towards them, and every deed cries
louder than a herald to him who searches all hearts...
   God himself is the prime author of beneficence, the rich
and generous provider of all that we need. But we, who are
taught in Scripture's every syllable to copy our Lord and
Maker in so far as the mortal may imitate the divine and
immortal—we snatch everything to our own enjoyment,
assigning some things to ourselves to live upon, hoarding
the rest for our heirs. Pitiless as we are, we care nothing for
the unfortunate, we give no kindly thought to the poor. A
man sees his fellow-man with no bread to eat, no food to
sustain life itself; yet far from hastening to help, far from
offering him rescue, he leaves him like a once sturdy plant to
wither unwatered pitifully away—and this even if he has
wealth to overflowing and might let the channels of his
abundance run forth to comfort many. The flow from one
river-source brings richness to many a spreading plain; so
the wealth of one household is enough to preserve multi-
tudes of the poor, if only a grudging uncharitable heart does
not fall like a stone to block the passage and thwart the
stream...

[God Wants Us to Have an Equal Share of His Goods]

You, therefore, who have been created rational beings, endued with mind to expound and interpret divine things, do not be enticed by what is but transitory, Strive to win those things which never forsake their holder. Live with restraint; do not think everything your own, but reserve a part for God's dear poor. All things belong to God, the Father of us and them. We are all of the same stock, all brothers. And when men are brothers, the best and most equitable thing is that they should inherit in equal portions. The second best is that even if one or two take the greater part, the others should have at least their own share. But if one man should seek to be absolute possessor of all, refusing even a third or a fifth to his brothers, then he is a cruel tyrant, a savage with whom there can be no dealing, an insatiate beast gloatingly shutting its jaws over the meal it will not share. Or rather he is more ruthless than any beast; wolf does not drive wolf from the prey, and a pack of dogs will tear the same carcass; this man in his limitless greed will not admit one fellow-creature to a share in his riches...

[Be Detached from Earthly Things and Be Ready]

Let us then, as rational beings, consider how fleeting our life is, how time, like the waters of a river, flows ceaselessly and irresistibly on, carrying everything upon it to the end which is death. It brings no enduringness, no security; would that it brought no reckoning either! But the grave thing is that for every hour we live, every word we utter, we must make our defence at an incorruptible tribunal. And therefore the blessed Psalmist, turning his thought to such things as these, desires to know the appointed time of his own end, and beseeches God that he may learn the number of his remaining days and so may prepare for his going forth—not confounded on a sudden like some unready traveller, casting round for the necessities of his journey after he is on his way. He says therefore: "O Lord, make me know my end and what is the measure of my days, that I may learn what is lacking to me. Behold, you have made my days as it were a handbreadth, and my time is as nothing before you"(Ps 38:5-6). See the sage care of a prudent soul, and this too in the royal dignity. He views as in a glass the King of kings and the Judge of judges, and he desires, first to order his living to the perfect pattern of the commandments, then to depart from here as a true citizen of the life there; may we all attain it also, by the grace and compassion of Jesus Christ our Lord, to whom be glory forever and ever.

4

ST. JOHN CHRYSOSTOM

By the sheer volume of his writings on social questions, John Chrysostom deserves a special chapter by himself. Sierra Bravo, in his collection of patristic texts on social and economic doctrine, devotes more than two hundred pages to him (*Doctrina Social y Economica de los Patres de la Iglesia*, pp. 306-535). Born in c. 347 and ordained a priest by Flavian, bishop of Antioch, he was appointed by his bishop to devote special attention to the ministry of preaching, a task he performed so well that he was given the name of Chrysostom, 'golden mouthed.' Against his wish, Chrysostom was made patriarch of Constantinople in 398 and immediately set about the work of reforming the moral and spiritual life of the city. His combination of honesty, asceticism, and tactlessness, joined with the hatred of Theophilus, patriarch of Alexandria and of Empress Eudoxia, brought about his ruin. He was deposed from his see in 403, but was shortly afterwards recalled by the court. But very soon his plain speaking incurred the wrath of Empress Eudoxia who succeeded in having him deposed the second time, exiled near to his native city Antioch, and finally to Pontus. He died before he arrived at his destination in 407.

Though Chrysostom wrote some treatises on special subjects (*On the Priesthood, On Monastic Life, On Virginity and Widowhood*, etc.) and a great number of

letters, most of his works are homilies, either exegetical in
the Old and New Testaments, or dogmatic (*On the
Incomprehensible Nature of God, Baptismal Catecheses,
Against the Jews*, etc.), or moral (*Lazarus and Dives, On
Alms*, etc.).

As far as social teaching is concerned, John Chrysostom may certainly be said to be the most brilliant and
eloquent exponent of the great themes of the Greek
patristic social doctrine. At the heart of his social thought
lies the double principle that sustains and nurtures common life: charity, which is embodied in compassion and
sharing; and solidarity, which expresses itself in the mutual interdependence of all human beings.

The bonds of charity that unite all human beings
together, according to Chrysostom, are many and varied:
their equality of nature, their common descent, their
family ties, their needs, their common language and
nationality. These bonds of love make the sharing of
one's possessions with others a serious obligation. Chrysostom considers riches as something essentially to be
shared. He repeatedly insists that the very purpose of the
possessions of riches is sharing, that it is the distribution
of riches, especially of superfluities, that makes them
good, that private ownership is something imperfect and
limited and should be legitimated by its being put to good
use through sharing.

Chrysostom was so zealous in exhorting almsgiving
and exalting the dignity of the poor and sometimes railed
so violently against riches that he has been accused of
being a demagogue and even a communist. Indeed certain texts of his seem to deny the right of private ownership. In his twelfth homily on the First Letter to Timothy,
for example, he affirms: "And observe that concerning
things that are common there is no contention, but all is
peaceable. But when one attempts to possess himself of
anything, to make it his own, then contention is introduced, as if nature herself is indignant. . . " Again, in the
same homily, we read a little earlier: "So destructive a
passion is avarice that to grow rich without injustice is

impossible.... The root and origin of riches must have been injustice." These affirmations, however, must be placed in their context, which does not intend to propose some form of economic communism, but an energetic exhortation of sharing as a solution to the problem of social inequalities.

Another notable aspect of Chrysostom's social doctrine is his elaborate teaching on work. In his thirty-sixth homily on the gospel of John, he draws a distinction between 'work' and 'toil,' according to which man in the earthly paradise would have to work since he was assigned the task of cultivating the earth, but not to toil. Toil is the consequence of sin. Nevertheless Chrysostom does not regard work as a shameful thing but as a means to discipline and correct the deviations of sin and as a way of obtaining the necessary things to help others. He also regards the primary purpose of work to be the production of necessary and useful, and not luxurious and superfluous things. In his fifteenth homily on the *Second Letter to the Corinthians*, he classifies the following professions according to their usefulness: agriculture, weaving, building, and shoe-making.

Finally, Chrysostom has also dealt with the problem of authority, civil government and law, especially in his twenty-third homily on the *Letter to the Romans*, the thirty-fourth homily on the *First Letter to the Corinthians*, and the fifteenth homily on the *Second Letter to the Corinthians*. He discusses the necessity of authority in social life, its origin, its purpose, its functions and benefits, the duty of submission to the government, the obligation of paying taxes, and the origin and knowability of natural law and its relation to conscience.

ON LAZARUS

[What the Rich Possess Belongs to the Poor]
Homily II, 4.[1] ... Strictly speaking, the rich man has not committed an act of injustice against Lazarus, since he did

---

[1]Text: PG 48.987.

not rob him of his possessions. His sin consisted rather in not giving part of his own possessions. Now if the one who does not give part of his own possessions is prosecuted by him whom he did not pity, what forgiveness can he obtain who steals possessions of others, since those whom he has oppressed will encircle him on all sides? He will need no witnesses, no prosecutors, no proofs, no evidence. The facts themselves, as they appear before our eyes. "Man and his works will appear before me," says the Lord.

Thus, not giving part of one's possessions to others is already a kind of robbery. If what I am telling you sounds perhaps rather odd, do not be surprised. I will adduce a text from the divine Scriptures which says that it is rapine, avarice and theft, not only taking possession of things belonging to others but also refusing to give part of one's possessions to others. What text is this? Reproaching the Jews through the mouth of the prophet, God says: "The earth has produced its fruits but you have not brought in tithes, and robbery of the poor dwells in your house" (Mal 3:10). "Because you have made the customary offerings," says the Lord, "you have taken away what belongs to the poor." This he says in order to make it clear to the rich that what they possess belongs to the poor, even when they receive the inheritance from their parents or come in for some money, whatever the source. Elsewhere he also says: "Rob not the poor man of his livelihood" (Sirach 4:1). A robber is one who takes things belonging to others, since robbery is taking and keeping what is not one's own. These texts therefore teach that if we refuse to give alms, we will be punished in the same way as robbers.

TO THE PEOPLE OF ANTIOCH

[Why There Are Things that Are Common and Things that Are Private]
Homily II, 6.[2] ... What does the Apostle mean when he says that "God provides us richly with all things for our use"

[2]Text: PG 49.43.

(1 Tm 6:17)? God gives us abundantly all things that are much more necessary than money, such as air, water, fire, sunshine and things of this kind. And yet it cannot be said that the rich has more sunshine than the poor, nor can it be said that the rich breathes more air than the poor. All these things are available to all, equally and in common. Why is it that the greatest and most necessary things, things that sustain our life, have been created by God for common use, and the least and most sordid thing, namely, money, is not common? Why, I would like to ask. To safeguard our life and to open for us a path to virtue. On the one hand if the necessities of life were not common, the rich, with their usual greediness, would perhaps take them away from the poor. In fact, if they have done so with money, how much more would they do with these things. On the other hand, if money were common and were available to all, then there would be no opportunity for almsgiving and no incentive for charity.

HOMILY ON PERFECT CHARITY

[Charity and Social Life]

1.[3] All good works are the fruit of charity... Now charity teaches us not only by words but also by deeds. In the first place, we ought to keep in mind the way in which we have been created. Indeed, after he had created the one man, God ordained that we should be born from him, so that we all should consider ourselves as one and try to practice charity for one another. In the second place, God in his wisdom fostered our mutual love through our treaties and commerce. Look how God has filled the universe with many goods, but to each part of the earth he has given its particular fruits. In this way, impelled by our needs we communicate with one another, give to others what we have overmuch and receive what we lack. Thus we increase our love for our brethren.

The same thing God has done with each human life. He

[3]Text: PG 56.279.

has not given to all of us to know everything, rather to one medicine, to another architecture, yet to another, art, so that we may love one another by necessity. The same thing is to be seen in the spiritual order, as St. Paul says: "To one the Spirit gives wisdom in discourse, to another the power to express knowledge; by the same Spirit another is given the gift of healing, and still another miraculous powers..."

HOMILIES ON THE GOSPEL OF MATTHEW

[Interest, Usury, and Almsgiving]
Homily V, 9.[4] Disperse therefore, that you may not lose; keep not, that you may keep; lay out, that you may save; spend, that you may gain. If your treasures are to be hoarded, do not hoard them yourself, for you will surely throw them away; entrust them, rather, to God, for then no one can make spoil of them... Lend, where there is no envy, no accusation, nor evil design, nor fear. Lend to Him who wants nothing, yet has need for your sake; who feeds all men, yet is hungry so that you may not suffer famine; who is poor so that you may be rich. Lend there where your return cannot be death, but life instead of death...

For nothing is baser, nothing is more cruel than the interest that comes from lending. For such a lender trades on other persons' calamities, draws profit from the distress of others, and demands wages for kindness, as though he were afraid to seem merciful. Under the mask of kindness he digs deeper their grave of poverty; when he stretches out his hand to help, he pushes them down; and when he receives them as it were in a harbor, he involves them in shipwreck as on a rock, or shoal, or reef.

Now the usurer will tell me: "Do you ask me to give another for his use that money that I have got together, and which is useful to me, and demand no reward?" No, I do not say this. On the contrary I do want that you should receive a reward; not however a mean nor small one, but far greater;

[4]Text: PG 57.61.

for in return for gold, I want you to receive heaven for interest. Why then shut yourself up in poverty, crawling about the earth, and demanding little for great? This is the lot of those who do not know how to be rich. For to God who in return for a little money is promising you the good things that are in heaven, you say: "Give me not heaven, but instead of heaven, the gold that perishes." This is for one who wishes to continue to live in poverty...

[Bad Example of the Christians
in Matters of Material Goods]
Homily XII, 5.[5] . . . Is it not the highest form of folly to heap up all your possessions where destruction and waste is the lot of all that is stored, and where things abide untouched and increase, there not to lay up even the least portion, and this when we are to live there for all eternity? This is the reason why the pagans do not believe what we say. Our actions and our works are the demonstrations which they are willing to receive from us; but when they see us building for ourselves fine houses, and laying out gardens and baths, and buying fields, they are not willing to believe that we are preparing for another sort of residence away from our city.

"For if this were so," they would say, "they would sell everything they have and deposit the money there beforehand." This is what they conjecture from the way things are usually done in this life. We see, indeed, that this is what those who are very rich do: they get themselves houses and fields and all the rest, chiefly in those cities in which they are to stay. But we do just the opposite; with all earnest zeal we get possession of the earth, which we are soon to leave; for a few acres and tenements we give up not only money but even our very blood, while for the purchase of heaven we do not endure to give even what is beyond our wants, and this though we are to purchase it at a small price, and to possess it forever, provided we had once purchased it.

Therefore I say we shall have to leave this world naked and poor, and suffer the utmost punishment. And we shall

[5]Text: PG 57.207.

suffer not only from our own poverty, but also for our making others to be such as ourselves. For when pagans see those that have partaken of so great mysteries earnest about these matters, much more will they cling to the things present.

[The Duty of the Rich to Make Good Use of His Possessions]
Homily XLIX, 3, 4.[6] ... For the temporal goods are but an appendage to the spiritual ones, so vile and trifling they are in comparison with these, however great they may be. Let us not therefore spend our energies on them, but regard both the acquisition and the loss of them with equal indifference, like Job who neither clung to them when present, nor sought them absent. On this account riches are called "chremata" (utilities), so that we should not bury them in the earth but should use them aright. Each artisan has his peculiar skill, so does the rich man. The rich man does not know how to work in brass, nor to frame ships, nor to weave, nor to build houses, nor any such thing. Let him then learn to use his wealth aright, and to pity the poor; so will he know a better art than all those.

For indeed this is the highest of arts. Its workshop is built in heaven. Its tools are not made of iron and brass, but of goodness and right will. Of this art Christ and his Father are the Teachers. "Be merciful," says he, "as your Father who is in heaven" (Lk 6:36). And what is indeed marvellous, being so superior to the rest, it needs no labor, no time for its perfection; it is enough to have willed, and the whole is accomplished. But let us see also its end, what it is. What then is the end of it? Heaven, the good things in the heavens, that ineffable glory, the spiritual bride-chambers, the bright lamps, the abiding with the Bridegroom, and other things, which no speech, nor even understanding, is able to set forth. Herein lies the immense difference between this art and the others. For most of the arts profit us for the present life, whereas this for the life to come also.

[6]Text: PG 58.500.

[The Excellence of the Art of Almsgiving]
Homily LII, 4.[7] ... Therefore justly will the rich, if they are wicked, be more punished than the poor, since they were not softened even by their prosperity. And tell me not that they gave alms, since if they did not give in proportion to their fortune, they will not escape punishment. Our alms are judged not by the measure of our gifts, but by the largeness of our heart. But if these suffer punishment, much more will those who are eager about superfluous things; who build houses of two or three stories, but despise the hungry; who give heed to covetousness, but neglect almsgiving...

5. ... Almsgiving is an art and better than all arts. For if the peculiarity of art is to issue in something useful, and nothing is more useful than almsgiving, it is obvious that this is both an art and better than all arts. For it makes for us not shoes, nor does it weave garments, nor build houses of clay, but procures life everlasting, and snatches us from the hands of death, and in either life shows us glorious, and builds the mansions that are in heaven and those eternal tabernacles...

And indeed of the arts of this life, each has and realizes one object only. Agriculture, for example, feeds us; weaving clothes us; or rather not so much as this, for each of them is in no way sufficient by itself to contribute to us its own part. Take, if you will, agriculture first. Without the smith's art from which it borrows spade, ploughshare, sickle, axe, and other things beside; without that of the carpenter, so as both to frame a plough, and to prepare a yoke and a cart to bruise the ears; and without the currier's, to make also the leather harness; and without the builder's, to build a stable for the bullocks that plough, and the houses for the farmer that sows; and without the woodman's, to cut wood; and without the baker's after all these, agriculture is nowhere to be found. And so the art of weaving, when it produces anything, calls for many arts, together with itself, to assist it in the works set before it; and if they are not present and

[7]Text: PG 58.522.

stretch forth the hand, this too stands, like the former, at a loss. Indeed every one of the arts stands in need of the other.

But when alms is to be given, we need nothing else; the disposition only is required. And if you say that money is needed, and houses and clothes and shoes, then read those words of Christ, which he spoke concerning the widow (Mk 12:43), and cease from this anxiety. For, however poor you are and even if you are poorer than the one who begs, cast in two mites and you will have fulfilled everything. Even when you have but a barley cake, and that is all you have, give it and you will have achieved the summit of this art.

[It is Easy for the Rich to Do Away with Poverty]
Homily LXVI, 3.[8] ... Let us consider these things then, my dear brethren, and let us discern the truth at length, though late, and let us grow sober. For I am now ashamed of speaking of almsgiving, because, though I have often spoken on this subject, I have achieved nothing worthy of the exhortation. Some increase indeed there has been, but not as much as I wished. I see you sowing, but not with a liberal hand. I therefore fear lest you also reap sparingly.

For as proof that we do sow sparingly, let us inquire, if you please, who are more numerous in the city, poor or rich; and who, neither poor nor rich, are the middle class. As for instance, a tenth part is rich, and a tenth is poor that has nothing at all, and the rest is middle class. Let us distribute then among the poor the whole multitude of the city, and you will see how great is our disgrace. For the very rich are indeed but few, but those who come next to them are many; again, the poor are much fewer than these. Nevertheless, although there are so many that are able to feed the hungry, many go to sleep in their hunger, not because those that have are not able with ease to succor them, but because of their great barbarity and inhumanity. For if both the wealthy, and those next to them, were to distribute among themselves those who are in need of bread and clothing,

[8]Text: PG 58.630.

scarcely would one poor person fall to the share of fifty men or even a hundred. Yet, they are waiting every day, despite the fact that there is a great abundance of those who can help them.

And that you may learn the inhumanity of the other, consider how the Church, whose revenue is one of the lowest among the wealthy, and not of the very rich, has assisted every day numberless widows and virgins, for indeed the list of them has already reached the number of three thousand. Together with these she assists those who are in prison, those who suffer in hospitals, those who are in convalescence, those who are away from home, those who are maimed, those who wait upon the altar; and with respect to food and clothing, those who happen to come every day. And yet, her substance is in no respect diminished. So that if ten men only were thus willing to spend, there would be no poor...

I am not constraining you to lessen your capital, not because I do not wish it, but because I see you are very recalcitrant. I am not then saying this. No. But give away the revenues, keep nothing of these. It is enough for you to have the money of your income pouring in on you as from a fountain; make the poor sharers with you, and become a good steward of the things God has given you...

[Social Function of Property]
Homily LXXVII, 3.[9] ... This parable (of the faithful servant, Mt 24:45-47) applies not to money only but also to speech, power, gifts, and every stewardship wherewith each is entrusted. It would suit rulers in the state also, for everyone is bound to make full use of what he has for the common good. If it is wisdom that you have, or power, or wealth, or whatever, let it not be for the ruin of your fellow-servants nor for your own ruin...

Let us who have money listen to these things as well. For Christ speaks not only to teachers but also to the rich. For

[9]Text: PG 58.706.

both have been entrusted with riches: the teachers with the more necessary wealth, the rich with the inferior one. While the teachers are giving out the greater wealth, you are not willing to show forth your generosity even in the lesser, or rather not generosity but honesty (for you are in fact giving things that belong to others), what excuse will you have?....

4. .... For you too are stewards of your own possessions, no less than he who dispenses the alms of the Church. Just as he has no right to squander at random and at hazard the things given by you for the poor, since they were given for the maintenance of the poor, so you may not squander your own. For even though you have received an inheritance from your father, and have in this way come to possess everything you have, still everything belongs to God... Therefore though he could have taken these possessions away from you, God left them so that you may have the opportunity to show forth virtue. Thus, bringing us into need one of another, he makes our love for one another more fervent...

6. .... For, if in worldly matters no man lives for himself, but artisan, soldier, farmer, and merchant, all of them contribute to the common good, and to their neighbor's advantage, much more ought we to do this in spiritual things. For this is most properly to live. He who lives for himself only and overlooks all others, is useless, he is not even a man, he does not belong to the human race.

HOMILIES ON THE GOSPEL OF JOHN

[The Origin of Social Inequalities]
Homily XV, 3.[10] ... God has given us but one dwelling-place, this world; he distributed all created things equally; kindled one sun for all; stretched above us one roof, the sky; set one table, the earth. And he also gave another much greater table than this (the Eucharist), but this, too, is one—those who partake of the mysteries understand what I

[10]Text: PG 59.102.

say. He has bestowed one manner of generation, the spiritual, for all; one fatherland for all, heaven; we all drink from the same chalice. He has not bestowed more abundant and more honorable largesse upon the rich and meaner and lowlier upon the poor, but has called all equally. He has provided temporal things as generously as spiritual.

Then, whence comes the great inequality of conditions in life? From the greed and arrogance of the rich. But, brethren, let us do away with this situation. While the general and more essential things are drawing us together to the same end, let us not be driven apart by earthly and mean things—I mean wealth, and poverty, and bodily kinship, and enmity, and friendship. All these things are shadow and less than shadow for those who have the bond of love from on high.

[Work and Toil]
Homily XXXVI, 3.[11] ... In the beginning, God gave us a life free from cares and exempt from toil. We did not rightly make use of the gift, but perverted our leisure and lost paradise. Therefore, he made our life thereafter a toilsome one...

"But why," you will ask, "are we now toiling?" Because you did not maintain an attitude of moderation towards not working hard. Rather, if the matter is closely studied there is yet another way by which laziness is active in corrupting us and causing us much trouble.

Now, if you please, suppose that we lock up a man, merely feeding him and keeping him sated with food, but not permitting him to walk or requiring him to work. Suppose we let him enjoy table and couch and continually live in luxury. What, indeed, would be more wretched than this life? However, you will say: "It is one thing to work and another to toil." Yet, in the beginning, it was possible to work without toil. "That was possible?" you will ask. Yes, it was, and God desired this, but you did not allow this. It was

---

[11] Text: PG 59.205.

for this reason that he set you to care for the earthly paradise, stipulating that you must work, but not mixing toil with work. If man had toiled from the beginning, he would not have inflicted toil as a punishment afterward. It is indeed possible to work and at the same time not to labor hard, as is the case with the angels...

[Covetousness is Idolatry]
Homily LXV, 3.[12] A terrible vice is the love of money, a terrible vice. It disables both eyes and ears, and makes men fiercer than wild beasts, not allowing them to consider conscience, friendship, or association, or the salvation of their own soul. On the contrary, once it has withdrawn them at once from all these things, like a harsh tyrant, it makes its captives slaves. Moreover, the dreadful part of this very bitter slavery is that it even persuades them to feel grateful for it, and the more they become enslaved in it, so much the more will the pleasure they take in it increase. As a result, the disease becomes incurable, the beast becomes hard to tame...

Therefore Paul calls it (the love of money) idolatry (cf. Col 3:5). Yet, not even by so doing did he deter men from acquiring it. Why did he say it is idolatry? Many possess riches and do not dare to make use of them, rather they regard them as sacred, passing them on intact to their children and their children's children, not daring to touch them, as if they were something consecrated to God. And if ever they were forced to use them, they feel as if they were doing something sacrilegious. Besides, as the pagan diligently cares for his idol, so you entrust your gold to bars and bolts, treasuring them in a chest instead of a shrine, and storing up the gold in vessels of silver...

[12]Text: PG 59.363.

HOMILIES ON THE ACTS OF THE APOSTLES

[No One, Whatever His Condition, Is Dispensed from Helping His Neighbor]
Homily XX, 4.[13] ... Nothing is more frigid than a Christian who does not care for the salvation of others. You cannot plead poverty here: for she that cast in her two mites will be your accuser (Lk 21:1). And Peter said: "Silver and gold I have none" (Acts 3:6). And Paul was so poor that he was often hungry and lacked the necessary food. You cannot plead lowness of birth: for they too were ignoble men, and of ignoble parents. You cannot allege want of education: for they too were "unlearned men" (Acts 4:13). Even if you are a slave therefore and a runaway slave, you can still do your part: for such was Onesimus... You cannot plead infirmity: for such was Timothy who often had infirmities...

Every one can profit his neighbor, if he will fulfill his part. Do you not see the unfruitful trees, how strong they are, how beautiful, how large, and smooth, and tall? But if we had a garden, we surely should much rather have pomegranates or fruitful olive trees than those trees which are delightful to the eyes but have but little profit. Such are those men who only consider their own interest, or rather, not even such, since these persons are only fit for burning, whereas those trees are at least useful for building houses and protecting those who live in them...

Do not say: "It is impossible for me to care for the others." If you are a Christian, it is impossible that it should be so. For as the natural properties of things cannot be made ineffectual, so it is here: the thing is part of the very nature of the Christian. Do not insult God. To say that the sun cannot shine would be to insult him. To say that a Christian cannot do good is to insult God and call him a liar. For it is easier for the sun not to give heat or not to shine than for the Christian not to send forth light; it is easier for the light to be darkness than for the Christian to be so...

[13]Text: PG 60.162.

HOMILIES ON THE LETTER TO THE ROMANS

[Origin, Nature, and Properties of Authority]
Homily XXIII, 1.[14] On this matter Paul discusses at length in other letters also. He requires that slaves be subjected to their masters as well as that subjects submit themselves to their rulers. And this he does to show that it was not for the subversion of political authority that Christ introduced his laws but for the better ordering of it, and to teach men not to undertake unnecessary and unprofitable wars. For we have enough struggles to contend with for the truth's sake to take on other useless ones... And to show that these requirements apply to all even for priest and monks, and not for men of secular professions only, he says: "Let every soul be subject to the higher powers," whether you be an apostle, or an evangelist, or a prophet, or anything whatsoever inasmuch as this subjection is not subversive of religion. And he does not say merely "obey," but "be subject."

The first foundation for such an order, its conformity to the logic of faith, is that all this is of God's appointment. "For there is no power," says he, "that does not come from God." What do you mean, Apostle? That every ruler is elected by God to the throne he occupies? No, this I do not say, answers the Apostle, I am not speaking about individual rulers, but about authority in itself. I mean to say that it is the will of God's wisdom that there should be authority, that some govern and others obey, and that things should not be carried on in confusion, the people swaying like waves in this direction and that. Hence Paul is not saying: "There is no ruler that is not appointed by God"; rather, he is speaking of power itself and says: "There is no power that does not come from God; it is he that establishes all the powers that be on earth."

Similarly when a certain wise man says: "It is by the Lord that a man is matched with a woman" (Prov. 19:14), he means that God establishes the institution of marriage, and

---

[14]Text: PG 60.613.

not that God joins together every man that comes to be with a woman. For we see that many men and women are joined for evil, even by the law of marriage, and this we should not ascribe to God... For since equality of power and honor leads many times to fighting, God has established different degrees and forms of subjection, as that, for instance, of husband and wife, of son and father, of old and young, of free and slaves, of ruler and ruled, of master and disciple. And why are you surprised in the case of mankind, when even in the body he has done the same things? For even here he has not made all parts of equal honor, but one less and another greater, some to rule and others to be ruled... Anarchy, wherever it may be, is an evil and a cause of confusion.

HOMILIES ON THE FIRST LETTER TO THE CORINTHIANS

[The Social Function of Riches]
Homily X, 3.[15] ... Speaking of faith, Paul says: "You are not your own," and "You were bought with a price" (1 Cor 6:19-20). All things, in fact, are God's. When then he calls and chooses to take things away from us, let us not, like ungrateful servants, flee away from him and steal our Master's goods. Your soul is not yours, much less are your riches your own. How is it then that you spend on what is unnecessary the things that are not yours? Do you not know that we will soon be on trial if we use them badly? But since they are not ours but our Master's, we should spend them for our fellow-servants...

Say not then: "I am but spending my own, and of my own I live a voluptuous life." It is not your own, but of others. Others', I say, because such is your own choice: for God's will is that those things should be yours which have been entrusted to you on behalf of your brethren. Now the things which are not your own become yours, if you spend them on

[15]Text: PG 61.86.

others. But if you spend them on yourself unsparingly, your own things become no longer yours. For since you use them cruelly and say that it is fair to spend your own things entirely for your exclusive enjoyment, I say they are no longer yours. For they are common to you and your fellow-servants, just as the sun is common, and the air, the earth, and all the rest... So also in regard of wealth. If you enjoy it alone, you have lost it, for you will not reap its reward. But if you possess it jointly with the rest, then will it be more your own, and then will you reap the benefit of it...

[How to Convince the Rich to Abandon Their Covetousness] Homily XI, 5.[16] ... Let us make use of the lessons of true wisdom and say that we do not forbid the seeking of riches as such, but of ill-gotten riches. For it is lawful to be rich, but without covetousness, without rapine, without violence, and without a bad reputation before all men. Let us first by means of arguments of true wisdom soothe those who seek riches, and for the moment not to talk to them about hell, since the sick man cannot bear as yet such discourse. Let us go to this world for all our arguments upon these matters and say: "Why do you choose to be rich through covetousness? To hoard up gold and silver for others and innumerable curses and accusations for yourself? The poor man whom you have defrauded is suffering anguish because of the lack of the necessities of life, and is lamenting, and drawing down upon you the curses of thousands. He may go about the market place at fall of evening and not knowing where he is going to spend the night. How can the unhappy fellow sleep, with pangs in the belly, tortured by hunger, while it is freezing and the rain coming down on him? And while you are coming home from the bath, clean and dandy, dressed in soft clothes, full of contentment and happiness, and hastening to sit down to splendidly prepared dinners, he is driven everywhere about the market place by cold and hunger, with his head hung low and his hands outstretched.

[16]Text: PG 61.94.

The poor man does not even have the courage to ask for the necessary food from one so well fed and so well rested, and often has to withdraw covered with insults.

When therefore, you have returned home, when you lie down on your couch, when the lights around your house shine bright, when your table is well prepared and plentiful, at that time remember that poor miserable man wandering about like dogs in the alleys, in darkness and in mire, and from these alleys he goes back, not to his house, his wife, or his bed, but to a pile of straw, like those dogs which we hear baying all through the night. And you, if you see but a drop of water falling from the ceiling, you would throw the whole house in confusion, calling for the slaves and disturbing everything, while he, laid in rags, and straw, and dirt, has to bear the bitter cold."

[The Essence of Christianity]
Homily XXV, 3.[17] ... This is the rule of the most perfect Christianity, its most exact definition, its highest point, namely, the seeking of the common good. Paul himself states it when he says: "Even as I also am of Christ"(1 Cor 11,1). For nothing can so make a man an imitator of Christ as caring for his neighbors. Indeed, even though you fast, or sleep on hard ground, or even suffer unto death, but should you take no thought for your neighbor, you have done nothing great; despite what you have done, you still stand far from this model of a perfect Christian.

HOMILIES ON THE SECOND LETTER TO THE CORINTHIANS

[The Art of Governing Compared with Other Arts]
Homily XV, 3.[18] ... Governing is an art, not merely a dignity, and an art above all arts. And if profane governing is an art and science superior to all others, much more is

[17]Text: PG 61.208.
[18]Text: PG 61.506.

governing in the Church. And the more the former is better than the rest, the more the latter is better than the former; rather, even much more. And, if you will, let us examine this argument more closely. There is an art of agriculture, of weaving, of building; these are very necessary arts indeed, since our life depends on them. Other arts surely are but ancillary to these: the coppersmith's, the carpenter's, the shepherd's. Further, among the arts, the most necessary of all is agriculture, which was even that which God first introduced when he had formed man. For without shoes and clothes it is possible to live; but without agriculture it is impossible...

You should be ashamed who need so many superfluous arts to survive, those of cooks, confectioners, embroiderers, and ten thousand other such people. You should be ashamed who introduce vain refinements... For God has made nature, quite independent, needing only a few things...

First then comes agriculture; second, weaving; third, building; and last of all, shoemaking. At least, among us, there are many, both servants and laborers, who live without shoes. These, therefore, are the useful and necessary arts. Now then let us compare them with the art of governing. I have singled out these arts that are the most important, so that, when it is seen that governing is superior to them, its victory over the rest may be unquestioned.

How, then, are we to show that it is more necessary than all others? Because without it there is no advantage in these. If you agree, let us leave aside the other three and focus our attention on the highest and the most important, agriculture. Where will be the advantage of the many hands of your laborers if they are at war with one another and plunder one another's goods? For it is the fear of the governing authority that restrains them and preserves the fruits of their labor. Destroy this authority and their work is reduced to nothing.

Now if we examine the question at greater depth, one will find yet another rule which is the parent and bond of this. What then may this be? It is that according to which each man should control and rule himself, chastising his vile passions, nourishing and promoting the growth of all the seeds of virtue with utmost care.

For there are indeed many kinds of government. One, by which men rule peoples and states, regulating their political life. Paul refers to this when he says: "Let every man be subject to the higher powers; for there is no authority that does not come from God" (Rom 13:1,4). Afterwards to show its usefulness, he adds: "Whoever governs is a minister of God for the good." And again: "He is a minister of God and avenger to punish with wrath him who does evil" (Rom 13:1-3).

A second, by which everyone that has reason governs himself. This, too, is mentioned by the Apostle when he says: "Do you have no fear of authority? Do what is good" (Rom 13:3) alluding to the one who governs himself.

There is, moreover, another government, higher than the political government. And what is it? That which is exercised in the Church. And this also is mentioned by Paul: "Obey them that have authority over you and submit to them, for they keep watch over you as men who must render an account" (Heb 13:17). This government is better than the political as heaven is better than earth, rather, even much more. For first of all, it considers principally not how it may punish sins committed, but how they may never be committed at all. Next, it does not seek to execute the culprit but to blot out the sins. The authority of the Church is not concerned with the things of this world, rather all its transactions are about the things in heaven... And therefore those who bear this authority have a greater honor committed to their hands than the viceroys, and even than those who wear imperial diadems, since they form men for greater things and for a greater destiny.

But neither those who exercise the political rule nor those who govern in the Church will be able to fulfill this charge unless they have first ruled themselves as they ought and have observed with all strictness the respective laws of their polity.

HOMILIES ON THE LETTER TO THE EPHESIANS

[Educate the Children in Using Riches]

Homily XXI, 2.[19] ... Let us consider everything as secondary to the provident care we should take of our children, and to our "bringing them up with the training and instruction befitting the Lord" (Eph 6:4). If from the very beginning they are taught to be a lover of true wisdom, then they have acquired a wealth superior to all other wealth and a glory superior to all other glory. You will achieve nothing as great by teaching them an art, and giving them that profane learning by which they will gain riches, as by teaching them the art of despising riches. If you desire to make them rich, do this. For the rich man is not he who desires many riches and is encircled with abundant wealth, but he who has need of nothing. Discipline your children in this, teach them this. This is the greatest riches. Do not seek how to give them reputation and high fame in profane learning, but consider deeply how you will teach them to despise the glory that belongs to this present life. In this way they will become more distinguished and more truly glorious. This is possible for the poor man and the rich man alike to accomplish...

Wealth is harmful, because it renders us unprepared for the vicissitudes of life. Let us therefore bring up our children to be such that they will be able to bear up against every trial, and not be surprised at what may come upon them...
And great will be the reward that will thus be reserved for us. For if men enjoy so great honor for making statues and painting portraits of kings, shall we, who adorn the image of the King of kings, (for man is the image of God) not receive ten thousand blessings if we produce a true likeness? For the likeness resides in the virtue of the soul, when we train our children to be good, to be meek, to be forgiving, (all these are attributes of God), to be beneficent, to be human; when we train them to take little account of this world. Let this then be our task, to mold and direct both ourselves and them according to what is right.

[19]Text: PG 62.151.

HOMILIES ON THE FIRST LETTER TO TIMOTHY

[Private Ownership is Stewardship, not Possession]
Homily XI, 2.[20] ... The wealth is not a possession, it is not property, it is a loan for use. For how can you claim that it is a possession if when you die, willingly or unwillingly, all that you have goes to others, and they again give it up to others, and these again to others. We are all sojourners; and the tenant of the house is perhaps more truly the owner of it, for when the owner dies, the tenant lives on and still enjoys the house and if the tenant has to pay for enjoying the house, the owner too has to pay for it to have it built and has to endure thousands of pains to have it fitted up. Property, in fact, is but a word; we are all owners but of other men's possessions.

Those things only are our own which we have sent before us to the other world. Our goods here are not our own; we have only a life interest in them; or, rather they fail us even here on earth. Only the virtues of the soul are properly our own, as almsgiving and charity. Worldly goods were called external things, even by those who are outside the Church, because they are external to us. But let us make them internal. For we cannot take our wealth with us when we depart from here, but we can take our charities. But let us rather send them before us so that they may prepare for us an abode in the eternal mansions (Lk 16:9)

Riches (χρήματα) are named from use (κεχρῆσθαι), not from ownership, and are not our own, and possessions are not a property but a loan. If not, then tell me through how many more hands it will pass. There is a well-known wise proverb (and popular proverbs, when they contain any wisdom, are not to be despised): "O field, how many men's have you been and how many more men's will you be?" This we should say to our houses and all our goods. Virtue alone is able to depart with us, and to accompany us to the world above. Let us then give up and extinguish that love of wealth, that we may kindle in us a desire for eternal things.

[20]Text: PG 62.555.

[It is Not Possible to Get Rich without Injustice]
Homily XII, 3.[21] ... But you who are experienced in
worldly affairs, do you not know how many men, after
infinite toils, have not enjoyed the fruits of their labors,
wither because they are prematurely cut off by death, or
overtaken by misfortunes, or assailed by disease, or ruined
by false accusers, or some other causes, which amidst the
variety of human casualties, has forced them to go empty-
handed?

But someone will object to me: "Don't you see the lucky
men who with little labor acquire the good things of life?"
But what good things? Money, houses, so many acres of
land, trains of servants, heaps of gold and silver? Can you
call these good things and not hide your head for shame?
How can a man, called to the pursuit of heavenly wisdom,
lust after worldly things, and name these valueless things
"goods"? If these things are good, then their possessors
must be called good. For is not he good who is the possessor
of what is good? But when the possessors of these things are
guilty of fraud and robbery, shall we call them good? For if
wealth is a good, but is increased by greed, the greedier a
man is, the better he must be. But is not this plainly a
self-contradiction? But suppose the wealth is not gained
wrongfully. But how is this possible? So destructive a passion is greed, that to grow rich without injustice is impossible. This Christ declared, saying: "Make to yourselves
friends of the mammon of unrighteousness" (Lk 16:9). But
what if, you say, a man succeeded to his father's inheritance? Then he received what had been gathered by
injustice...

[The True Meaning of Private Property]
4. Tell me, then, where do you get your riches from? From
whom did you receive it and from whom did he receive who
transmits it to you? "From my father and he from my
grandfather." But can you, going back through many gener-

<hr>

[21]Text: PG 62.562.

ations show that the riches were justly acquired? No, you cannot. The root and origin of them must have been injustice. Why? Because God in the beginning made not one man rich and another poor. Nor did he afterwards take and show to one treasures of gold, and deny the other the right of searching for it. Rather, he left the earth free to all alike. How come then, if it is common, you have acres and acres of land, while your neighbor has not a portion of it? "My father transmitted them to me," you say. But whom did he receive them from? "From my grandfather." But you must go back and find the original answer.

Jacob made himself rich, but he gained wealth as a reward for his just labors. However, I will not urge this argument too closely. Let us say that riches should be justly gained and without rapine. For you are not responsible for the covetous acts of your father. Your wealth may be derived from rapine; but you did not commit the act of robbery, that his gold was dug up somewhere out of the earth. What then? Is wealth therefore good? By no means! "But it is not bad either," you say. Yes, it is not bad or evil if you are not avaricious and distribute it to the poor. "But if I do not do evil, even though I do not do good, it is not bad," you retort. True. But is not this an evil, that you alone should have the Lord's property, that you alone should enjoy what is common? Is not "the earth God's, and the fullness thereof?" If then our possessions belong to one common Lord, they belong also to our fellow-servants. The possessions of the Lord are all common. Do we not see this the established rule in great houses? To all is given an equal share of provisions, because they proceed from the treasures of the Lord. And the house of the master is open to all. The King's possessions are all common: cities, market places, and public walks. We all share them equally.

Observe the wise dispensation of God. To put mankind to shame he has made certain things in common, such as the sun, air, earth, water, heaven, sea, light, stars. Their benefits are dispensed equally to all as brethren. We are all formed with the same eyes, the same body, the same soul, the same structure in all respects, all things from the earth, all men from one man, and all in the same habitation. But these are not enough to shame us. He has also made other things common, as we have said: baths, cities, market places, walks.

Observe further now concerning things that are common, there is no contention, but everything is peaceful. But as soon as someone attempts to possess himself of anything to make it his own, then contention is introduced, as if nature itself protests against the fact that, whereas God brings us together in every way, we are eager to divide and separate ourselves by appropriating things, using those cold words "mine and yours." Then struggles and hatred arise. But where this does not happen, no strife or struggles appear.

Hence it is to be concluded that common sharing is more convenient and more conformable to our nature. Why is it that there is never a dispute about a market-place? Is it not because it is common to all? But about a house, about a property, about money, disputes never come to an end. Things that necessary are set in common, whereas in the least things, we do not observe community and equality. Yet God has opened freely to all those greater things so that we may learn to share in common these inferior things. Nevertheless, for all this, we have not learnt the lesson.

5

THE GOLDEN AGE OF LATIN PATRISTIC LITERATURE

As the Greek patristic age reached its apogee in the East with the Cappadocian Fathers and John Chrysostom between the fourth and the fifth centuries, in the West, roughly during the same time, Latin patristic literature achieved its highest glory with Ambrose, Jerome, and Augustine. In this chapter we will study the social teachings of Ambrose and Jerome. Augustine, both for the bulk of his writings and the importance of his doctrine, deserves a separate treatment in the next chapter.

Part One: Ambrose of Milan

Ambrose (c. 337-397), bishop of Milan, a doctor of the Church, was preeminently a pastor, a successful man of action, an energetic administrator, endowed with an iron will, a great sense of discipline, and a superb practical turn of mind. He also exercised an extensive political activity, under various forms, with Gratian, Justina, Valentinian II, and Theodosius.

On social teachings his most significant works include *On Naboth, On Tobit* and *On Duties. On Naboth* is a sharp critique against the rapaciousness of the rich, based upon an episode in the life of Naboth reported in the First Book of Kings, chapter 21. In *On Tobit* Ambrose argues against the practice of lending with interest. In both these works the influence of Basil's ideas is apparent. *On Duties* is the first treatise on Christian ethics with its scheme taken from Cicero's work of the same name (*De Officiis*). Its moral concepts are derived from stoicism but thoroughly transformed by the Christian faith. Of Ambrose's social doctrine we will discuss three points: justice, private property, and the relationship between Church and State.

Justice, according to Ambrose, is primarily a social virtue. He declares that the two principles that govern and sustain society are justice and good-will. The former implies wisdom, the latter, goodness (*On Duties*, I, 28, 130). Justice is one of the four cardinal virtues that secure the common good. "No virtue produces more abundant benefits than equity or justice, which is more concerned with others than with oneself, neglecting one's own advantages and preferring the common good," affirms Ambrose in *Paradise*, 3, 18. In *On Duties* he repeatedly insists on the nll"(*On Duties*, III, 4, 25). The obligation of looking for the common good is founded in the natural law itself; differently from the animals men must seek the welfare of others: "We are bound by the law of nature to act for the good of all" (*Ibid.*). Ambrose's concept of justice is, therefore, very close to our notion of "social justice" today.

Ambrose's teaching on private property has been the subject of conflicting interpretations. Dudden, in his *The Life and Times of St. Ambrose*, Vol. II, Oxford, 1935, suggests that for Ambrose private ownership is contrary to divine and natural laws and is the consequence of human greed. There are quite a few passages that seem to substantiate this interpretation. Some representative samples are given here. "The world was created for all in general, yet a handful of the rich endeavor to make it their own preserve" (*On Naboth*, 11). "When giving to the poor you are not giving him what is yours, rather you are paying back to him what is his. Indeed what is common to all and has been given to all to make use of, you have usurped for yourself alone. The earth belongs to all, and not only to the rich; yet those who do not enjoy it are far fewer than those who do. You are paying back, therefore, your debt; you are not giving gratuitously what you do not owe" (*Ibid.*, 53). "Moreover it is unjust that he who is completely equal to you should not be assisted by his fellow man, especially given the fact that our Lord God has willed that this earth should be a common possession of all and that its fruits should be made available to all. On the contrary, greed has distributed the rights of possessions" (*Commentary on Psalm* 118, Homily 8, 22). "Next they (the philosophers) considered it consonant with justice that one should treat common, that is, public property as public, and private as private. But this is not even in accord with nature, for nature has poured forth all things for all for common use. God has ordered all things to be produced, so that there should be good in common to all, and that the earth should be a kind of common possession for all. Nature, therefore, has produced a common right for all, but greed (*usurpatio*) has made it a right for a few" (*On Duties*, I, 28, 132).

No doubt these texts should be carefully interpreted in their immediate contexts and in the general framework of Ambrose's social teaching. To understand them correctly one should remember that Ambrose, like other Fathers, did not elaborate a full-fledged system of social thought in which every term (e.g. private, public, right of ownership, use, sharing) is clearly defined. What Ambrose intends to affirm in these texts is that all the goods of the earth are created for the use of all human beings (not in the sense that they are indiscriminately and commonly "owned" by all); that all human beings have a natural right to make use of them; that the right of private ownership is not unconditional, exclusive, and absolute, but essentially limited; that there is a strict duty of justice, and not merely of charity, to share these goods with others. There is no doubt in Ambrose's mind that "private ownership" in the exclusive and absolute form is the result of sin and greed, and therefore the only way of overcoming this form of private ownership is unselfish communication and sharing.

As bishop of Milan, Ambrose was in close contact with the emperors, who frequently resided in his see. Incidents involving him and them are well known: his struggle over the Altar of Victory against Symmachus and Justina; the refusal to hand over the Pontian Basilica, and the New Basilica to the Arians at the request of Justina; his diplomatic missions to Maximus; his protest against Theodosius's order to rebuild the synagogue at Callinicum; his excommunication of Theodosius because of his excessive punishment of the people of Thessalonica.

Ambrose has not written a special treatise on the relationship between Church and State; his thoughts on this topic are expressed as remarks drawn from him by political events or made in the course of his Scriptural exegesis. The State as such is good and intended by God. In principle it precedes the Fall and is natural. However, because of sin, society is no longer what it should be; some of its institutions, like slavery and private ownership in its absolute and exclusive form, are the result of the Fall. So indeed is monarchy. While the State itself is natural, coercive power is the fruit of sin, not, however, as an invention by the devil but as the divinely approved remedy for sin. Thus where there is a monarch, he must be accepted as the power ordained of God and given his due.

There are thus two distinct societies, the Church and the State. What is the relationship between these two bodies? It is recalled that, when the Roman empire became Christian, Constantine thought of himself as responsible to God for the welfare of both Church and State. Eusebius of Caesarea elaborated this conception into a theology of the superiority of imperial power over the Church. Athanasius and Basil protested against this conception, but without result. In the West, Hosius of Cordova and Hilary of Poitiers also voiced energetic protestations against it.

But it was not until Ambrose came that the Church's right of independence from the State in its own domain was fully asserted in theory and practice. He makes a distinction between the State, *respublica*, and Church, *religio*. The latter possesses the right of liberty in matters of faith (*causa Dei, causa fidei, causa religionis*). This right of liberty means in practice that the representatives of the Church, its episcopacy (*sacerdotium*) and its hierarchy (*ordo ecclesiasticus*), must be free from State supervision and lay authority. The bishops can be judged only by their fellow bishops, not by the emperors. On the contrary, in matters of faith, the Christian emperors are subject to the bishops. "The emperor, in fact, is in the Church, not over the Church" (*Sermo contr. Aux.* 36). "Divine things are not subject to the emperor's authority" (*Letter* 20, 8). Lastly, the churches and all ecclesiastical buildings are not subject to the emperor's authority: "To the emperor belong the palaces; to the bishop, the churches" (*Letter* 20, 19).

Moreover, while the Christian emperor must not interfere with the affairs of the Church, he should help put the decisions of the Church into practice, even by force, and should protect the true religion and the true Church by prohibiting pagan cults and punishing heretics. The Church, in its turn, as the guardian of the moral law, will through the bishops guide the emperor in his decisions so that they may be in accordance with the moral norms, and if necessary, it will use its own kind of force, spiritual sanctions, excommunication, the threat of damnation. Thus Ambrose, in fact, excommunicated Theodosius, Maximus, and Eugenius. For the emperor, as a Christian, is within the Church, and, as a layman, is subordinate to the bishop.

Ambrose's doctrine of the relationship between Church and State does not therefore advocate two mutually exclusive spheres, but an interpenetration of Church and State. It is true, however, that in this mutual relationship, the ultimate authority lies in the hands of the Church, since now the sovereign is not responsible directly to God but to the Church. And not rarely had the Church to tell the faithful whether or not the sovereign had acted rightly and consequently whether or not they should obey him. It is an open question whether a bishop or a body of bishops will ever have sufficient knowledge and wisdom to declare with absolute certitude and without possibility of error that the sovereign in a concrete instance has acted wrongfully and therefore is no longer entitled to the obedience of his subjects.

THE HEXAMERON

[The Primitive Political Order and the Present One]
V, 15, 52.[1] In the beginning men exercised their political power given to them by nature, following the example of bees, so that work and dignity were common. Individuals learnt to share their duties and divide their authority and rewards, so that no one was excluded either from honors or from work. This was the most perfect state of things inasmuch as no one could become arrogant by possessing power permanently or crushed by a prolonged submission. Promotion is made without envy, according to the order of the offices and the measure of time. Offices that are given by rotation are more tolerable; no one would dare to lay too heavy a burden on another who would succeed him in his office and from whom he could receive in turn much harm. No burden would seem too heavy to anyone if he knows that he will eventually obtain honor.

But then, men, in their lust for power, began to claim undue authority and no longer wished to give up what they had obtained. Military service, which was a common right, became a burden; the order of succession to power disap-

[1]Text: CSEL 32.1.178.

peared, each one was free to seize for himself what he could get; offices became more difficult to bear, and because they were not voluntarily undertaken, they suffered neglect... Anything, however easy, can become difficult when it is forced. Thus uninterrupted work and submission tended to destroy interest and love, and prolonged and continuous possession of power produced insolence. What man whom you meet would voluntarily give up his power and renounce his great kingdom and freely change himself from being first into being last? Not only do we fight for the highest offices, but also for the intermediate ones, and we even dispute about the first places at banquets. And if we happen to occupy some position of responsibility, we will not wish to give it up. On the contrary, in ancient times, we find equality in work and humility in power.

PARADISE

[The Virtue of Justice, Foundation of Society]
III, 18.[2] The fourth river is the Euphrates, which in Latin means 'fecundity and abundance of fruits.' It is the symbol of justice, the food of every soul. No virtue produces more abundant benefits than equity or justice, which is more concerned with others than with itself, neglecting its own advantages, and preferring the common good... Justice is the most important virtue because it represents the concord of all the other virtues... Justice is not divisible into parts. It is, as it were, the mother of all virtues.

ON NABOTH

[Ambition and Greed of the Rich]
1.[3] The story of Naboth, ancient though it may be, is of perennial application. Daily the rich and prosperous covet other people's goods, daily they endeavor to dispossess the

---

[2]Text: CSEL 32.1.276.
[3]Text: CSEL 32.2.469.

humble, robbing the poor of their possessions, their little ancestral plot of ground. Discontented with what they have, they feel their craving enkindled by any property of their neighbors. So that Ahab is not one person, someone born long ago; every day, alas, the world sees Ahabs born, never to die out—or if one such die, a multitude rises up instead, and the spoilers still outnumber the spoiled. And Naboth is not one person either, a poor man who was once murdered; every day some Naboth is done to death, every day the poor are murdered...

2. You rich, how far will you push your frenzied greed? Are you alone to dwell on the earth? Why do you cast out men who are fellow-creatures and claim all creation as your own? Earth at its beginning was for all in common, it was meant for rich and poor alike; what right have you to monopolise the soil? Nature knows nothing of the rich; all are poor when she brings them forth. Clothing and gold and silver, food and drink and covering—we are born without them all; naked she receives her children into the tomb, and no one can enclose his acres there. A little turf suffices for poor and rich, and the earth which proved too narrow for the appetites of the living is wide enough at last for the rich and all that is his.

Nature, impartial at our coming, is impartial at our going; she bears us all equal, and entombs us equal in her bosom. Who can tell class from class among the dead? Open the earth again and find your rich man if you may; excavate a tomb a short while after, and if you know the man that you see, prove by token that he was poor. The sole difference is that the rich has more to waste away with him; the silken garments and cloth of gold swathing his body are lost for the living without helping the dead. Being rich, he has perfumes lavished on him, but that does not stop the stench; he wastes the sweetness that might be used by others and is none the sweeter for it himself. And he leaves behind him heirs to bicker...

4. But in his lifetime even, why whould he think he has everything in plenty? You, the rich man who call yourself rich, you do not know how needy you are, how truly necessitous you feel. The more you have, the more you want, and however much you win, in your own eyes you are poor still. Rapacity is not quenched by gain; it is fanned the more... Holy Scripture shows us how wretchedly poor a rich man may be, how abject a beggar he may be.

5. Ahab was king of Israel, Naboth a poor man. (Cf. 1 Kgs 21). The one enjoyed a whole kingdom's affluence, the other possessed a little holding. Naboth coveted none of the rich man's estates; Ahab considered himself in want because his poor neighbor had a vineyard. Which of them do you think was poor?...

But let us pass to the words of Scripture. "And some time after this, as Naboth the Jezraelite had a vineyard in Jezrael near the palace of Ahab, king of Samaria, Ahab said to Naboth: 'Give to me your vineyard, that I may make of it a garden of herbs, because it is near my house, and I will give you for it another vineyard; or if it seems good to you, I will give you money for the vineyard, and I will make of it a garden of herbs.' Naboth said to Ahab: 'God forbid that I should give you the inheritance of my fathers.' Ahab went home disturbed; he lay on his bed and covered his face and would not eat" (1 Kgs 21:1-4)... What has the king to say? Listen. 'Give to me'; are not these the words of the poor, of some beggar in the streets? 'Give to me.' Give to me—I am in want; give to me—I am without other means of livelihood; give to me—I have not wherewith to eat or drink, to keep or to clothe myself, not a loaf, not a coin, nothing at all. Give to me—the Lord has given to you, and you can, and should, give to me; to me he has given nothing. Give to me; I am helpless unless you give. Give to me; it is written, 'give alms.' How servile, how despicable is all this! There is no feeling of humility in it, only a burning greed. But what effrontery too in the servile words! Give me *your* vineyard, he says; he acknowledges that it is not his, that he has no claim to it, but he asks for it nevertheless. "And I will give you for it another vineyard." The rich man disdains as worthless what is his own, and covets as something most precious what is another's. "Or if it seems good to you, I will give you money." He quickly covers his first mistake, and offers money instead of another vineyard; his own properties are to reach out everywhere, and no one else should have property at all...

11.[4] "And I will make of it a garden of herbs." This was the aim, then, of all his wild frenzy; space was needed for common herbs. Such are you, rich; you are not so anxious to own for use—rather you wish to shut others out. You are more concerned to rob the poor than to gain anything for yourselves. It is an affront to you, so you thin, if a poor man has something a rich man might care to own, and anything that belongs to others you consider a loss to you. What pleasure can come to you from this waste of nature's wealth? The world was created for all in general, yet a handful of the rich endeavor to make it their own preserve.

12... "Woe," cries the prophet, "to them that join house to house, field to field" (Is 5:8); and he indicts them for a covetousness which defeats its own ends. They flee from a life with other men, and hence they expel their neighbors; but flight proves impossible, for when they have expelled these they find others, and after a new expulsion they cannot but come on new neighbors still; after all, they cannot dwell on the earth alone...

13. We have heard the rich man's words in seeking another's property; hear now the poor man's in defending his own: "God forbid that I should give you the inheritance of my fathers." He shuns Ahab's money like the plague...

14. The covetous king's spirit was troubled at the words; and he lay on his bed, covered his face and would not eat. The rich take to mourning if they are baulked of their plunder; if

[4]Text: CSEL 32.2.473.

a poor man will not cede his property, they cannot hide the vehemence of their grief. They long for sleep, they cover their faces, they cannot bear the thought that something somewhere belongs to another, the knowledge that something in the whole world is not theirs, the news that some neighbor has property, the voice of the poor defying them...

15. "He would not eat"; because he wanted another's bread. The bread that rich men eat belongs to others more than to them, for they live on plunder, and what they pay comes from what they pillage. Or one may say that in eating no bread he meant to inflict death on himself because something was denied him.

16. Contrast with all this the state of Naboth. He has nothing; for him there can be no question of any self-chosen fast, unless it be to God; the only fasting he does comes of necessity. Thus you, rich, steal everything from the poor, rather than they who suffer the penalty of want. They fast if they have not; you fast when you have. Hence you exact a penalty from yourselves before you impose it on the poor, and the pains of dire need are thrust upon you by your very temper of mind.

The poor have nothing to enjoy; you will neither enjoy what you have nor let others do so. You dig up gold from the mines only to bury it again, and how many men's lives with it.

17. And for whom is your wealth kept? You read of the rich miser: "He lays up treasure and knows not for whom he stores it" (Ps 38:7). Your heir awaits it in idleness, or he grumbles and complains that you take a long time dying. He resents the time while his heritage is increasing, and longs for the moment when he can squander it. A sad thing indeed, when you receive no gratitude even from the one who benefits by your labors! It is for his sake that you starve yourself dismally for days, afraid of meals and their drain on your provisions; for his sake you will fast every day.

18. I know of a rich man who, when he left for the country, would have small-sized loaves brought him from town, then count them over, so that one could tell from the number of loaves how many days he would stay in the country. His barn he kept locked and would not open it, so that his possessions would not diminish. He allowed himself one loaf a day, hardly enough for even a miser's appetite. I was told too—and I believe it—that if at a meal an egg were brought him, he would complain that it meant a chicken lost. I record this to bring home to you that God's justice punishes you in kind, using your abstinences to avenge the tears of the poor...

[The Hypocrisy of the Rich Man's Fasting]
44.[5] How vividly does the Scripture portray the rich and their ways! They are disconsolate if they cannot rob their neighbors, they refuse to eat, they fast—not to lessen their crime but to accomplish it. At such times you see them joining the congregation at church—dutiful, demure, regular—hoping to win the grace to effect their evil purpose. But God says to them: "This is not the fast that I have chosen, that you bow your head like a reed or be in sackcloth or ashes. You shall not call this an acceptable fast... But loose every bond of wickedness, undo the knots of covenants made by force, let the afflicted go free, tear up very unjust writing. Break your bread to the hungry; and bring the needy and homeless into your house... " (Is 58:5-7).

45. You the rich, do you hear what the Lord God says? And yet you come to church, not to give to the poor but to take away. You fast, not that the cost of your meal may go to those in want, but that you may gain something in plunder from them. What do you mean with your letter and paper, your seal and writing, your legal bond? Did you not hear the words: "Loose every bond of sickness, undo the knots of

[5]Text: CSEL 32.2.492.

covenants made by force, let the afflicted go free, tear up every unjust writing"? You show me your tablets; I pronounce the words of God's law. You write with ink; I cite the oracles of the prophets, written with the spirit of God. You invent false witness; I call to witness your own conscience, which utters against you a judgment you cannot escape or evade, and whose testimony you will not be able to gainsay in the day when God manifests the secrets of men. You say: "I will pull down my barns." The Lord says: Rather let all the store in them be turned to the service of poor and needy. You say: "I will build greater, and gather there all that accrues to me." The Lord says: "Break your bread to the hungry." You say: "I will take the poor man's house from him." The Lord says: "Bring the needy and homeless into your house." How can you ask that God should hear you favorably when to God himself you give no hearing?

If the rich man's whim is not humored, subterfuge is contrived and refusal of what he asks is held to be an affront to God.

[Sharing of Riches Is a Duty of Justice]
53.[6] What you, rich, give to the needy brings profit to yourself; for yourself too your possession is increased when it is diminished. You yourself are fed by the bread you give to the poor, because whoever has mercy on the poor is himself sustained by the fruits of his compassion. Mercy is sown on earth and sprouts in heaven; what is planted in the poor produces in front of God. "Do not say, I will give tomorrow," says the Lord (Prov 3, 28). If he does not suffer that you say: "I will give tomorrow," how can he bear you to answer: "I will not give"? When giving to the poor you are not giving him what is yours; rather you are paying back to him what is his. Indeed what is common to all and has been given to all to make use of, you have usurped for yourself alone. The earth belongs to all, and not only to the rich; yet those who do not enjoy it are far fewer than those who do.

[6]Text: CSEL 32.2.498.

You are paying back, therefore, your debt; you are not giving gratuitously what you do not owe...

[The Rich and the Poor Are Equal]
54. What reason then do you rich have for being proud? How can you say to the poor man, "Don't touch me."? Were you not conceived in the womb and born as the poor was? Why do you flaunt your noble stock? Among you and your like the ancestry of a dog is traced like a wealthy man's, and a horse's fine breed is boasted of like a consul's. This horse has such and such a sire, such and such a dam, another can vaunt his ancestry two or three generations back. But all this is no help in the race; speed, not breed, wins the prize, and one with a famous name is all the more disgraced if he loses. You then, my rich man, take care that the virtues of your fathers are not put to shame in you; otherwise they too may have to bear the reproach: "Why did you choose *him*, why make *him* your heir?" It is no credit to an heir to have gilded ceilings or slabs of porphyry. The praise for this must not go to men, but to mine and quarry where men are punished. It is the poor who dig for gold, though to them the gold is denied, and they toil in the search for what they cannot keep.

55. But I find it strange that you rich should brag of gold, since it is rather a stumbling block than ground for praise: "Gold also is a stumbling block, and woe to them that seek after it." Again, there is a blessing for the rich man "who has been found without blemish and who has not gone after gold or put his trust in treasure of money." But it seems he is hard to find, for the writer wishes to be shown such a man: "Who is he, that we may praise him?" His actions are to be praised as rare rather than accepted as customary. Thus a man who remains commendable amid riches is a man truly perfect and one to be glorified—"he who might have transgressed and did not transgress, and might have done evil and did it not" (Sirach, 31:7-10).

[The Heartlessness of the Rich—
The Right Use of Possessions]
56. ... You give coverings to walls and bring men to nakedness. The naked cries out before your house unheeded; your
fellow-man is there, naked and crying, while you are per-
plexed by the choice of marble to clothe your floor. A poor
man begs for money in vain; your fellow-man is there,
begging bread, and your horse champs gold between his
teeth. Other men have no corn; your fancy is held by precious ornaments. What a judgment you draw upon yourself!
The people are starving, and you shut your barns; the people
are groaning, and you toy with the jewel upon your finger.
Unhappy man, with the power but not the will to rescue so
many souls from death, when the price of a jewelled ring
might save the lives of a whole populace...'

58. You who bury your gold in the ground, you are the
keeper and steward of your wealth, not its lord and master.
But where your treasure is, there is your heart also, and your
heart is there with the gold, buried in the ground. Sell your
gold rather, and purchase salvation; sell your jewels and
purchase the kingdom of God; sell your land and purchase
eternal life! What I say is true, for I cite the words of truth
itself: "If you want to be perfect, sell all you have and give to
the poor, and you will have treasure in heaven" (Mt 19:21).
And be not sorrowful at this saying, lest of you also it should
be said: "Only with difficulty will a rich man enter into the
Kingdom of God" (Mt 20:23). Rather, as you read these
words, consider how your wealth may be snatched from you
by death, wrested from you by the power of some greater
one; consider too how you are asked to give little for much,
the transitory for the eternal, treasure of money which is
corruptible for the treasure of grace which lasts. Consider
how you are not the sole owner of these things—the moth
shares them with you, and wealth-consuming rust. Such
company avarice has given you. Then mark what manner of
debtors are bound to you by gratitude. "The bountiful in
bread will be blessed by the lips of the just, and there will be
testimony of his goodness" (Sirach, 31:28). God the Father

becomes your debtor, paying interest as to a kindly lender for the gift whereby you help the poor. God the Son also; he says. "I was hungry, and you gave me to eat; thirsty and you gave me to drink; a stranger, and you brought me in; naked, and you covered me" (Mt 26:35-36). For whatever has been given to each of the least, this he says has been given to him...

ON THE DUTIES OF THE CLERGY

[Mercy and Its Advantages]
I, 11, 38.[7] Mercy, also, is a good thing, for it makes men perfect insofar as it imitates the perfect Father. Nothing graces the Christian soul so much as mercy. It is exercised chiefly towards the poor; you should consider them as sharers with you in the common fruits of the earth, which brings them forth for the use of all. Consequently you should distribute to the poor what you have and in this way help your fellow-men and companions. You give money, the poor man receives life; the money you give is his livelihood; your money is his property.

39. Further he gives more to you than you to him, since he is your debtor in regard to your salvation. If you clothe the naked, you clothe yourself with righteousness. If you welcome the stranger into your home and receive the needy, they will procure for you the friendship of the saints and an eternal dwelling-place. That is no small recompense. You sow earthly things and receive heavenly rewards...

[The Demands of Social Justice]
I, 28, 130.[8] Justice, then, concerns the society and the community of the human race. For what holds society together is divided into two parts: justice and good-will. The latter is also called liberality and kindness. Justice seems to me the

[7]Text: PL 16.34.
[8]Text: PL 16.61.

loftier, liberality the more pleasing, of the two. The one gives judgment, the other shows goodness.

131. But what the pagan philosophers take to be the first duty of justice is not acceptable to us. They maintain, in fact, that the first expression of justice is to hurt no one, unless one is provoked to do so by the wrongs received. This opinion is contradicted by the authority of the Gospel. For the Scripture wills that we should imitate the spirit of the Son of man, who came to give grace, not to bring harm (Lk 9:56).

132. Next they considered it consonant with justice that one should treat common, that is, public property as public, and private as private. But this is not even in accord with nature, for nature has poured forth all things for all for common use. God has ordered all things to be produced, so that there should be food in common to all, and that the earth should be a kind of common possession for all. Nature, therefore, has produced a common right for all, but greed has made it a right for a few. Here, too, we are told that the Stoics taught that all things that the earth produces have been created for the use of man, and that men have been born for the sake of men, so that one may be of mutual advantage to another . . .

135. Thus, in accordance with the will of God and the bonds of nature, we ought to assist one another, to vie with one another in doing good works, to lay, as it were, all our advantages before all, and (to use the words of the Scripture) to bring help to each other from a feeling of devotion or of duty, by giving money, or by doing something, one way or another, so that among us the good of the society may be increased. Let no one shirk from these duties for fear of danger but let him consider all affairs of the society, whether good or evil, as their own concern. Thus Moses was not afraid to undertake terrible wars for his people's sake, nor did he fear the armies of the mightiest kings, nor yet was he frightened by the savagery of barbarian nations. He put

aside the though of his own safety so as to give freedom to his people.

[The Use of Sacred Gold Vessels for Charitable Purposes]
II, 28, 136.[9] It is a very great incentive to mercy to share in other people's misfortunes, to help them as far as our means allow, and sometimes even beyond them. For it is better for mercy's sake to take up a case, or to suffer hatred rather than to show lack of feeling. So I once brought hatred on myself because I broke up the sacred vessels to redeem captives—a fact that could displease the Arians. It was not the act itself that displeased them; rather it was a pretext they could use to blame me. Who indeed can be so hard, so cruel, and so cold-hearted as to be displeased by the fact that a man is saved from death, or a woman from barbarian rapes, things that are worse than death, or boys and girls and infants from the pollution of idols, whereby through fear of death they were defiled?

137. Though we did not act thus without good reason, yet we have pursued this matter with the people so as to confess and to proclaim again and again that it was far better to preserve souls than gold for the Lord. For He who sent the apostles without gold also founded the Church without gold. The Church possesses gold, not to store it up, but to distribute it and to use it to help those in want. What need is there to guard what, if kept, is of no use to anyone? Do we not know how much gold and silver the Assyrians carried off from the Lord's temple? Is it not far better that the priests should melt it down to support the poor, if other supplies fail, than to have it plundered and defiled by a sacrilegious enemy? Would not the Lord himself say: "Why did you allow so many needy to die of hunger? Surely you do have gold. You should have given them food and sustenance. Why are so many captives brought to the slave market and why are so many unredeemed left to be killed by

[9]Text: PL 16.139.

the enemy? It would be better to preserve living vessels than gold ones."

[The Common Good is the Good of Each]
III, 4, 25.[10] It is clear, then, that we should consider and admit that what benefits the individual is the common good and should judge nothing as useful unless it benefits all. For how can one be benefitted alone? What is useless to all is harmful. I certainly cannot conceive that what is useless to all can be of use to anyone at all. For if there is but one law of nature for all, there is also but one state of usefulness for all. And we are bound by the law of nature to act for the good of all. It is not, therefore, right for the person who wishes the interests of another to be considered according to nature, to injure him against the law of nature.

ON TOBIT

[Usury and Lending with Interest]
2.7.[11] If I lend money without exacting interest, I act justly. Indeed lending with the expectation of interest is unjust, but lending itself is not, as it is written "Lend to your neighbor in his hour of need" (Sirach, 29:2). David too has said: "The just man is kindly and lends" (Ps 37:21). But the other kind of lending, that which is done in order to gain profit, is rightly condemned as abominable and is forbidden by the Law (Cf. Deut 23:19). Tobit shuns taking interest: he instructs his son not to despise God's commandments, to give alms from his possessions, not to lend his money with interest, not to turn his face from any of the poor (Cf. Tb 4:6-9). Whoever gives this advice condemns interest-taking, which is for many the way to make a profit and the occasion to do commerce. Usury is forbidden to the saints.

8. The more blameworthy is usury, the more admirable is the one who abstains from it. If you have money, give it

[10]Text: PL 16.152.
[11]Text: CSEL 32.2.521.

away. The money that you keep idle, make it useful for others. Give it with the intention of not recovering it; and if it is returned to you, do not receive profit from it. If the borrower cannot pay your money back to you, let him repay you his gratitude; if you are cheated of your money, you will acquire justice, because he is just who has compassion and lends. If you lose your money, you will gain mercy, as it is written: "He is merciful who lends to his neighbor" (Sirach 29:1).

[The Rich Lend for Their Own Profits]
11.[12] You rich, such are indeed your favors! You give little and demand much in return. This is your compassion: you plunder even when you say you are giving help. For you even the poor are a source of profit. You subject the poor to usury; you know how to oblige them to pay you interest even when they do not have enough to look after their basic needs. Truly compassionate you are! You grant them freedom and then bind them to yourselves; you oblige them to pay you interest even when they have nothing to eat. Can one imagine anything more perverse? The poor ask for medicine and you offer them poison; they beg for bread and you give them a sword; they plead for freedom and you subject them to slavery; they implore to be freed from their bonds and you entrap them in an inescapable net.

LETTERS

[The Right Use of Riches]
2, 11.[13] Let your people not desire many things; a few things are already many to them. Poverty and riches are words which imply want and satiety. He is not rich who does not have everything he desires, nor is he poor who has. Let no one despise a widow, or cheat an orphan, or defraud his neighbor. Woe to him who has amassed a fortune by deceit and builds a city in blood, that is, his soul. For it is the soul

[12]Text: CSEL 32.2.523.
[13]Text: PL 16.881.

that is built like a city. Greed does not build it, but sets it on fire and burns it... The riches of a man ought to work towards the redemption of his soul, not to its destruction. Wealth is redemption if one uses it well; it is a snare if one does not know how to use it. For what is a man's money if not provision for his journey? A great amount is a burden; a moderate sum is sufficient. We are pilgrims in this life; many are walking along, but we must make a good journey in order to have Christ as our fellow-traveler who spent his life on earth doing good.

[The Evil of Avarice]
2, 15. Happy is the man who has been able to cut out the root of vices, avarice. Surely he will not fear the balance of justice. Avarice generally dulls men's senses and perverts judgments, so that they think profit as piety and money as reward of prudence. But great is the reward of piety and the advantage of moderation; the possession of these virtues is sufficient. For, what do superfluous riches profit in this world if they do not assist our birth and impede our dying? Naked we are born into this world, we leave it in destitution, and we are buried without our inheritance.

[Follow the Example of Christ]
2, 26. Let your people seek the riches of good works and be rich in character. The beauty of riches is not in the purses of the rich, but in their support of the poor. In the weak and needy, riches shine brighter. Let the wealthy learn to seek not their own interests, but those which are Christ's, so that Christ may seek them out and bestow his possessions on them. He spent his blood for them; he poured his Spirit; he offers them his kingdom. What else can he give who has given himself? Or what will the Father refuse to give, who delivered his only-begotten Son to death for us? Therefore, admonish them to serve the Lord in purity and grace, to lift up their eyes to heavenly things with all the intensity of their minds, to count nothing as gain except what profits eternal life, since all the gain of this world is the loss of souls...

[The State Should Defend Christianity, the True Religion,
by Not Erecting the Altar of Victory]
17, 9.[14] Suppose today some pagan emperor (which God
forbid!) were to set up an altar to idols and compel Christians to gather there, to be present while sacrifices are being
offered, to be choked with ashes from the altar, with the
cinders of sacrilege, with smoke from the brazier, to vote in
a Senate-House in which they take the oath at the altar of an
idol before they are asked for their votes (for as they understand it, the altar is placed there so that every meeting shall
deliberate under oath to it), and all this despite the present
Christian majority in the Senate. Would that not be
regarded as persecution by a Christian who was compelled
to attend the Senate with such a choice before him? And
compulsion is often used. Christians are forced to attend
under penalties. Now that you are the emperor, are Christians to be forced to swear by an altar? An oath is an
acknowledgment of divine power in him whom you invoke
to guarantee your good faith. With *you* as emperor, are
there petitions and demands that you should order the
erection of an altar and provide funds for profane
sacrifices?

10. No such decree can be made without sacrilege. Therefore
I beg you not to decree or order it, and not to put your
signature to any decrees of the kind. As a bishop of Christ, I
appeal to your faith. We should all have joined in appealing
to you, all the bishops, had not the news that something of
the sort had been put forward in your Consistory, or been
requested by the Senate, come so suddenly and been so hard
to believe.

[Ambrose's Refusal to Hand over the New Basilica
to the Arians. Limits of the Power of the State]
20, 19. The order comes: "Hand over the basilica." I reply:
"It is not lawful for me to hand it over, nor good for your

---

[14]Text: PL 16.963.

Majesty to receive it. If you have not right to violate the house of a private citizen, do you think that you can appropriate the house of God?" It is alleged that the emperor has the right to do anything, that everything belongs to him. I answer: "Do not burden yourself with the idea that you have any right as emperor over the things of God. Do not exalt yourself; if you wish to remain emperor, submit yourself to God. It is written: "Give to God the things that are God's, to Caesar the things that are Caesar's."

To the emperor belong the palaces; to the bishop, the churches. You have been entrusted with jurisdiction over public buildings, but not over sacred ones. Again it is said that the order came from the emperor: "I, too, ought to have a basilica." I replied: "It is not lawful for you to have one. What have you to do with an adulteress? She is an adulteress who is not joined to Christ by lawful union!"

[Ambrose Refused to Be Judged by the Civil Court.
Bishops Should Be Judged by Bishops Only]
21. Bishop Ambrose to the most gracious Emperor and most blessed Augustus Valentinian.

1.[15] Dalmatius, tribune and secretary, cited me by order of your Grace, as he alleged, requiring me to choose judges, as Auxentius had done. He did not mention the names of those who have been asked for, but added that the disputation would take place in the Consistory, with your Piety as the final arbiter.

2. To this I have, I believe, a sufficient answer. No one should regard me as contumacious when I assert what your father, of august memory, not only answered by word of mouth but also sanctioned by law, that in a matter of faith or ecclesiastical discipline the judge must not be inferior in office or different in standing. These are the words of the rescript, and they mean that he wished bishops to be judged by bishops. Again, if a bishop was to be prosecuted on other charges, and a matter of conduct was to be examined, he

[15]Text: PL 16.979.

wished that this also should come before a court of bishops.

3. Who, then, has answered your Grace contumaciously? He who desires to see you like your father, or he who would have you different from him? Or are there, perhaps, some who set no store by that great emperor's opinion, despite the fact that his faith was proved by the constancy of his profession and his wisdom proclaimed by the improvement in the state of the country?

4. When did your gracious Majesty ever hear of laymen judging bishops in a matter of faith? Are we so prostrate with flattery as to forget the rights of a bishop so that I should contemplate entrusting to others what God has given to me? What will happen next, if a bishop is to be instructed by a layman? The layman holding forth, the bishop listening, the bishop learning from the layman! In view of the holy Scriptures and the precedents of antiquity, it is impossible to deny that in a matter of faith—in a matter of faith, I repeat—it is the practice for bishops to judge the Christian emperors, and not emperors bishops.

5. God willing, you will one day reach a riper age, and then you will know what to think of a bishop who allows laymen to trample on his episcopal rights. Your father, a man of mature years, by the favor of God, used to say: "It is not for me to judge between bishops." Now your Grace is saying: "I must be the judge." He, baptized in Christ as he was, thought himself unequal to the responsibility of such a judgment. Do you, Sir, who have yet to earn the sacrament of baptism, take upon yourself to pronounce judgment concerning the faith, when you do not yet know the sacraments of the faith?

Part Two: Jerome

Jerome's life (347-419) and writings bring together the most important events and personalities of the patristic era. He was born into the period when Christianity emerged as the legitimate religion, witnessed the definitive establishment of orthodox Christianity in the Empire, and died shortly after the sack of Rome by Alaric. He was brought into contact with several eminent Fathers. He often referred to Ambrose in his writings, carried on an important correspondence with Augustine, studied under Gregory of Nazianzus, and was acquainted with Gregory of Nyssa.

Not an original thinker nor an able social organizer, Jerome's chief claim to fame is his translation of the Bible into Latin (the Vulgate) and his attempt to introduce the ascetic life into the West. As far as social teaching is concerned, Jerome's ideas are neither profound nor brilliant. In his letter to Demetrias (Letter 130), he affirms that the possession of earthly goods is not contrary to the Gospel and that the advice to sell all one's possessions and to distribute them to the poor is not obligatory to all. Nevertheless he strongly encourages the sharing of one's possessions with others. Besides his 125 letters which give us inestimable information on persons and events, one of Jerome's most interesting works pertinent to our subject is his *Homily on Luke 16:19-31*. The story of the Rich Man and Lazarus has been commented upon by John Chrysostom among many others. It is interesting to compare Jerome's commentary with that of John Chrysostom given in chapter IV.

LETTERS

[Avoid Avarice and Covetousness]

22, 31.[16] You must also avoid the sin of covetousness, not merely by refusing to appropriate what belongs to others—such an act is punished by the laws of the state—but also by not holding on to your own property, which has now become no longer yours. "If you have not been trustworthy with someone else's money," says the Lord, "who will give you what is your own?" (Lk 16:12). Gold and silver is someone else's, ours is the spiritual heritage. Elsewhere it is written: "The ransom of a man's life is his riches" (Prov 13:8). Further: "No man can serve two masters, for either he will hate the one and love the other; or else he will hold to the one and despise the other. You cannot serve God and Mammon" (Mt 6:24). Riches, that is, for in Syrian language, Mammon means riches. The "thorns" that choke our faith are the excessive concern for our bodily sustenance. The root of covetousness is the preoccupation with worldly things proper to pagans...

32. ... The love of money is the root of all evil, and the Apostle speaks of covetousness as idolatry (Cf. Col 3:5). "Seek first the kingdom of God and all these things shall be added to you" (Mt 6:33). The Lord will never allow a just man to die of hunger. "I was young," says the Psalmist, "and now am old, yet have I not seen the righteous forsaken nor his children begging bread" (Ps 37:25).

[Poverty and Perfection]

130, 14.[17] I think it is unnecessary to warn you against covetousness, since it is the way of your family both to have riches and to despise them. The Apostle tells us that covetousness is idolatry, and to him who asked the Lord the question: "Teacher, what good must I do to possess everlasting life?", the Lord replied: "If you want to be perfect, go,

[16]Text: CSEL 54.191.
[17]Text: CSEL 56.193.

sell all your possessions, and give to the poor, and you will have treasure in heaven. Afterward, come back and follow me" (Mt 19:16,21). This is the perfection of apostolic action and virtue: to sell all that one has and to distribute to the poor, and thus freed from all earthly encumbrance to fly up to the heavenly realms with Christ. To us, or I should rather say, to you, a careful stewardship is entrusted, although in such matters full freedom of choice is left to every individual, whether old or young.

Christ said: "If you want to be perfect." What he means is: I do not compel you. I do not command you, but I set the palm of victory before you, I show you the prize. It is for you to decide whether you will enter the arena and win the crown. Let us consider how wisely Wisdom has spoken. "Sell all your possessions." To whom is this command given? Of course, to the ones to whom it was said: "If you want to be perfect." Sell not a part of your possessions but "all your possessions." And when you have sold them, what then? "Give to the poor." Not to the rich, not to your relatives, not to minister to self-indulgence, but to relieve the needs of others. It makes no difference whether a man is a priest, or a relative, or an acquaintance, you should think of nothing but his poverty. Let your praises come from the stomachs of the hungry and not from the rich banquets of the overfed...

Others may build churches, may adorn their marble columns, may deck the unconscious capitals with gold and precious ornaments, may cover church doors with silver and decorate the altars with gold and gems. I do not blame those who do these things. I do not repudiate them. Everyone must follow his own conscience. And it is better to spend one's money thus than to hoard it up and brood over it. Your duty, however, is of a different kind. It is yours to clothe Christ in the poor, to visit him in the sick, to feed him in the hungry, to shelter him in the homeless, particularly such as are of the household of the faith, to support communities of virgins, to take care of God's servants, of those who are poor in spirit, who serve the same Lord as you day and night, who while they are on earth live the angelic life and speak only of the praises of God. Having food and clothing they rejoice and count themselves rich. They seek for nothing more, contented if only they can persevere in their way of life. For as soon as they begin to seek more they are shown to be undeserving even of those things that are needful.

HOMILY ON LUKE 16:19-31: THE RICH MAN AND LAZARUS[18]

[The Rich Man and Lazarus]
"There was a certain rich man." When the Lord had declared: "No man can serve two masters; you cannot serve God and mammon," and the greedy Pharisees had rebuked him, he set before them an example, or rather, a truth, in the form of an example and parable. Strictly speaking, it is not really a parable when the names of the characters are given. A parable gives an example, but does not allow identification. Where Abraham is mentioned by name, and Lazarus, the prophets, and Moses, there Lazarus is genuine; if Abraham is a true person, so also is Lazarus. We have read who Abraham was; we have not read of Lazarus, but he who made Lazarus, also made Abraham. If he speaks of Abraham as a real person, then we understand Lazarus, also, as a living reality, for fiction is not congruous with the real.

"There was a certain rich man." Just think of the kindness of the Lord! Lazarus, the beggar, is called by his name because he was a saint, but the man who is rich and proud is not deemed worthy of a name. "There was a certain rich man." I say, 'certain,' because he has passed like a shadow. "There was a certain rich man who used to clothe himself in purple and fine linen." Ashes, dust, and earth, he covered up with purple and silk. "Who used to clothe himself in purple and fine linen, and who feasted every day in splendid fashion." As his garments, so his food; and with us, likewise; as our food, so our garments.

"There was a certain poor man, named Lazarus." The

---

[18]This homily is not found in Migne, but is included in the Supplement PLS.

meaning of Lazarus' name is 'boe-houmenos,' one who has been helped; he is not a helper, but one who has been helped. He was a poor man and, in his poverty, the Lord came to his assistance. "Who lay at his gate, covered with sores." The rich man, in purple splendor, is not accused of being avaricious, nor of carrying off the property of another, nor of committing adultery, nor, in fact, of any wrongdoing; the evil alone of which he is guilty is pride. Most wretched of men, you see a member of your own body lying there outside at your gate, and have you no compassion? If the precepts of God mean nothing to you, at least take pity on your own plight, and be in fear lest you become such as he. Why do you save what is superfluous to your pleasures? Give in alms to your own member what you waste. I am not telling you to throw away your wealth. What you throw out, the crumbs from your table, offer as alms.

[The Pitiful Condition of Lazarus and His Reward]
   "Who lay at his gate." He was lying at the gate in order to draw attention to the cruelty paid to his body and to prevent the rich man from saying, I did not notice him; he was in a corner; I could not see him; no one announced him to me. He lay at the gate; you saw him every time you went out and every time you came in. When your throngs of servants and clients were attending you, he lay there full of ulcers. If your eyes disdained to look upon putrid flesh, did not your ears, at least, hear his plea? "Who lay at his gate, covered with sores." He did not have just one sore, his whole body was sores, so that the magnitude of his suffering might arouse your utmost compassion. "Who lay at his gate, covered with sores, and longing to be filled with the crumbs that fell from the rich man's table." There is some relief to sickness if one has resources, but if you add poverty to extreme weakness the infirmity is doubled. Sickness is always fastidious and cannot take anything indelicate; it is nauseated by it. How much real suffering that causes! In the midst of so many wounds, he does not, however, think of the pain of his afflictions, but of the pangs of hunger. "Longing to be filled with the crumbs that fell from the rich man's table." In a

certain way, he is saying to the rich man: The crumbs from your table are enough for me; what you brush off the table are enough for me; what you brush off the table, give in alms; draw profit from your losses. "Even the dogs would come and lick his sores." What no man deigned to bathe and touch, gentle beasts lick.

"It came to pass that the poor man died and was borne away by the angels into Abraham's bosom; but the rich man also died and was buried; and in hell lifting up his eyes..." We have heard what each has suffered on earth; let us consider how they fare in the nether world. The temporal has passed and is over; what follows is for all eternity. Both are dead; the one is met by angels, the other with torments; the one is borne away on the shoulders of angels, the other goes to his punishment; the one, Abraham receives into his bosom of happiness; the other, hell devours. Lazarus "was borne away by the angels." Great sufferings are suddenly exchanged for delights. He is carried by angels and born away without even the effort of walking. He is carried after his great trials because he was exhausted. "Was borne away by the angels." One angel was not enough to carry the pauper, but many came to form a chorus of jubilation. "Was borne away by angels." Every angel rejoices to touch so precious a burden. With pleasure, they bear such burdens in order to conduct men into the kingdom of heaven. He was escorted and carried into the bosom of Abraham, not to the side of Abraham, but into the bosom of Abraham, that Abraham might caress him, revivify him; that he might hold him in his bosom and, like a tender and compassionate father, warm him back to life again.

[The Fate of the Rich Man]
"The rich man also died and was buried"; earth has returned to its earth. "In hell, lifting up his eyes." Note the import and appropriateness of each word. "In hell, lifting up his eyes." Lazarus was above; he was below; he lifted up his eyes to behold Lazarus, not to despise him. "Lifting up his eyes, being in torments." His whole being was in anguish; his eyes alone were free, free to gaze upon the happiness of the

other man. He was allowed the liberty of his eyes to be tortured the more, because he does not enjoy what the other had. The riches of others are torments to those who are in poverty. "Lifting up his eyes, being in torments." The one many angels carry away; the other is held fixed in never-ending torments. Being in torments: the Gospel did not say in torment, but in torments, for such are the rewards of covetous wealth. He saw Abraham afar off; he looked up at him only to increase his torture. "Lazarus in his bosom." Abraham's bosom was the poor man's Paradise. 'Abraham afar off and Lazarus in his bosom.' Someone may say to me: Is Paradise in the nether world? I say this, that Abraham's bosom is true Paradise, but I also grant that the bosom of a holy man is Paradise.

"He cried out and said," (excruciating pain increases the volume of the voice) "Father Abraham, have pity on me." 'Father Abraham.' Even though I am in the grip of torments, nevertheless, I call upon my father. Just as the son who squandered all his possessions calls his father, even so I call you father, despite my punishments. By nature, I call you father, even though I have lost you as father through sin. Have pity on me. "In the nether world who gives you thanks?" Vain is your repentance in a place where there is no room for repentance. Torments, not the disposition of your soul, force you to repent. "Have pity on me." A saint, indeed, is Abraham, holy and blessed, and all of us are in haste to enter his bosom, but I am not so sure that it is possible for anyone in hell or in heaven to feel pity. The Creator pities His creature; one Physician came to restore the dead, for the others could not.

"Send Lazarus to dip the tip of his finger in water." 'Send Lazarus.' You are mistaken, miserable man; Abraham cannot send, but he can receive. "To dip the tip of his finger in water." Recall your lifetime, rich man; you did not conde-scend to see Lazarus and now you are longing for the tip of his finger. 'Send Lazarus.' You should have done that for him while he lived. "To dip the tip of his finger in water." See the conscience of the sinner; he does not dare ask for the whole finger. "Cool my tongue, for I am tormented in this flame." Cool my tongue, for it has uttered many a proud word. Where there is sin, there is also the penalty for sin. "To cool my tongue, for I am tormented in this flame." How evil the tongue can be, James has told us in his Letter: "The tongue also is a little member, but it boasts mightily." The more it has sinned, the more it is tormented. You long for water, who formerly were so fastidious at the mere sight of smeary and spattered dishes.

Abraham said to him, "Son, remember that you in your lifetime have received good things." Be sure you know what he means: good things to you; but they are not good. You have received what you thought were good, but you cannot have been a lord upon earth and reign here too. It is not possible to have wealth both on earth and in hell. 'Lazarus in like manner evil things.' If ever we are sick, if we are beggars, if we are wasting away in sickness, if we are perishing from the cold, if there is no hospitality for us, let us be glad and rejoice; let us receive evil things in our lifetime. When the crushing weight of infirmity and sickness bears down upon us, let us think of Lazarus. "Besides all that, between us and you a great gulf is fixed." It cannot be bridged, removed, or levelled. We can see it, but cannot cross it. We see what we have escaped; you see what you have lost; our joy and happiness multiply your torments; your torments augment our happiness.

[The Rich Man's Slavery to the Senses]

He said, "Then, father, I beseech you." The miserable creature does not cease to call him father. "Then, father, I beseech you." You should have called him father in former times, for he was your true father. Did you acknowledge your father, you who despised your brother? "To send him to my father's house." Notice the perversity; not even in pain does he speak truth. You see what he says: "Then, father, I beseech you." Your father, then, is Abraham; how can you say, therefore, send him to my father's house? You have not forgotten your father; you have not forgotten that he who was your father has destroyed you. Because he was your father, you have five brothers. You have five brothers: sight, smell, taste, hearing, touch. These are the brothers to whom formerly you were enslaved; they were your brothers. Since they were the brothers you loved, you could not love your brother, Lazarus, Naturally, you could not love him as brother, because you loved them. Those brothers have no love for poverty. Your sight, your sense of smell, your taste, your sense of touch, was your brother. These brothers of yours loved wealth; they had no eye for poverty. "I have five brothers, that he may testify to them." They are the brothers who sent you into these torments; they cannot be saved unless they die. "Lest they too come into this place of torments." Why do you want to save those brothers who have no love for poverty? It must needs be that brothers dwell with their brother.

"Abraham said to him, 'They have Moses and the Prophets, let them hearken to them.'" Why do you ask that Lazarus go? 'They have Moses and the Prophets.' Besides, Moses and the prophets went about in goatskins, wandering in their caves and in holes in the ground; they were poor men just like Lazarus, and they suffered calamities and endured hunger. Why do you ask me to send Lazarus? They have Lazarus in Moses and the prophets. Moses was Lazarus; he was a poor man; he was naked. He esteemed the poverty of Christ greater riches than the treasures of Pharaoh. They also have the prophets. They have Jeremia who is thrown into a cistern of mud and who fed upon the bread of tribulation. They have all the prophets; let them hearken to them. Every day Moses and the prophets are preaching against your five brothers; let them teach them; let them instruct them. Let them summon the eye; and what do they say to it? Do not look upon the carnal, but discern the spiritual. "What we have seen with our eyes," says the apostle, "what we have heard, what our hands have handled: of the Word of God." He instructs the ear, too, the sense of smell, of taste. All the prophets and all the saints teach these brothers.

6

ST. AUGUSTINE OF HIPPO

Augustine (354-430) is certainly the greatest Latin Father and one of the greatest theologians of all times. The Bishop of Hippo has exerted an incredibly powerful influence on the culture, theology, and religious attitude of the Western world. As a bishop, he ably performed the heavy task of administering his diocese, including that of building an almshouse for the poor and at least five basilicas. He also preached incessantly, paying special attention to catechising the poor and ignorant. He took an active part in many African councils at Carthage and Milevis. As teacher of the faith he combatted many heresies, especially manichaeism, donatism, and pelagianism. Above all, Augustine has written innumerable works the bulk of which would be equal to some fifteen volumes in a standard encyclopedia.

Of course, Augustine is better known in the history of theology as the Doctor of Grace, but in his writings he has discussed practically every important topic of Christian philosophy and theology. Though he has not systematically developed a body of social doctrine, Augustine provides several key concepts, dispersed throughout his writings, which serve as a structure for his social teaching. Of these we will mention only those which are germane to our theme: social order, private property, and the relation between Church and State.

A. In Augustine, order is "the distribution which allots things equal and unequal, each to its own place" (*City of God*, XIX, 13). This order is found in the material universe when the irrational and inanimate beings are subjected to man (cf. *Ibid.*, XIX, 15). It is found in man himself when his soul rules over his body, his reason over his other parts, and in reason itself, when the contemplative part rules over the active part (cf. *Against Faustus*, XXII, 27). And lastly, it is found among human beings in their relationship with one another. This relationship constitutes the social order. Man, for Augustine, is social by nature: "Since every human being is a part of the human race, and human nature is something social and possesses the capacity for friendship as a great and natural good, for this reason God wished to create all men from one, so that they might be held together in their society, not only by the similarity of race, but also by the bond of blood relationship" (*The Good of Marriage*, 7).

This social order is realized in three forms: family, city or state, and the universal society of mankind: "After the state or city comes the world, the third circle of human society—the first being the house, and the second the city" (*City of God*, XIX, 7). Each of these forms possesses a structure of which authority and law are the basic elements. Temporal authority and law must follow the eternal law, the latter being "that law by which it is just that everything be ordered in the highest degree" (*On Free Choice of the Will*, I, 6). At the core of the social order, however, lies charity. Law and authority should not be a despotic and absolute rule but must be informed by love for all: "There is no one in the human race that does not deserve our love, if not because of his love for us, then because of our common nature" (Letter 130, 13).

Together with charity, justice is the condition and foundation of peace. Peace is, for Augustine, the "tranquility of order" (*City of God*, XIX, 13). This peace is of different kinds: domestic, civil, and heavenly. It must be achieved in the body, in the soul, between the body and the soul, between man and God, between man and man (cf. *City of God*, XIX, 13). Freedom itself, according to Augustine, is a consequence of charity. This is the meaning of his famous dictum: "Love, and do what you will" (*Commentary on the Letter of John*, VII, 8).

B. Whereas Augustine's teaching on man's social relationship centers around the notion of order, his teaching on riches and the right of ownership is based upon the concept of right use. The latter is ultimately identical with order, since right use is nothing other than orderly utilization of the means to achieve the end. Augustine draws an important distinction between use (*uti*) and enjoy (*frui*): "To enjoy anything means to cling to it with affection for its own sake. To use a thing is to employ what we have received for our use to obtain what we want, provided that it is right for us to want it" (*On Christian Doctrine*, I, 4). Things, and among them, riches are to be "used," that is, they should be considered as means to obtain what we love. We encounter here the notion of instrumentality of riches, which we have already seen in the Greek Fathers, particularly Clement of Alexandria and John Chrysostom.

If instead of "using" the things, we "enjoy" them, that is, love them for their own sake, we "abuse" them, according to Augustine. It is indeed in the correct "enjoying" and "using" of things that virtue and vice lie. Virtue consists in "enjoying" things that are to be "enjoyed" and in "using" things that are to be "used," whereas vice is to "enjoy" what is to be "used" and to "use" what is to be "enjoyed" (cf. *On Christian Doctrine*, I, 3). A use of things is correct when "the soul remains in the law of God and is subjected to the one God with a full love and administers all the things given to it, without anxiety or passion, that is, according to God's precepts" (*Commentary on the Genesis*, I, 3). A bad use is made of things when the user "clings to them with love and is entangled by them, that is, he becomes subject to those things which ought to be subject to him, and creates for himself goods whose right and proper use require that he himself be good" (*On Free Choice of the Will*, I, 13).

Augustine recognizes the right of private ownership but considers it justified only if the possessions are correctly used and are limited to basic necessities. Augustine has a strict concept of necessities; for him what is over and above necessary food and clothing is superfluous. And what is superfluous must be given to others, as he repeatedly insists: "See to it not only that little will suffice you but also that God will not demand much of you. Seek only what he has given you, and from it take only what you need. All the rest is superfluous; it is necessary for others. The superfluities of the rich are the necessities of the poor. When you possess superfluities, you possess the goods of others" (*Commentary on Psalm 147*, 12).

For Augustine, therefore, the purpose of material goods is to meet the basic needs of mankind. A person may legitimately possess them with this aim in mind. But when they are misused, or when they become superfluous, there is lacking an essential condition for a rightful ownership, and consequently whoever possesses them loses his title to them and must give them to others (cf. Sermon 50, 4). There results from this a strict moral obligation of sharing the superfluities. This insistence on sharing the earthly goods can be said to be the most distinguishing feature of Augustine's social teaching. He believes that not sharing one's superfluities with the needy is equivalent to fraud (cf. Sermon 206, 2) and theft (cf. Sermon 178, 3-4).

There are two passages in Augustine's works, namely, *On the Gospel of John*, Tractate VI, 25-26, and Letter 93, XII, 50, which seem to suggest that Augustine holds a purely positivistic concept of private property. He seems to affirm that the right of private ownership depends on imperial laws, and not on the nature of man. The context of these two passages, however, invalidates such an interpretation. In his debate with the Donatists who claimed to have a legitimate ownership of their churches, Augustine argued that their contention could be justified either by the Scripture or by human laws, that is, the imperial laws. The first alternative is ruled out, since the Scripture does not specify in the concrete who shall own what. If, on the other hand, the Donatists have recourse to the human laws, then their argument is self-defeating since the imperial laws deny them the possession of the things of which they claim ownership. It is clear, therefore, that in these texts Augustine is not defending the theory that private property is justified only by imperial laws; rather, he is using an *argumentum ad hominem* to deny the Donatists' claim.

C. Finally, we will briefly mention Augustine's view of the state and the relationship between it and the Church. Augustine sees man in his fallen condition as profoundly vitiated by sin, driven by the burning desire of self-aggrandizement, by the relentless lust for domination over other men, and by the insatiable appetite for fame and glory. Being social animals, men necessarily live together in society, but because they are corrupted, they need the state to hold their violent passions in check. The purpose of the state is therefore to maintain earthly peace. This external peace and order, which is absolutely necessary for all men, is termed the peace of Babylon, and is not the same as the true peace of the city of God. The state achieves its purpose primarily through the use of coercion and the fear of punishment. But even this purpose, according to Augustine, is accomplished only in a most imperfect fashion, since those who bear political power are only fallible and sinful men.

Despite their imperfections, however, rulers, who are ordained by God to be the ministers of his wrath and a terror to evildoers, must be obeyed and respected, except when they order something clearly contrary to God's commands. Even in this case, however, the subject has no right to rebel against the ruler; rather, he must be willing to accept the punishment inflicted upon him by the ruler for his disobedience, and pray that God will forgive his oppressor.

Augustine also teaches that it is the Christian's duty to participate in the work of the state as emperor, official, judge, soldier, or jailer. This teaching represents no doubt a departure from the position of the New Testament regarding the role of the Christian in the state. Moreover, Augustine's most radical reversal of the traditional attitude of Christians toward the state and its rulers came when in the course of his struggle against the Donatists, he finally changed his mind and maintained that the political authorities had not only the right but also the obligation to use their power to punish those who, in the judgment of the Church, were guilty of heresy and schism. These and many other teachings of Augustine on the Church and state are instances of his realistic attempt to adapt the message of the Gospel to the ever-changing circumstances of his times.

Part One: Social Writings

ON FREE CHOICE OF THE WILL

[Eternal Law and Temporal Law]
I, VI, 15.[1] Augustine: Therefore, if you agree, let us call a law temporal when, although it is just, it can justly be changed in the course of time.

Evodius: Let us agree to this term.

A: What of the law called the supreme reason, which ought always to be obeyed, the law through which evil men deserve a wretched life and good men a happy one, and through which, finally, the law that we have just called temporal is rightly passed and rightly changed? Can any thinking person fail to realize that it is immutable and eternal? Can it

[1]Text: CCL 29.220.

ever be unjust that the evil are wretched and the good happy, or that the well-ordered and prudent people should elect their own officials while the wicked ones should be deprived of this power?

E: I see that this law is eternal and immutable.

A: I think too that you understand that in temporal law there is nothing just and lawful which men have not derived from eternal law. If a nation at one time confers offices justly and at another time, still quite justly, does not confer offices, this change, although it is temporal, is just; for it has been derived from eternal law, under which it is always just for responsible people to confer offices and for irresponsible people to be unable to do so. Or do you have a different view?

E: I agree.

A: To put in a few words, as best as I can, the notion of eternal law that has been impressed upon our minds: it is that law by which it is just that everything be ordered in the highest degree. If you have an objection, state it now.

E: I have no objection, for what you say is true.

A: Therefore, although there is one law according to which all the temporal laws for governing men are changed, the eternal law itself cannot be changed, can it?

E: I understand that it cannot be changed. No power, no chance, no misfortune can ever bring it about that it is not just for everything to be ordered in the highest degree.

[Eternal, Temporal Laws and the Correct Use of Riches] I, XV, 31.[2] Augustine: Since it is clear that some men love eternal things while others love temporal ones, and since we

[2]Text: CCL 29.232.

have agreed that there exist two laws, the eternal and the temporal—if you have any idea of justice, who do you judge ought to be subject to eternal law, and who to temporal?

Evodius: I think that what you ask is easy. It is obvious that happy men, because they love eternal things, act under the eternal law, while unhappy men are subject to the temporal law.

A: Your judgment is correct, provided that you hold fast to what reason has now clearly demonstrated: that those who serve temporal law cannot be free of the eternal law from which, we said, are derived all the things that are just or justly changed; and those who abide by the eternal law through good will do not need temporal law. You understand this quite well, it appears.

E: I do.

A: The eternal law, therefore, orders us to turn our love away from temporal things, and to turn it, once purified, to things eternal.

E: Yes, it does.

A: What then do you think that the temporal law commands, except that men should possess those things which may be called ours for a time (when men cling to them out of desire) by that right by which peace and human society are preserved—insofar as they can be preserved amid these circumstances? And these are, first, the body, together with what are called its goods, such as good health, keen senses, strength, beauty; certain of these are needed in the useful arts and therefore are to be more highly valued, while others are of less value. Next there is freedom—not, indeed, true freedom, which is reserved for those who are happy and who abide by eternal law; rather, I am speaking now of that freedom which men who have no masters think they possess, and which men who wish to be free of human masters

202 *St. Augustine of Hippo*

desire. Next, there are parents, brothers, husband or wife, children, kindred, relatives, friends, and those who are bound to us by some bond of intimacy. Then, too, there is the state itself, which is usually held to have the place of a parent. There are also honors, praise, and what is called popular favor. Lastly, there are possessions—a term which includes all the things that we rightfully own, over which we seem to have the power of selling or giving away.

To explain how the law distributes to each man his own property is difficult and lengthy, and is clearly not at all necessary for our discussion. It is enough to understand that the power exercised by this law does not go beyond the depriving and removal of these things, or some of them, from those whom it punishes. It maintains order through fear, twisting and turning to what it wants the minds of those unhappy men whom it has been adapted to rule. Since men fear to lose temporal goods, in using them they observe a certain moderation suited to the bond of whatever kind of society can be established by men of this sort. They do not punish the sin of loving temporal goods except when the temporal goods are dishonestly taken from others. Therefore, see how we have come to the point you thought so far away; for we had planned to inquire how far the law which governs states and the people of this world has the right to punish.

E: I see that we have come to this point.

A: Therefore, you also understand that if men did not love what can be taken away from them against their will, there would be no punishment, either in the form of an injustice done to them, or by way of a just penalty inflicted upon them.

E: I understand this also.

A: Thus some men make evil use of these things, and others make good use. And the man who makes evil use clings to them with love and is entangled by them (that is, he becomes subject to those things which ought to be subject to him, and creates for himself goods whose right and proper use require that he himself be good); but the man who uses these rightly proves that they are indeed goods, though not for him (for they do not make him good or better, but become better because of him). Therefore he is not attached to them by love, lest he make them limbs, as it were, of his spirit (which happens if he loves them), and lest they weaken him with pain and wasting when they begin to be cut off from him. Instead, let him be above temporal things completely. He must be ready to possess and control them, and even more ready to lose and not to possess them. Since this is so, you do not think, do you, that silver or gold should be blamed because of greedy men, or food and wine because of gluttons and drunkards, or womanly beauty because of adulterers and fornicators? And so on with other things, especially since you may see a doctor use fire well, and the poisoner using bread for his crime.

E: This is most true. The things themselves are not to be blamed, but rather the men who make evil use of them.

THE WAY OF LIFE OF THE CATHOLIC CHURCH

[Possession of Riches and Perfection]
I, 23, 42.[3] If anyone considers dispassionately and serenely all the words of Job, he will see the worth of those things over which men wish to gain power, and to which they are so attached by cupidity that they become slaves to mortal things even as they imprudently seek to master them. Having lost all his riches and been reduced suddenly to extreme poverty, Job kept his soul so undisturbed and fixed upon God as to show that earthly things were not important in his sight, but that he was greater than they and God greater than he. If the men of our day could be of such mind, we would not have to be so insistently forbidden in the New

[3]Text: PL 32.1329.

Testament to possess these goods in order to reach perfection. For to possess such things without clinging to them is much more praiseworthy than not to possess at all.

[Christianity and Possession of Goods]

I, 35, 77.[4] Meanwhile, Manichaeans, why continue your outbursts? Why allow yourselves to be blinded by party prejudice? Why do you carry on such tedious defense of such errors? Seek for fruit in the field and grain on the threshing floor; they will be found without difficulty and will even offer themselves to the seeker. Why gaze so intently on the sweepings? Why frighten ignorant men away from the abundance of a fertile garden by pointing to the roughness of the hedge? There is a sure entrance known only to a few by which one can come in, but you either do not believe it exists or do not wish to discover it. In the Catholic Church, there are great numbers of the faithful who do not use worldly goods; there are others who use them as though not using them, as the Apostle said, (1 Cor 7:31). This has been proved in times when Christians were forced to worship idols. For how many men of wealth, how many rural householders, and merchants, and soldiers, how many civic leaders, and even senators, persons of both sexes, suffered for the true faith and religion, giving up all those vain and temporal goods which they used but were not enslaved to, thus proving to unbelievers that they possessed these goods and were not possessed by them.

78. Why do you maliciously claim that the faithful who have been renewed in baptism ought no longer to beget children, or to possess lands or houses or money? St. Paul permits these things. For, it cannot be denied that he wrote to the faithful the following, after enumerating the various evildoers who shall not possess the kingdom of God: "And such were some of you, but you have been washed, you have been sanctified, you have been justified in the name of our Lord

[4]Text: PL 32.1342.

Jesus Christ, and in the Spirit of our God" (1 Cor 6:11). Surely, no one would venture to understand by the washed and sanctified anyone but the faithful and those who have renounced this world.

LETTERS

[Goods Are Legitimately Possessed by Divine or Human Law]
93 (Addressed to Vincent, a Donatist bishop)
50.[5] Hear, at least through me, the voice of the Lord's grain, toiling amidst the chaff until the final winnowing on the Lord's threshing floor, which is the wide world, where "God hath called the earth from the rising of the sun even to the going down thereof" (Ps 49:1), where even the children praise the Lord. Hear this voice: Whoever by reason of this imperial edict persecutes you, not to correct you through love, but to show hatred to you as an enemy, displeases us. And although no one justly possesses earthly goods except by divine law, by which the just possess all things, or by human law, which it is the power of earthly kings to enact, and since you wrongly call yours goods which you do not possess justly, and which you have been ordered by the laws of earthly kings to give up, it will be useless for you to say: "We have toiled to amass them" when you read the text: "The just shall eat the labors of sinners" (Prov 13:22). However, if by reason of this law which the kings of the earth, the servants of Christ, have enacted to restrain your impiety, anyone covets your lawful property, he incurs our disapproval. Finally, if anyone holds the goods of the poor, or the basilicas of the people, which you held under the name of the Church, which goods are owed exclusively to the Church, the true Church of Christ, and if he holds them through cupidity, not through justice, he also incurs our disapproval.

[5]Text: CSEL 34.493.

[Possessions Become Good through the
Goodness of Their Possessors]
130 (Addressed to Proba).
3.[6] Through love of this true life you ought, then, to consider
yourself desolate in this world, no matter what happiness
you enjoy. For, just as that is the true life in comparison with
which this other, which is so much loved, is not to be called
life, however pleasant and prolonged it may be, so that is the
true comfort which God promised by the Prophet saying: "I
will give them true comfort, peace upon peace" (Is 57:18,19).
Without this comfort there is more grief than consolation to
be found in earthly comforts, whatever they may be. Certainly, as far as riches and high-ranking positions and other
things of that sort are concerned—things which mortals
think themselves happy to possess, because they have never
partaken of that true happiness—what comfort can they
bestow, when it is a far better thing not to need them than to
excel in them, and when we are tortured by the craving to
possess them, but still more by the fear of losing, once we do
possess them? Not by such goods do men become good, but
having become good otherwise, they make these things
good by their good use of them. Therefore, there is no true
comfort in these things; rather, it is found where true life is.
A man's happiness necessarily must come from the same
source as his goodness.

[Sufficiency and Superfluities]
12.[7] Is it agreed, then, that over and above that temporal
welfare men may wish for positions of rank and authority
for themselves and their families? Certainly, it is proper for
them to wish for these things, not for the sake of the things
themselves, but for another reason, namely, that they may
do good by providing for the welfare of those who live under
them. But it is not proper to covet them out of the empty
pride of self-esteem, or useless ostentation, or hurtful van-

[6]Text: CSEL 44.42.
[7]Text: CSEL 44.53.

ity. Therefore, if they wish for themselves and their families only what is sufficient of the necessaries of life, as the Apostle says: "But godliness with contentment is a great gain. For we brought nothing into this world, and we can carry nothing out; but having food and wherewith to be covered, with these we are content. For they that will become rich fall into temptation, and the snares of the devil and into many unprofitable and hurtful desires, which drown men into destruction and perdition. For the desire of money is the root of all evils, which some coveting have erred from the faith and have entangled themselves in many sorrows" (1 Tim 6:6-10)—this sufficiency is not an improper desire in whoever wishes this and nothing more; whoever does wish more does not wish this, and therefore does not wish properly. He wished this and prayed for it who said: "Give me not riches (or) beggary; give me only enough of the necessaries of life, lest being filled I should become a liar and say: 'Who sees me'? or become poor, I should steal and forswear the name of my God" (Prov 30:8,9). Surely you see that this sufficiency is not to be coveted for its own sake, but to provide for health of body and for clothing which accords with man's personal dignity, and which makes it possible for him to live with others honorably and respectably.

Among all these objects, man's personal safety and friendship are desired for their own sake, whereas a sufficiency of the necessaries of life is usually sought—when it is properly sought—for the two reasons mentioned above, but not for its own sake. Now, personal safety is closely connected with life itself, and health, and integrity of mind and body. In like manner, friendship is not confined by narrow limits; it includes all those to whom love and affection are due, although it goes out more readily to some, more slowly to others, but it reaches even our enemies, for whom we are commanded to pray. Thus, there is no one in the human race to whom love is not due, either as a return of mutual affection or in virtue of his share in our common nature. But, those who love us mutually in holiness and chastity give us the truest joy. These are the goods we must pray to keep when we have them, to acquire when we do not have them.

[The Bad Use of Goods Deprives the Possessor
of His Right of Ownership]
153. (Addressed to Macedonius)
26.[8] And now, if we look carefully at what is written: "The
whole world is the wealth of the faithful man, but the
unfaithful one has not a penny"(Prov 17:6), do we not prove
that those who seem to rejoice in lawfully acquired gains,
and do not know how to use them, are really in possession of
other men's property? Certainly, what is lawfully possessed
is not another's property, but 'lawfully' means justly and
justly means rightly. He who uses his wealth badly possesses
it wrongfully, and wrongful possession means that it is
another's property. You see, then, how many there are who
ought to make restitution of another's goods, although
those to whom restitution is due may be few; wherever they
are, their claim to just possession is the proportion to their
indifference to wealth. Obviously, no one possesses justice
unlawfully: whoever does not love it does not have it; but
money is wrongly possessed by bad men while good men
who love it least have the best right to it. In this life the
wrong of evil possessors is endured and among them certain
laws are established which are called civil laws, not because
they bring men to make a good use of their wealth, but
because those who make a bad use of it become thereby less
harmful to others. This comes about either because some of
them become faithful and fervent—and these have a right to
all things—or because those who live among them are not
hampered by their evil deeds, but are tested until they come
to that City where they are heirs to eternity, where the just
alone have a place, the wise alone leadership, and those who
are there possess what is truly their own. Yet, even here, we
do not intercede to prevent restitution from being made,
according to earthly customs and laws, although we should
like you to be indulgent to evil-doers, not to make them take
pleasure or persist in their evil, but because, whenever any of

[8] Text: CSEL 44.426.

them become good, God is appeased by the sacrifice of mercy, and if evil-doers did not find Him merciful there would be no good men.

[Possibility of Salvation of the Rich.
Property and Family]
157 (Addressed to Hilarius)
23.[9] Listen, now, to something about riches in answer to the next inquiry in your letter. In it you wrote that some are saying that a rich man who continues to live rich cannot enter the kingdom of heaven unless he sells all he has, and that it cannot do him any good to keep the commandments while he keeps his riches. Their arguments have overlooked our fathers, Abraham, Isaac, and Jacob, who departed long ago from this life. It is a fact that all these had extensive riches, as the Scripture faithfully bears witness, yet He who became poor for our sakes, although He was truly rich, foretold in a truthful promise that many would come from the east and the west and would sit down not above them, nor without them, but with them in the kingdom of heaven (cf. Mt 8:11). Although the haughty rich man, who was clothed in purple and fine linen and feasted sumptuously every day, died and was tormented in hell, nevertheless, if he had shown mercy to the poor man covered with sores who lay at his door and was treated with scorn, he himself would have deserved mercy. And if the poor man's merit had been his poverty, not his goodness, he surely would not have been carried by angels into the bosom of Abraham who had been rich in this life. This is intended to show us that on the one hand it was not poverty in itself that was divinely honored, nor, on the other, riches that were condemned, but that the godliness of the one and the ungodliness of the other had their own consequences, and, as the torment of fire was the lot of the ungodly rich man, so the bosom of the rich Abraham received the godly poor man. Although Abraham lived as a rich man, he held his riches so lightly and thought

[9]Text: CSEL 44.472.

them of so little worth in comparison with the commandments of God that he would not offend God by refusing to
sacrifice, at His bidding, the very son whom he had hoped
and prayed for as the heir of his riches (cf. Gen 22:1-10).

24. At this point they probably say that the patriarchs of old
did not sell all they had and give it to the poor, because the
Lord had not commanded it. The New Testament had not
yet been revealed, as it was fitting it should not be until the
fullness of time had come, so neither was it fitting that their
virtue should be revealed; yet God knew that they could
easily exercise this virtue interiorly, and He bore such striking witness to them that, although He is the God of all the
saints and of all just men, He deigned to speak of them as
His particular friends: "I am the God of Abraham, and the
God of Isaac and the God of Jacob: this is my name forever"
(Ex 3:15). But, after "the great mystery of godliness was
manifested in the flesh" (1 Tim 3:16), and the coming of
Christ was made visible by the calling of all nations—and
the patriarchs, too, had believed in Him but had preserved
the faith, so to speak, in the root of the olive tree, of which
the fruit was to be manifested in its own time, as the Apostle
says (cf. Rom 11:17)—then, the rich man was told: "Sell all
whatsoever you have, and give to the poor, and you shall
have treasure in heaven: and come, follow me" (Mt 18:21).

25. If they say this, they seem to speak with reason. But they
should hear and take account of the whole, not open their
ears to half of it and close them to the other half. To whom
did the Lord give this commandment? Why, to the rich man
who was asking His advice on how to receive eternal life, for
he had said to the Lord: "What shall I do that I may receive
life everlasting"? (Mt 19:16-22). He did not answer him: "If
you wish to enter into life, sell all that you have," but: "If you
wish to enter into life, keep the commandments." And when
the young man said that he had kept the commandments
which the Lord had quoted to him from the Law, and asked
what was still lacking to him, he received this answer: "If

you wish to be perfect, go, sell all that you have and give to the poor." And, lest he might think he was losing what he so dearly loved, He said: "And you shall have treasure in heaven." Then He added: "And come, follow me," that no one who might do this should think it would bring him any reward unless he followed Christ. But the young man went away sad, so anyone can see how he kept those commandments of the Law, for I think he spoke with more pride than truth when he answered that he had kept them. However, it is a fact that the good Master distinguished between commandments of the Law and that higher perfection; for in the one place He said: "If you wish to enter into life, keep the commandments," but in the other: "If you wish to be perfect, sell all you have," and the rest. Why, then, do we refuse to admit that the rich, although far from that perfection, nevertheless enter into life if they keep the commandments, and give that it may be given to them, forgive that they may be forgiven?

26. We believe that the Apostle Paul was the minister of the New Testament when he wrote to Timothy, saying: "Tell the rich of this world not to be proud, nor to trust in so uncertain a thing as wealth. Let them trust in the living God who gives us abundantly all things to enjoy. To do good, to be rich in good works, to give easily, to communicate to others, to lay up in store for themselves a good foundation against the time to come, that they may lay hold on the true life" (1 Tim 6:17-19). In the same way, it was said to the young man: "If you wish to enter into life." I think that, when he gave those instructions to the rich, the Apostle was not wrong in not saying: "Tell the rich of this world to sell all they have, give to the poor and follow the Lord," instead of: "Not to be proud, not to trust in so uncertain a thing as wealth." It was his pride, not his riches, that brought the rich man to the torments of hell, because he despised the good poor man who lay at his gate, because he put his hope in uncertain riches, and thought himself happy in his purple and fine linen and sumptuous banquets...

29. Let the rich hearken to this: "What is impossible for men is easy for God," and whether they retain riches and do their good works by means of them, or enter into the kingdom of heaven by selling them and distributing them to provide for the needs of the poor, let them attribute their good works to the grace of God, not to their own strength. What is impossible for men is easy, not for men, but for God. Let your friends hear that, and, if they have already sold all their goods and distributed them to the poor, or are still making plans and arrangements to do so, and in this way are preparing to enter into the kingdom of heaven, let them not attribute this to their own strength, but to the same divine grace. For, what is impossible for men is easy, not for them, because they are men, but for God. The Apostle also says this to them: "With fear and trembling, work out your salvation. For it is God who works in you both to will and to accomplish, according to His good will" (Phil 2:12). True, they say that by selling their goods they have followed the Lord's counsel of perfection, since it is there added: "And come, follow me." Why, then, in the good works which they do, do they rely entirely on their own will, and fail to hear the reproach and testimony of the Lord, whom they say they are following: "Without me, you can do nothing"? (Jn 15:5).

30. If, when the Apostle said: "Tell the rich of this world not to be proud, not to trust in so uncertain a thing as wealth," he meant that they should sell all they had and gain their reward by distributing it to the needy, then, in what follows: "to give easily, to communicate to others, to lay up in store for themselves a good foundation against the time to come," if he believed that otherwise they could not enter into the kingdom of heaven, he was deceiving those whose homes he so carefully set in order, warning and instructing how wives should behave to their husbands and husbands to wives, children to parents, parents to children, servants to masters, masters to servants, for how could any of this be done without a home and family possessions?. . .

34. Everyone who renounces this world renounces without question everything that is in it, that he may be Christ's disciple. For, when He had pronounced the parable of the charges necessary for building a tower, and of the preparation for war of one king against another, He added: "Whoever does not renounce all that he possesses cannot be my disciple" (Lk 16:33). A person renounces his riches, if he has any, either by not loving them and distributing them to the needy, thereby to be lightened of useless burdens, or by loving Christ more and transferring his hope from them to Him, so using them as to give easily, to share, to lay up a good store in heaven, and to be ready to give them up as he would his parents and children and wife if he were faced with the alternative of not having them unless he gave up Christ. For, if he renounces the world on any other terms when he draws near to the sacrament of faith (baptism), he does what blessed Cyprian mourned over in the case of the lapsed, saying: "They renounce the world in word only, not in deed" (Letter 11:1). Surely it is to such a one, who at the approach of temptation is more afraid of losing his wealth than of denying Christ, that these words apply: "Here is a man who began to build and was not able to finish" (Lk 14:30). He is also the one who, while his adversary is yet afar off, sends an embassy desiring peace, that is, at the approach and threat of temptation, before it hurts him, he agrees to give up Christ and deny Him rather than be deprived of what is dearer to him. And there are many such who even think that the Christian religion ought to help them to increase their riches and multiply earthly delights.

35. But this class does not include the rich Christians who, although they possess riches, are not possessed by them, because they have renounced the world in truth and in their heart, and who put no hope in such possessions. These use a sound discipline in training their wives, their children, and their whole household to cling to the Christian religion; their homes, overflowing with hospitality, "receive the just man in the name of a just man that they may receive the

reward of a just man"(Mt 10:41); they give their bread to the
hungry, they clothe the naked, they ransom the captive, "to
lay up in store for themselves a good foundation for the time
to come that they may lay hold on the true life"(1 Tim 6:19).
If it happens that they have to suffer the loss of their money
for the faith of Christ, they hate their riches; if this world
threatens them with bereavement or with separation from
their families, they hate their parents, brothers, children,
wives; finally, if there is question of an agreement with their
adversary about the very life of their body, they go so far as
to hate their own life, rather than risk being forsaken by a
forsaken Christ. Why? Because on all these points they have
received a commandment that they cannot otherwise be
Christ's disciples.

36. But this commandment that they must hate even their
own life for the sake of Christ does not mean that they own it
as something that can be sold, or that they can lay hands on
themselves and destroy it, but that they are ready to lose it
by dying for the name of Christ rather than live a dying life
by denying Christ. In the same way, the riches which they
were not ready to sell at the summons of Christ they must be
ready to lose for Christ, lest by losing Christ they lose
themselves with their riches. We have striking examples of
this in the wealthy of both sexes raised on high by the glory
of martyrdom. Thus, many who had previously shrunk
from the perfection to be attained by selling their goods
were suddenly made perfect by imitating the Passion of
Christ, and those who clung to their riches through the
frailty of flesh and blood, when suddenly faced with sin,
have resisted for the faith even unto blood. There are others
who have not won the crown of martyrdom, who have not
taken to heart the high and noble counsel of perfection by
selling their goods, yet they are free of deeds deserving
damnation; they have fed Christ hungry, given drink to Him
thirsty, clothed Him naked, received Him a wanderer, and,
although they will not sit with Christ on a throne when He
comes to judge, they will stand at His right to receive the
judgment of mercy: "Blessed are the merciful for they shall

obtain mercy" (Mt 5:7), and "Judgment without mercy to him that has not done mercy, but mercy exalts itself above judgment" (James 2:13).

37. Henceforth, let those objectors cease to speak against the Scriptures; let them, in their sermons, encourage men to higher things without condemning lower ones. For, they are unable to preach holy virginity in their exhortations without condemning the marriage bond, although the Apostle teaches that "everyone has his proper gift from God, one after this manner, another after that"(1 Cor 6:13). Let them, then, walk in the path of perfection by selling all their goods and spending them on works of mercy, but, if they are truly the poor of Christ, and if they store up, not for themselves but for Christ, why should they pronounce punishment on His weaker members before they have attained to the seats of judgment? If they are the kind of men to whom the Lord says: "You shall sit on twelve seats, judging the twelve tribes of Israel" (Mt 19:28), and of whom the Apostle says: "Know you not that we shall judge angels?" (1 Cor 6:13), let them rather make ready to receive into everlasting mansions, not the accursed, but the charitable rich who have made friends of them through the mammon of iniquity (cf. Lk 16:9). I think that some of those who babble these ideas without restraint or reason are supported in their needs by rich and religious Christians. We may say that the Church has its own soldiers and its own provincial officers, of whom the Apostle says: "Who serves as a soldier at any time at his own charges?" It has its vineyard and its planters, its flock and its shepherds, of whom the Apostle goes on to say: "Who plants a vineyard and eats not the fruit thereof? Who feeds a flock and drinks not of the milk of the flock?" (1 Cor 9:7). Yet, to offer such arguments as they offer would not be to plant a vineyard, but to uproot it; it would not be to gather the flock for the pasture, but to drive the sheep from the flock to destruction.

38. As those who are fed and clothed at the expense of the charitable rich—for they accept nothing for their own necessities except from those who sell their goods—are not judged and condemned by the more perfect members of Christ who furnish their own needs with their own hands—a higher virtue which the Apostle strongly commends (cf. Acts 20:34)—so they in turn ought not to condemn as Christians of lower grade those from whose resources they are supplied; but by right living and right teaching they rather should say to them: "If we have sown unto you spiritual things, is it a great matter if we reap your carnal things?" (1 Cor 9:11). The servants of God who live by selling the honest works of their own hands could, with much less impropriety, condemn those from whom they receive nothing than could those others who are unable to work with their hands because of some bodily weakness, yet who condemn the very ones at whose expense they live.

CHRISTIAN INSTRUCTION

["Use" and "Enjoy"]
I, 3, 3.[10] There are, then, some things which are to be enjoyed, others which are to be used, others which are enjoyed and used. Those which are to be enjoyed make us happy. Those which are to be used help us as we strive for happiness and, in a certain sense, sustain us, so that we are able to arrive at and cling to those things which make us happy. But, if we who enjoy and use things, living as we do in the midst of both classes of things, strive to enjoy the things which we are supposed to use, we find our progress impeded and even now and then turned aside. As a result, fettered by affection for lesser goods, we are either delayed in gaining those things which we are to enjoy or we are even drawn away entirely from them.

4. To enjoy anything means to cling to it with affection for its own sake. To use a thing is to employ what we have

[10]Text: CCL 32.8.

received for our use to obtain what we want, provided that it is right for us to want it. A bad use ought rather to be termed an abuse. Suppose, then, we were travelers in a foreign land, who could not live in contentment except in our own native country, and if, unhappy because of that traveling abroad and desirous of ending our wretchedness, we planned to return home, it would be necessary to use some means of transportation, either by land or sea, to enable us to reach the land we were to enjoy. But, if the pleasantness of the journey and the very movement of the vehicles were to delight us and turn us aside to enjoy the things which we ought, instead, merely to use, and were to confuse us by false pleasure, we would be unwilling to end our journey quickly and would be alienated from the land whose pleasantness would make us really happy. Just so, wanderers from God on the road of this mortal life, if we wish to return to our native country where we can be happy, we must use this world, and not enjoy it, so that the 'invisible attributes' of God may be clearly seen, "being understood through the things that are made" (Rom 1:20), that is, that through what is corporeal and temporal we may comprehend the eternal and spiritual.

OUR LORD'S SERMON ON THE MOUNT

[Give to Everyone but Not Everything]
I, 20, 67.[11] But since it is a small matter merely to abstain from injuring, unless you also confer a benefit as far as you can, our Lord goes on to say: "Give to everyone that asks you, do not turn your back on the borrower" (Mt 6:42). "To everyone that asks you," says he; not: everything to him that asks. You should therefore give what you can honestly and justly give. What if someone should ask money so that he may use it to oppress the innocent? What if, in short, he should ask you to commit impure acts? But not to give many examples, which are in fact innumerable, that certainly is to be given which may hurt neither yourself nor the other

[11]Text: CCL 35.76.

party, as far as can be known or calculated by man. If someone is justly denied what he asks, you are required by justice to explain to him why his request has been denied, so that you may not send him away empty. Thus you will give to everyone that asks you, though you will not always give what he asks. You will sometimes give something better when you have set him right who was making unjust requests.

[Lend without Interest]
68. Then, as to the Lord's saying: "Do not turn your back on the borrower," it is to be referred to the attitude of the mind, for God loves a cheerful giver (2 Cor 9:7). Everyone who accepts anything, borrows, even if he himself does not have to pay for it; for inasmuch as God pays back more to the merciful, whoever does a kindness lends at interest. If, however, the word 'borrower' should be taken to mean only those who accept anything with the intention of repaying it, then we must understand that the Lord has included two ways of doing a favor. Either we give gratuitously what we give as an act of benevolence, or we lend to one who will repay us. Frequently men who, in consideration of the divine reward, are disposed to give gratuitously, become slow to give what is asked in loan, as if they were destined to receive nothing in return from God, since he who receives pays back the thing which is given him. Rightly, therefore, does the divine authority exhort us to this way of bestowing a favor, saying: "Do not turn your back on the borrower," that is, do not alienate your good will from him who asks it, both because your money will be useless, and because God will not pay you back, since the borrower has done so. But when you give a favor from a regard to God's precept, your deed cannot be unfruitful with Him who gives these commands.

ON THE GOSPEL OF SAINT JOHN

[The Right of Possession Is Based on Human Laws]
Tractate VI, 25.[12] Failing everywhere else, what do they (the Donatists) now allege against us, not knowing what to say? They have taken away our houses, they have taken away our estates. They bring forward wills. "See, Gaius Seius made a grant of an estate to the church over which Faustinus presided." Of what church was Faustinus bishop? What is the church? To the church over which Faustinus presided, said he. But Faustinus presided not over a church, but over a sect. The dove, however, is the Church. Why do you protest? We have not devoured houses; let the dove have them. Let us inquire who the dove is, and let her have them. You know, my brethren, that those houses of theirs are not Augustine's. And if you do not know it and think that I take pleasure in possessing them, God knows what I think of them and what I suffer on their account. He knows my groaning, since he has deigned to impart to me something of the dove.

Behold, there are these estates. By what right do you assert your claim to them? By divine right or by human right? Let them answer: Divine right we have in the Scriptures, human right in the laws of kings. By what right does every man possess what he possesses? Is it not by human right? For by divine right: "The earth is the Lord's and the fullness thereof " (Ps 24:1). The poor and the rich God made of one clay; the same earth supports alike the poor and the rich. By human right, however, one says: "This estate is mine, this house is mine, this servant is mine." By human right, however, is by right of the emperors. Why so? Because God has distributed to mankind these very human rights through the emperors and kings of this world.

Do you wish us to read the laws of the emperors and to act by the estates according to these laws? If you found your possession on human right, let us recite the laws of the emperor; let us see whether they would allow the heretics to possess anything. But you say: What is the emperor to me? It is by his right that you possess the land. Take away rights created by emperors, who will dare say: "That estate is mine, or that slave is mine, or this house is mine"? If, however, men possess these goods because they have received rights from the emperors, do you want us to read the laws, so that you may be glad that you possess even a single garden, and attribute it to nothing but the clemency of the dove that you are permitted to remain in possession even there? There are indeed laws well known to all in which the emperors have directed that those who, being outside the communion of the Catholic Church, usurp to themselves the name of Christians, and are not willing in peace to worship the Author of peace, may not dare to possess anything in the name of the Church.

26. But you reply: "What have we to do with the emperor?" We have already said that we are treating of human right. Now the Apostle would have us obey kings and honor them, saying: "Honor the king" (1 Pet 2:17). Do not say then: "What have I to do with the king?", since in that case what have you to do with the possession? It is by rights derived from kings that possessions are enjoyed. You have said: "What have I to do with kings?" Do not say then that the possessions are yours, since it is to those same rights, by which men enjoy their possessions, that you have referred them.

Do you claim to found your possessions of divine right? Well, then, let us consult the Gospel; let us see how far extends the Catholic Church of Christ, upon whom the dove came which said: "This is he that baptises," and while the Scripture says: "My dove is one, the only one of her mother" (Cant 6:9). Why have you lacerated the dove? Rather, why have you lacerated your own bowels? For while you are torn to pieces, the dove continues, whole and entire. Therefore, by brethren, if, every argument of theirs being refuted, they have nothing further to say, I will tell them what to do: Let them come to the Catholic Church, and together with us,

they will have not only the earth, but also Him who made
heaven and earth.

EXPOSITIONS ON THE PSALMS

[For Whom Do the Rich Store Their Goods?]
Exposition of Ps 39:7.[13] "He lays up treasure, and knows not
for whom he gathers it." Folly and vanity! "Blessed is the
man whose hope is the Lord, who has not cast his eyes on
vanities and on lying follies." "Wild talk," you think (I speak
to one who has a hankering for treasure himself); "such
words are nothing but old wives' tales." You are a careful,
sensible man; every day you devise new means of money-
making—from business, from farming, perhaps from plead-
ing and legal practice, perhaps from soldiering; and there is
usury besides. You are shrewd; you use every act you know
to add coin to coin and to shroud your gainings in jealous
secrecy. Robbing others, you are anxious not to be robbed
yourself; you fear to suffer the wrong you do, though your
suffering does not atone for your sin. But, of course, with
you there is no suffering; you are a cautious man, and as
good at keeping money as at getting it; you know where to
invest your wealth, with whom to trust it, how none of your
gathering need be lost. Well, I ask you in your shrewdness
and carefulness: Granted your gathering and storing are
proof against any loss, tell me for whom you store your
treasure. There are other evils that go with this vanity of
your covetousness; these I leave; I neither stress them nor
tax you with them. The one point I make, the one question I
put, is that brought up by the reading of the psalm. Granted,
you gather and lay up treasure. I do not say: "Beware lest in
gathering you should be gathered up yourself; beware lest
greed may have dulled your hearing or understanding"; I
will put it more plainly. I do not say, then: "Beware lest in
your zeal to despoil the lesser you become the spoil of the

---

[13]Text: CCL 38.

greater; unwittingly, unbeknown to yourself, you live in a sea where the bigger fish eat up the smaller." I pass that by; I pass by the difficulties and dangers that beset the quest for money, the trials of those who gather it, the risks that they face at every turn, the mortal fears that haunt them continually; and this I pass by. Granted, you gather wealth unopposed, you store it unmolested. But examine that shrewdness, that wisdom which emboldens you to deride my words and account them folly; then tell me; You lay up treasure; for whom do you think to gather it? I see what you mean to answer (do you think it escaped the psalmist?); you will tell me, "My children; I am storing it for them." To screen your iniquity you make a plea of fatherly love. "I am storing it for my children." Granted you are; was this plea then unknown to Idithun? He knew it assuredly, but held such things to belong to the days of old, and spurned them because he was hastening towards the new.

I return to probe this matter of you and your children. You who store and they whom you store for are doomed to pass away; or rather (for 'doomed to pass' implies some permanence now), you and they are already passing. Take this very day; from the sermon's opening words to this moment we have been growing older, though you are not conscious of it. So with the hair of your head; it grows unnoticed, but grow it does—now in church, while you are standing there, while you say or do anything; there is no sudden growth of it to send you to the barber's. Thus in all of us time goes fleeting by, whether our mind is on it or whether it is busied elsewhere—it may be with something wrong. You are passing away, and the child you store for is passing too. Hence I ask you first: This child you store for—are you sure he will inherit? And again, if he is not yet born, are you sure he will be? You store for children who may never be born or never inherit; your treasure is stored, but not in its rightful place.

[Store Up Your Goods in the Right Place: Heaven]
You are servant to one of great estate; you have also goods of your own; and your lord's counsel could never mean the

loss of his servant's goods. All that you have and love was given you by him, and he would not have you lose his own gift, since indeed he is ready to give you himself. More; he would not have you lose even his temporal gift. There is plenty of it, it is overflowing, it may surely be held to have reached excess; even so, says your lord, I would not have you lose it. "What then am I to do?" Remove it; the place you have put it is unsafe. If you consult your own covetousness even, you may find that it too is satisfied by my counsel. You wish to keep without loss what you have already; I am showing you where you may secure it. Do not lay up treasure on earth, not knowing for whom you gather it or how its owner and keeper may squander it. He who lays hold of it may be himself laid hold of; or while you store it for him you may lose it yourself before he comes.

Hence I counsel your anxiousness: "Lay up for yourselves treasures in heaven." Here on earth if you wished to guard wealth you would look about you for a storehouse; you might mistrust your own house because of the servants; you might take your goods to the bankers' quarter, where mishaps are less likely, thieves can scarcely get in, and everything is securely guarded. Yet why should you take this measure except that you have no better storehouse: What if I offer you a better? This shall be my advice: "Do not commit your goods to the banker, he is not to be trusted; there is another whom you may trust, commit them to him. He has great storehouses where wealth can never be lost; he is rich beyond all the rich." At this you will say perhaps: "I shall never dare to ask such a one to guard my goods." But what if he invites you? Know him for what he is; this person of great estate is your own Lord, and he speaks thus: "My servant, I would not have you lose your goods; learn from me where to store them. Why keep them where you may lose them, and—loss or no loss—where you yourself cannot always be? There is another place; I will take you thither. Let your wealth precede you; fear no loss; I who gave it will guard it for you."

[Store Up Your Possessions in a Safe Place
by Giving Them to the Poor]
Such are your Lord's words. Question your faith; will you
trust him? You will say: "What I cannot see is as good as
lost; I must see my wealth here." But at that rate you will
neither see it here nor possess anything there. You have
treasures—no matter what—buried underground; when
you leave the house you do not take them with you. You
came here to hear a sermon, to reap some spiritual wealth,
but your thoughts are with the temporal; well, have you
brought it with you? At this very moment you cannot see it.
You think you have it at home, where you know you have
put it, but are you sure that you have not lost it? Many a man
before now has gone home and not found what he had
hoarded.—Did some covetous hearts beat faster then?
When I spoke of returning to emptied hoards, I think there
was a whispering in each of them: "Heaven forbid, Bishop;
wish us better fortune; say a prayer for us; heaven forbid
such disaster should happen; I trust in God that I shall find
my treasure safe." You trust in God then, and do not trust
God himself? "I trust in Christ that what I left will be safe
and sound, that none will go near it, none will take it." If you
trust in Christ you think you need fear no loss at home; still
less need you fear if you trust him further and store your
goods where he counsels you. Are you sure of your servant
and doubtful of your Lord, sure of your house and doubtful
of heaven? "But I," you ask me, "how can I put treasure in
heaven?" You have heard my counsel; store your treasure
where I have said; the way of its reaching heaven I do not
mean you to know. Put it in the hands of the poor; give it to
those in need; what matter to you how it reaches there? Shall
I not deliver what I am given? Have you forgotten my
words: "When you have done it to one of the least of mine,
you have done it unto me"?

Suppose that some friend of yours had vats, cisterns or
other vessels skilfully made for storing wine or oil; and
suppose yourself in search of somewhere to hide or store
your produce. He might say to you: "I will store it for you."
He would have secret channels and passages to the vessels,

and through them the liquid visibly poured would travel invisibly. Again, he might say to you: "Pour out here what you have"; and you, finding that this was not the place where you thought to put it, might be afraid to pour. But your friend, knowing the hidden workings beneath his grounds, would surely bid you: "Pour it and set your mind at rest; it passes from here to there; you cannot see how, but you may trust me; I am the builder."

He by whom all things were made has built mansions for all of us, and lest we should lose our goods on earth he would have them go before us there. If you store them on earth, tell me for whom you gather them. You have children, you answer. Number one more among them; let one portion be Christ's.

SERMONS

[Lent Is the Special Time for Doing Acts of Charity]
206, 1.[14] With the completion of the year's cycle, the season of Lent has come, at which time I am constrained to exhort you because you owe the Lord works in harmony with the spirit of the season, works which, nevertheless, are useful not to the Lord, but to you. True, other seasons of the year ought to glow for the Christian by reason of his prayers, fasts, and almsdeeds; but this season ought to arouse even those who are sluggish at other times. In fact, those who are quick to attend to these works at other times should now perform them with even greater diligence. Life in this world is certainly the time of our humiliation as these days signify when the sufferings of the Lord Christ, who once suffered by dying for us, are renewed each year with the recurrence of this holy season. For what was done once and for all time so that our life might be renewed, is solemnly celebrated each year so that its memory may be kept fresh. If, therefore, we ought to be humble of heart with sentiments of most sincere piety throughout the entire period of our earthly sojourn

[14]Text: PL 38.1041.

when we live in the midst of temptations, how much more necessary is humility during these days when we not only pass the time of our humiliation by living, but manifest it by special devotion: Christ's humility has taught us to be humble because He yielded to the wicked by accepting His death; the exaltation of Christ lifts us up because by rising again He blazed the way for His devoted followers. For, "if we have died with him, we shall also live with him; if we endure, we shall also reign with him" (2 Tim 2:11-13). One of these conditions we now celebrate with due observance in view of His approaching Passion; the other we shall celebrate after Easter when His Resurrection is, as it were, accomplished again. Then, after the days of this humiliation will be the time of our glorification. Although now is not yet the time to experience this exaltation, it gives us pleasure to anticipate it in our considerations. Now, therefore, let us voice our lamentations more insistently in prayers; then we shall exult more exuberantly in praise.

[Failure to Share the Surplus Goods
with Others Is Like Theft]
2. Let us by our prayers add the wings of piety to our almsdeeds and fasting so that they may fly more readily to God. Moreover, the Christian soul understands how much he should avoid stealing another's goods when he realizes that failure to share his surplus with the needy is like to theft. The Lord says: "Give, and it shall be given to you; forgive, and you shall be forgiven" (Lk 6:37,38). Let us graciously and fervently perform these two types of almsgiving, that is, giving and forgiving, for we, in turn, pray the Lord to give us good things and not to requite our evil deeds. "Give, and it shall be given to you," He says. What is truer, what is more just, than that he who refuses to give should cheat himself and not receive? If a farmer is not justified in gathering a harvest when he knows he has sowed no seed, how much more unreasonable for him who has refused to hear the petition of a poor man to expect a generous response from God? For, in the person of the poor, He who experiences no hunger wished Himself to be fed. Therefore, let us not spurn

our God who is needy in His poor, so that we in our need may be filled in Him who is rich. We have the needy, and we ourselves have need; let us give, therefore, so that we may receive. In truth, what is it that we give? And in return for that pittance which is meagre, visible, temporal, and earthly, what do we desire to receive? What the "eye has not seen nor ear heard, nor has it entered into the heart of man" (1 Cor 2:4). Without the assurance of God it would have been effrontery to wish to gain such treasures in return for such paltry trifles, and it is effrontery to refuse to give to our needy neighbor these things which we would never have possessed except for the bounty of Him who urges us to give. With what confidence do we hope to see Him giving to our neighbor and to us, if we despise His commands in the least details? "Forgive, and you shall be forgiven," that is, pardon and you shall be pardoned. Let servant be reconciled to fellow servant lest he be justly punished by the Lord. In this kind of almsgiving no one is poor. Even he who has no means of livelihood in this world may do this to insure his living for eternity. Gratuitously this alms is given; by being given away it is increased; and it is not consumed except when it is not shared. Therefore, let those enmities which have lasted even to this day be broken up and ended. Let them be ended lest they end you; let them be no longer held lest they hold you; let them be destroyed by the Redeemer lest they destroy you, the retainer.

[Fasting and the Practice of Other Virtues]
3. Let not your fasting be of the kind condemned by the Prophet when he said: "Not this fast have I chosen, says the Lord" (Is 58:5). For He denounces the fasts of quarrellers and seeks those of the devout. He denounces those who oppress and seeks those who release. He denounces those who stir up hostilities and seeks those who set free. For, during these days, you restrain your desires from lawful pursuits that you may not do what is unlawful. At no time will he be addicted to wine or adultery who is now continent in marriage. Thus, by humility and charity, by fasting and almsgiving, by temperance and forgiveness, by sharing

blessings and by not retaliating for evils, by declining from wickedness and by doing good, our prayer seeks and attains peace. For prayer, supported as it were on the wings of virtues, speeds upwards and is easily borne into heaven whither Christ, our peace, has preceded.

[Almsgiving and Humility]
239, 4.[15] If Elias needed nothing, did Christ need anything? My brethren, the Scriptures admonish us for this very reason: God frequently brings need upon His servants, whom He is able to feed, so that He may find devoted souls. Let no one be proud because he gives to the poor; Christ was poor. Let no one be proud because he receives a wayfarer; Christ was a wayfarer. The One who accepts is richer than he who gives. He who received possessed all things; he who gave gave to Him from whom he had received what he gave. Let no one, then, be proud when he gives to the poor, my brethren. Let him not say in his mind: "I give, he accepts; I receive him, he needs shelter." Perhaps he is superior to you in some respect in which you are lacking. Perhaps he whom you receive is just; he lacks bread, but you lack truth; he lacks a roof, but you lack heaven; he lacks money, but you lack justice.

[Lend without Interest]
Lend your money; pay out what you receive. Do not be afraid that God will judge you if you lend your money. By all means, by all means, lend your money. But God says to you: "What do you wish?" Do you wish to exact usury? What does 'to exact usury' mean? To give less and receive more. Then God says to you: "Behold, give to me; I receive less and I give more. What do I say? Yes, I give a hundredfold and life everlasting." He to whom you seek to give your money so that it may increase, the man whom you thus seek, rejoices when he gets the money and weeps when he returns it; he begs to get the money, but he calumniates you to avoid

[15]Text: PL 38.1128.

repaying it. Yes, indeed, give to the man and do not turn
away from him who seeks a loan. But take only so much as
you have given. Let him to whom you have given not weep;
otherwise, you have spoiled an act of kindness. And if what
you gave and what he received is due and he, perhaps, does
not have it at hand, just as you gave it to him when he asked
for it, so now wait since he does not have it; he will pay you
when he does have it. Do not make new troubles for him
whose burdens you once lightened. Behold, you have given
money, and now you are demanding it; but he does not have
it to give to you. He will pay you when he does have it. Do
not shout and say: "Am I asking for a loan? I am seeking
only what I gave; what I have given, that I will get back."
You are right; but he does not have the money. You are not a
money-lender, yet you wish him to whom you furnished the
money to have recourse to a money-lender in order to pay
you. If you are not making your demand because of the
interest, so that you may not be looked upon as a money-
lender, why do you wish him to put up with another money-
lender because of you? You are putting pressure on him, you
are tightening your hold on him even though you are
demanding only what you gave. Moreover, by stifling him
and by making difficulties for him, you have not bestowed a
kindness but, instead, you have brought much distress upon
him. Perhaps, you may say: "He has the wherewithal to pay.
He has a home; let him sell it. He has possessions; let him sell
them." When he sought help from you, he did so in order not
to sell; let him not, because of your importunity, do that
which you helped him to avoid. God orders and God wills
that this attitude be taken toward all men.

[Lending to the Poor Is Lending to God]
5. But are you avaricious? God says to you: "Be avaricious!
Be just as avaricious as you can, but come to terms with Me,
for I made My rich Son poor for your sake." Truly, when
Christ was rich, He became poor on account of us. Do you
seek gold? He made it. Do you seek silver? He made it. Do
you seek a household? He made it. Do you seek flocks? He
made them. Do you seek possessions? He made them. Why

do you seek only what He made? Seek Him who made all these things. Consider how He loved you: "All things were made through him, and without him nothing was made" (Jn 1:3). All things, He Himself among them, were made by Him. He who made all things was Himself made among them. He who made man was Himself made Man; He was made what He made, so that what He made might not perish. He who made all things was made among all things. Consider riches; what is richer than He by whom all things were made? Yet, although He was rich, He took mortal flesh in a virgin's womb. He was born as an infant; He was wrapped in swaddling clothes; He was laid in a manger; He patiently waited for the normal periods of life; He, by whom all seasons were made, patiently endured the seasons. He was nursed; He cried; He appeared as an infant. He lay there, yet He was reigning; He was in the manger, yet He sustained the world; He was nursed by His Mother and adored by the Gentiles; He was nursed by His Mother and adored by angels; He was nursed by His Mother, and announced by a gleaming star. Such riches and such poverty! Riches, that you might be created; poverty, that you might be redeemed. Therefore, the fact that He as a poor Man was granted hospitality as a poor Man was the result of the condescension of the recipient, not of the wretchedness of the needy.

THE CHRISTIAN LIFE

[A Christian in Name and in Deed]
6. Let us not flatter ourselves in the mere fact that we are called Christians; rather, let us believe that we deserve to be judged if we assume a name to which we have no claim. Or, if anyone is so unbelieving, so unfaithful, so persistent, so obstinate, so bold, that he does not fear the imminent anger and indignation of God the Judge, let him at least feel abashed before human judgments. Let him realize how dull, how foolish, and how senseless he is considered even by other people, since his vanity and madness are so great that · he takes upon himself a name to which he is not entitled.

For, who is so conceited and so pitiable that he would dare to establish himself as a lawyer if he is uneducated? Who is so mad and bereft of reason that he would proclaim himself a soldier if he does not know how to use arms? One does not choose such a name without reason. To be called a cobbler, one must repair shoes; to be looked upon as an artisan or workman, one must produce proof of his art; to be recognized as a trader, one exhibits costly objects originally purchased at smaller price. From examples of this sort we realize that there is no name without the corresponding act and, furthermore, that every name is derived from the antecedent act. Now, then, are you called a Christian when you perform no distinctively Christian acts? The name Christian connotes justice, goodness, integrity, patience, chastity, prudence, humility, kindliness, innocence, and piety; how do you defend your assumption of that name when your conduct manifests so few out of so many virtues? He is truly a Christian who is one not in name only but also in deed; who imitates and follows Christ in all respects; who is holy, innocent, undefiled, chaste; in whose heart evil finds no room, since this heart is dominated by piety and by a goodness which, knowing only how to bring help to all, knows not how to harm or injure anybody. He is a Christian who, according to the example of Christ, is accustomed to do good to those who oppose him and to pray for his persecutors and his enemies rather than to hate them. Whoever is quick to hurt or harm another person lies when he calls himself Christian; he is truly a Christian who can say in all honesty: "I have harmed nobody; I have lived in justice with all men."

[A True Christian Accepts Christ's Teaching
and Imitates His Love]
14. Let no one, therefore, deceive or lead another person astray, for, unless a man has been just, he does not have life in him; unless he has observed the commandments of Christ in every respect, he cannot have part with Him; unless he has despised earthly possessions, he will not gain heavenly ones; unless he has scorned human considerations, he will not

have divine blessings. Let no one declare himself to be a
Christian unless he both follows the teaching of Christ and
imitates His example. Do you think that man is a Christian
who nourishes no needy person with his bread, who
refreshes no thirsty person with his wine, whose table no one
shares, under whose roof no stranger or wayfarer abides,
whose garments clothe no naked person, whose helping
hand assists no pauper, whose blessings no one experiences,
whose mercy no one feels, who imitates the good in no way
but rather laughs and mocks and persistently harasses the
poor? Far be such an attitude from the minds of all Christians, far be it that any person of this sort be termed a
Christian, far be it that such a one should be called the child
of God. He is a Christian who follows the way of Christ,
who imitates Christ in all things, as is written: "He who says
that he abides in Christ ought himself to walk just as he
walked" (1 Jn 2:6). He is a Christian who shows mercy to all,
who is not disturbed by any injury, who does not permit the
poor to be oppressed in his presence, who assists the
wretched and succors the needy, who sympathizes with the
sorrowful and feels the grief of another as his own, who is
reduced to tears by the weeping of another, whose house is
common property for all, whose door is never closed to
anyone, whose table is shared by every poor person, whose
food is offered to all, whose goods all share and no one feels
slighted, who serves God day and night, who meditates
upon and considers His precepts ceaselessly, who makes
himself poor in this world so that he may become rich in the
eyes of God, who suffers himself to be considered of no
account among men so that he may be acceptable before
God and the angels, who seems to hold nothing concealed in
his heart, whose soul is simple and spotless, whose conscience is faithful and pure, whose whole thought is directed
to God and whose whole hope is in Christ, who desires
heavenly rather than earthly possessions, who despises
earthly goods so that he may acquire divine. As for those
who love this world and who are content and well pleased
with this life, hear what the Scripture says to them: "Do you

not know that the friendship of this world is enmity with God? Therefore, whoever wishes to be a friend of this world becomes an enemy of God" (James 4:4).

Part Two: Political Writings

CITY OF GOD

[The Social Nature of Man]

XII, 28.[16] True religion therefore rightly acknowledges and teaches that the Creator of the universe is the same as the Creator of all living creatures, that is, of both souls and bodies. Among those creatures of earth man is pre-eminent, being made in the likeness of God. And, for the reason I have mentioned, though there may be other and weightier reasons that are hidden from us, man was created as one individual; but he was not left alone. For the human race is, more than any other species, at once social by nature and anti-social by sin. And the most salutary warning against this perversion or disharmony is given by the facts of human nature. We are warned to guard against the evil of dissension, or to remedy it when once it has appeared, by remembering that first father of our race, who was created by God as one individual with this intention: that from that one individual a multitude might be propagated, and that this fact should teach mankind to preserve a harmonious unity in plurality. Furthermore, the fact that a woman was made for the first man from his own side shows us clearly how affectionate should be the union of man and wife (cf. Gen 2:22).

[16]Text: CCL 48.384.

[The Origin of the Earthly and Heavenly Cities]
XIV, 28.[17] We see, then, that the two cities have issued from two kinds of love: the earthly city was created by self-love reaching the point of contempt for God, the Heavenly City by the love of God carried as far as contempt of self. In fact, the earthly city relies on itself, the Heavenly City relies on the Lord (2 Cor 10:17). The former looks for glory from men, the latter finds its highest glory in God, the witness of a good conscience. The earthly lifts up its head in its own glory, the Heavenly City says to its God: "My glory, you lift up my head" (Ps 3:3). In the former, the lust for domination rules over its princes as over the nations it subjugates; in the other both those placed in authority and those subject to them serve one another in love, the rulers by their counsel, the subjects by obedience. The one city loves its own strength shown in its powerful leaders; the other says to its God: "I will love you, my Lord, my strength" (Ps 18:1).

Consequently, in the earthly city its wise men who live by men's standards have pursued the goods of the body or of their own mind, or of both. Or those of them who were able to know God "did not honor him as God, nor did they give thanks to him, but they dwindled into futility in their thoughts, and their senseless heart was darkened in asserting their wisdom"—that is, exalting themselves in their wisdom, under the domination of pride—"they became foolish, and changed the glory of the imperishable God into an image representing a perishable man, or birds or beasts or reptiles"—for in the adoration of idols of this kind they were either leaders or followers of the general public—"and they worshipped and served created things instead of the Creator, who is blessed for ever" (Rom 1:21ff). In the Heavenly City, on the contrary, there is no merely human wisdom, but there is a piety which rightly worships the true God, and looks for its reward in the fellowship of the saints, not only holy men but also holy angels, "so that God may be all in all" (1 Cor 15:28).

[17]Text: CCL 48.451.

[The Peace of the Universe Maintained
by a Law of Nature]
XIX, 13.[18] The peace of the body, then, is the ordered
equilibrium of all its parts; the peace of the irrational soul is
a duly ordered repose of the appetites; the peace of the
rational soul is the duly ordered agreement of knowledge
and action. The peace of body and soul is the duly ordered
life and health of a living creature; peace between mortal
man and God is an ordered obedience, guided by faith, in
subjection to an eternal law; peace between men is an
ordered and regulated fellowship; the peace of a home is the
ordered agreement among those who live together about
giving and obeying orders; the peace of the political community is an ordered harmony of authority and obedience
between citizens; the peace of the Heavenly City is a perfectly ordered and perfectly harmonious fellowship in the
enjoyment of God, and a mutual fellowship in God; the
peace of the whole universe is the tranquillity of order—and
order is the arrangement of things equal and unequal in a
pattern which assigns to each its proper position...

[God's Gifts Should Be Rightly Used]
God, then, created all things in supreme wisdom and
ordered them in perfect justice; and in establishing the
mortal race of mankind as the most beautiful of earthly
things, he has given to mankind certain good things suitable
to this life. These are: temporal peace, in proportion to the
short span of a mortal life—the peace that consists in bodily
health, security, and in fellowship with one's kind; and
everything necessary to safeguard or recover this peace—
those things, for example, which are appropriate and
accessible to our senses: light, speech, air to breathe, water
to drink, and whatever is suitable for the feeding and clothing of the body, for the care of the body and the adornment
of the person. And all this is granted under the most equitable condition: that every mortal who uses aright such goods,

[18]Text: CCL 48.678.

goods designed to serve the peace of mortal men, shall receive more abundant and better goods, namely, the peace of immortality, and the glory and honor appropriate to it in a life which is eternal for the enjoyment of God and of one's neighbor in God; whereas he who wrongly uses those earthly goods shall lose them, and shall not receive the better gifts of heaven.

[Order and Peace in the Human Society]
XIX, 14.[19] We see, then, that all man's temporal goods are to be used in order to enjoy the earthly peace in the earthly city; whereas the Heavenly City they are used in order to enjoy the eternal peace. Thus, if we were irrational animals, our only aim would be the adjustment of the parts of the body in due proportion, and the appeasing of the appetites—only, that is, the comfort of the flesh, and an adequate supply of pleasures, so that bodily peace might promote the peace of the soul. For if bodily peace is lacking, the peace of the irrational soul is also hindered, because it cannot achieve the quieting of its appetites. But the two together promote that peace which is a mutual concord between soul and body, the peace of an ordered life and of health. For living creatures show their love of bodily peace by their avoidance of pain, and by their pursuit of pleasure to satisfy the demands of their appetites they demonstrate their love of peace of soul. In just the same way, by shunning death they indicate quite clearly how great is their love of the peace in which soul and body are harmoniously united.

But because there is in man a rational soul, he subordinates to the peace of the rational soul all that part of his nature which he shares with the beasts, so that he first engages in deliberation and acts in accordance with his mind in order to achieve that ordered agreement of cognition and action which we called the peace of the rational soul. For with this end in view he ought to wish to be spared the distress of pain and grief, the disturbances of desire, the

[19]Text: CCL 48.680.

dissolution of death, so that he may come to some profitable knowledge and may order his life and moral standards in accordance with this knowledge. But he needs divine direction, which he may obey with resolution, and divine assistance that he may obey it freely, to prevent him from falling, in his enthusiasm for knowledge, a victim to some fatal error, through the weakness of the human mind. And so long as he is in this mortal body, he is a pilgrim in a foreign land, away from God; therefore he walks by faith, not by sight (cf. 2 Cor 5:6). That is why he views all peace, of body or of soul, or of both, in relation to that peace which exists between mortal man and immortal God, so that he may exhibit an ordered obedience in faith in subjection to the eternal Law.

Now God, our master, teaches two chief precepts, love of God and love of neighbor; and in them man finds three objects for his love: God, himself, and his neighbor; and knows that he is not wrong in loving himself so long as he loves God. It follows, therefore, that he will be concerned also that his neighbor should love God, since he is told to love his neighbor as himself; and the same is true of his concern for his wife, his children, for the members of his household, and for all other men, so far as is possible. And, for the same end, he will wish his neighbor to be concerned for him, if he happens to need that concern. For this reason he will be at peace, as far as lies in him, with all men, in that peace among men, that ordered harmony; and the basis of this order is the observance of two rules: first, to do no harm to anyone, and secondly, to help everyone whenever possible. To begin with, therefore, a man has a responsibility for his own household since, obviously, both by natural and human law, he has easier and more immediate contact with them; he can exercise his concern for them. That is why the Apostle says: "Anyone who does not take care of his own people, especially those in his own household, is worse than an unbeliever—he is a renegade" (1 Tim 5:8). This is where domestic peace starts, the ordered harmony about giving and obeying orders among those who live in the same house. On the one hand the orders are given by those who are concerned for the interests of others; thus the husband gives orders to the wife, parents to children, masters to servants. On the other hand those who are the objects of this concern obey orders; for example, wives obey husbands, the children obey their parents, the servants their masters. But in the household of the just man who "lives on the basis of faith" and who is still on pilgrimage, far from that Heavenly City, even those who give orders are the servants of those whom they appear to command. For they do not give orders because of a lust for domination but from a dutiful concern for the interests of others, not with pride in taking precedence over others, but with compassion in taking care of others.

[Man's Natural Freedom and the Slavery Caused by Sin] XIX, 15.[20] This relationship is prescribed by the order of nature, and it is in this situation that God created man. For he says: "Let him have lordship over the fish of the sea, the birds of the sky... and all the reptiles that crawl on the earth" (Gen 1:26). He did not wish the rational being, made in his own image, to have dominion over any but irrational creatures, not man over man, but man over beasts. Hence the first just men were set up as shepherds of flocks, rather than as kings of men, so that in this way also God might teach us that the normal hierarchy of creatures is different from that which punishment for sin has made necessary. For, when subjection came, that condition is justly imposed on the sinner. That is why we do not hear of a slave anywhere in the Scriptures until Noah, the just man, punished his son's sin with this word (Gen 9:25). This son therefore deserved this name because of his misdeed, not because of his nature. The origin of the Latin word for slave, *servus*, is believed to be derived from the fact that those who by the laws of war could rightly be put to death by the conquerors, became *servi*, slaves, when they were preserved, receiving this name from their preservation. But even this enslave-

20Text: CCL 48.682.

ment could have happened only as a result of sin. For whenever a just war is fought, the opposing side must be in the wrong, and victory, even when the victory falls to the wicked, is a humiliation visited on the conquered by divine judgment, either to correct or punish their sins. We have a witness to this in Daniel, a man of God, who in captivity confesses to God his own sins and the sins of his people, and in devout grief testifies that they are the cause of that captivity (cf. Dan 9:3-15). The first cause of slavery, then, is sin, whereby man was subjected to man in the condition of bondage; and this can only happen by the judgment of God, with whom there is no injustice, and who knows how to allot different punishments according to the deserts of the offenders.

Now, as our Lord above says, "Everyone who commits sin is sin's slave" (Jn 8:34), and that is why, though many devout men are slaves to unrighteous masters, yet the masters they serve are not themselves free men; "for when a man is conquered by another he is also bound as a slave to his conqueror" (2 Pet 2:19). And obviously it is better to be slave to a human being than to a lust; and, in fact, the most pitiless domination that devastates the hearts of men is that exercised by this very lust for domination, to mention no others. However, in that order or peace in which men are subordinate to other men, humility is as salutary for the servants as pride is harmful to the masters. And yet by nature, in the condition in which God created man, no man is the slave either of man or of sin. But it remains true that slavery is penal in character and is ordained by that law which enjoins the preservation of the order of nature, and forbids its disturbance. In fact, if nothing had been done to contravene that law, there would have been nothing to require the discipline of slavery as a punishment. That explains also the Apostle's admonition to slaves, that they should be subject to their masters, and serve them loyally and willingly (cf. Eph 6:5). What he means is that if they cannot be set free by their masters, they themselves may thus make their slavery, in a sense, free, by serving not with the slyness of fear, but with the fidelity of affection, until all injustice disappears and all human lordship and power is annihilated, and God is all in all (cf. 1 Cor 15:24,28).

[Equity in the Relation between Master and Slave]
XIX, 16.[21] To be sure, our holy fathers in the faith had slaves, but they so managed the peace of their households as to make a distinction between the situation of children and the condition of slaves only in respect of the temporal goods of this life. On the contrary, in the matter of the worship of God—in whom we must place our hope of everlasting goods—they were concerned, with equal affection, for all the members of their household. This is what the order of nature prescribes, so that this is the source of the name *paterfamilias*, a name that has become so widely accepted that even those who exercise unjust rule rejoice to be called by this title. On the other hand, those who are genuine 'fathers of their household' are concerned for the welfare of all in their households in respect of the worship and service of God, as if they were all their children, longing and praying that they may come to the heavenly home, where it will not be a necessary duty to give orders to men, because it will no longer be a necessary duty to be concerned for the welfare of those who are already in the felicity of that immortal state. But until that home is reached, the fathers have an obligation to exercise the authority of masters greater than the duty of slaves to put up with their condition as servants.

However, if anyone is, through his disobedience, an enemy to the domestic peace, he is reproved by a word, or by a blow, or any other kind of punishment that is just and legitimate, to the extent allowed by human society; but this is for the benefit of the offender, intended to readjust him to the domestic peace from which he had broken away. For just as it is not an act of kindness to help a man, when the effect of the help is to make him lose a greater good, so it is not a blameless act to spare a man, when by so doing you let

[21]Text: CCL 48.683.

him fall into greater sin. Hence the duty of a blameless person includes not only doing no harm to anyone but also restraining a man from sin or punishing his sin, so that either the man who is chastised may be corrected by his experience, or others may be deterred by his example. Now a man's house ought to be the beginning, or rather a small component part of the civil community, and every beginning is directed to some end of its own kind, and every component part contributes to the completeness of the whole of which it forms a part. In other words, domestic peace contributes to the peace of the city—that is, the ordered harmony of those who live together in a house in the matter of giving and obeying orders, contributes to the ordered harmony concerning authority and obedience obtaining among the citizens. Consequently it is fitting that the father of a household should take his rules from the law of the city, and govern his household in such a way that it fits in with the peace of the city.

[Peace in the Heavenly Society and
Peace in the Earthly City]
XIX, 17.[22] But a household of human beings whose life is not based on faith is in pursuit of an earthly peace based on the things belonging to this temporal life, and on its advantages, whereas a household of human beings whose life is based on faith looks forward to the blessings which are promised as eternal in the future, making use of earthly and temporal things like a pilgrim in a foreign land, not as snares or obstructions to block their way to God, but simply as supports which help him more easily to bear the burdens of the corruptible body which weighs heavy on the soul; and not to increase its burdens. Thus both kinds of men and both kinds of households alike make use of the things essential for this mortal life; but each has its own very different end in making use of them. So also the earthly city, whose life is not based on faith, aims at an earthly peace, and it limits the goal of its peace, of its harmony of authority and

[22]Text: CCL 48.683.

obedience among its citizens, to the voluntary and collective attainment of objectives necessary to mortal existence. In contrast, the Heavenly City, or rather that part of it which is on pilgrimage in this condition of mortality, and which lives on the basis of faith—must make use of this peace also, until this mortal state, for which this kind of peace is essential, passes away. And therefore, it leads what we may call a life of captivity in this earthly city as in a foreign land, although it has already received the promise of redemption, and the gift of the Spirit as a kind of pledge of it; and yet it does not hesitate to obey the laws of the earthly city by which those things which are designed for the support of this mortal life are regulated; and the purpose of this obedience is that, since this mortal condition is shared by both cities, a harmony may be preserved between them in things that are relevant to this condition...

[The Peace of the Heavenly City Is the only True Peace]
While this Heavenly City, therefore, is on pilgrimage in this world, she calls out citizens from all nations and so collects a society of aliens, speaking all languages. She takes no account of any difference in customs, laws, and institutions, by which earthly peace is achieved and preserved—not that she annuls or abolishes any of those, rather, she maintains them and follows them (for whatever divergences there are among earthly peace), provided that no hindrance is presented thereby to the religion which teaches that the one supreme and true God is to be worshipped. Thus even the Heavenly City in her pilgrimage here on earth makes use of the earthly peace and defends and seeks the compromise between human wills in respect of the provisions relevant to the mortal nature of man, so far as may be permitted without detriment to true religion and piety. In fact, that City relates the earthly peace to the heavenly peace, which is so truly peaceful that it should be regarded as the only peace deserving the name, at least in respect of the rational creation. For this peace is the perfectly ordered and completely harmonious fellowship in the enjoyment of God, and of each other in God. When we arrive at that state of peace,

there will be no longer a life that ends in death, but a life that is life in sure and sober truth; there will be no animal body to 'weigh down the soul' in its process of corruption; there will be a spiritual body with no cravings, a body subdued in every part to the will. This peace the Heavenly City possesses in faith while on its pilgrimage, and it lives a life of righteousness, based on this faith, having the attainment of that peace in view in every good action it performs in relation to God, and in relation to a neighbor, since the life of a city is inevitably a social life.

LETTERS

[Whether Heretics Should Be Persecuted:
Augustine's Earlier View on Tolerance]
44, 7-11.[23] Fortunius began to insist that I should answer categorically this question: Whether the persecutor or the persecuted is in the right? I replied that the question was not fairly stated: it might be that both were in the wrong, or that the persecution might be made by the one who was the more righteous of the two parties; and therefore it was not always right to infer that one is on the better side because he suffers persecution, although that is almost always the case. When I perceived that he still laid great stress upon this, wishing to have the justice of the cause of his party acknowledged as beyond dispute because they had suffered persecution, I asked him whether he believed Ambrose, bishop of the Church of Milan, to be a righteous man and a Christian. He was compelled to deny expressly that that man was a Christian and a righteous man; for if he had admitted this, I would at once have objected to him that he thought it necessary for him to be rebaptized. When, therefore, he was compelled to pronounce concerning Ambrose that he was a not a Christian nor a righteous man, I related the persecution which he endured when his church was surrounded with soldiers. I also asked whether Maximianus, who had

[23]Text: CSEL 34.114.

made a schism from their party at Carthage, was in his view a righteous man and a Christian. He could not but deny this. I therefore reminded him that he had endured such persecution that his church had been razed to the foundations. By these instances I tried to persuade him, if possible, to give up affirming that the suffering of persecution is the most infallible mark of Christian righteousness.

He also related that, in the beginning of their schism, his predecessors, being anxious to devise some way of hushing up the fault of Caecilianus, lest a schism should take place, had appointed over the people belonging to his communion in Carthage an interim bishop before Majorinus was ordained in opposition to Caecilianus. He alleged that this interim bishop was murdered in his own meeting-house by our party. This, I confess, I had never heard before, though so many charges brought by them against us have been refuted and disproved, while greater and more numerous crimes have been alleged by us against them. After having narrated this story, he began again to insist on my answering whether in this case I thought the murderer or the victim the more righteous man; as if he had already proved that the event had taken place as he had stated. I therefore said that we must first ascertain the truth of the story, for we ought not to believe without examination all that is said; and that even were it true, it was possible either that both were equally bad, or that one who was bad had caused the death of another yet worse than himself. For, in truth, it is possible that the one who rebaptizes the whole man is more guilty than him who kills the body only.

After this there was no occasion for the question which he afterwards put to me. He affirmed that even a bad man should not be killed by Christians and righteous men; as if we called those who in the Catholic Church do such things righteous men. Moreover, such a statement is easier for them to affirm than to prove to us, since they themselves, with few exceptions, bishops, presbyters, and clergy of all kinds, go on gathering mobs of most demented men, and causing, wherever possible, so many violent massacres and devastations to the injury not of Catholics only, but sometimes even of their own partisans. In spite of these facts, Fortunius, affecting ignorance of their most villainous doings, which were better known by him than by me, insisted upon my giving an example of a righteous man putting even a bad man to death. This was, of course, not relevant to the matter in hand; for I conceded that wherever such crimes were committed by men having the name of Christians, they were not the actions of good men. Nevertheless, in order to show him what was the true question before us, I answered by inquiring whether Elijah seemed to him to be a righteous man; to which he could not but asset. Thereupon I reminded him how many false prophets Elijah slew with his own hand (cf. 1 Kings 18:40). He saw plainly therein, as indeed he could not but see, that such things were then lawful to righteous men. For they did these things as prophets guided by the Spirit and sanctioned by the authority of God, who knows infallibly to whom it may be even a benefit to be put to death. He therefore required me to show him any righteous person who in the New Testament times had put any one, even a criminal and impious man, to death.

I then attempted to show that it was not right either for us to reproach them with atrocities of which some of their party had been guilty, or for them to reproach us if any such deeds were found by them to have been done on our side. For I granted that no example could be produced from the New Testament of a righteous man putting any one to death. But I insisted that by the example of our Lord Himself, it could be proved that the wicked had been tolerated by the innocent. For he allowed His own betrayer, who had already received the price of His blood, to remain undistinguished from the innocent who were with Him, even up to that last kiss of peace. He did not conceal from the disciples the fact that in the midst of them was one capable of such a crime; nevertheless, He administered to them all alike, without excluding the traitor, the first sacrament of His body and blood (cf. Mt 26:20-28).

From this we passed on to something else, many on both sides discoursing to the best of their ability. Among other things it was alleged that our party was still intending to persecute them; and he (Fortunius) said that he would like to see how I would act in the event of such persecution, whether I would consent to such cruelty, or withhold from it all countenance. I said that God saw my heart, which they could not see; and that they had hitherto had no ground for apprehending such persecution, which if it did take place would be the work of bad men, who were, however, not so bad as some of their own party. I further pointed out that it was not incumbent on us to withdraw ourselves from communion with the Catholic Church on the ground of anything done against our will, and even in spite of our opposition (if we had an opportunity of testifying against it), since we had learned that toleration for the sake of peace which the apostle prescribes in the words: "Forbearing one another in love, endeavoring to keep the unity of the Spirit in the bond of peace" (Eph 4:2,3). I affirmed that they had not preserved this peace and forbearance, when they had caused a schism, within which, moreover, the more moderate among them now tolerated more serious evils, lest that which was already a fragment should be broken again, although they did not, in order to preserve unity, consent to exercise forbearance in smaller things. I also said that in the ancient economy the peace of unity and forbearance had not been so fully declared and commended as it is now by the example of the Lord and the charity of the New Testament; and yet prophets and holy men were wont to protest against the sins of the people, without endeavoring to separate themselves from the unity of the Jewish people, and from communion in partaking along with them of the sacraments then appointed.

["Compel Them to Come in": Augustine's Later Advocacy of Force and Compulsion]
93, 5-10.[24] To Vincentius, My Brother Dearly Beloved, Augustine sends greetings.

You are of opinion that no one should be compelled to follow righteousness; and yet you read that the householder

[24]Text: CSEL 34.449.

said to his servants, "Whomsoever you shall find, compel them to come in" (Lk 14:23). You also read how he who was at first Saul, and afterwards Paul, was compelled, by the great violence with which Christ coerced him, to know and to embrace the truth; for you cannot but think that the light which our eyes enjoy is more precious to men than money or any other possession. This light, lost suddenly by him when he was cast to the ground by the heavenly voice, he did not recover until he became a member of the Holy Church. You are also of opinion that no coercion is to be used with any man with a view to deliver him from the fatal consequences of error; and yet you see that, in examples which cannot be disputed, this is done by God, who loves us with more real regard for our profit than any other can. And you also hear Christ saying: "No man can come to me except the Father draw him" (Jn 6:44), which is done in the hearts of all those who, through fear of the wrath of God, come near to Him. You know also that sometimes the thief scatters food before the flock that he may lead them astray, and sometimes the shepherd brings wandering sheep back to the flock with his rod.

Did not Sarah, when she had the power, choose rather to afflict the insolent bondwoman? And truly she did not cruelly hate her whom she had formerly by an act of her own kindness made a mother; but she put a wholesome restraint upon her pride (Gen 16:5). Moreover, as you well know, these two women, Sarah and Hagar, and their two sons Isaac and Ishmael, are figures representing spiritual and carnal persons. And although we read that the bondwoman and her son suffered great hardships from Sarah, nevertheless the Apostle Paul says that Isaac suffered persecution from Ishmael: "But as then he that was born after the flesh persecuted him that was born after the Spirit, even so it is now" (Gal 4:29). Thus those who have understanding may perceive that it is rather the Catholic Church which suffers persecution through the pride and impiety of those carnal men whom it endeavors to correct by afflictions and terrors of a temporal kind. Whatever therefore the true and rightful Mother does, even when something severe and bitter is suffered by her children at her hands, she is not rendering evil for evil, but is applying the benefit of discipline to counteract the evil of sin, not with the hatred which seeks harm, but with the love which seeks to heal. . .

Let us learn, my brother, in actions which are similar to distinguish the intentions of the agents; and let us not, shutting our eyes, deal in groundless reproaches, and accuse those who seek men's welfare as if they did them wrong. In like manner, when the same apostle says that he had delivered certain persons unto Satan, that they might learn not to blaspheme (cf. 1 Tim 1:20), did he render to these men evil for evil, or did he not rather esteem it a good work to correct evil men by means of the evil one?

If to suffer persecution were in all cases a praiseworthy thing, it would have sufficed for the Lord to say, "Blessed are they which are persecuted," without adding "for righteousness' sake" (Mt 5:10). Moreover, if to inflict persecution were in all cases blameworthy, it would not have been written in the sacred books, "Whoever privately slanders his neighbor, him will I persecute" (Ps 101:5). In some cases, therefore, both he that suffers persecution is in the wrong, and he that inflicts it is in the right. But the truth is that always both the bad have persecuted the good, and good have persecuted the bad: the former doing harm by their unrighteousness, the latter seeking to do good by the administration of discipline; the former with cruelty, the latter with moderation; the former impelled by lust, the latter under the constraint of love. For he whose aim is to kill is not careful how he wounds, but he whose aim is to cure is cautious with his lancet; for the one seeks to destroy what is sound, the other that which is decaying. The wicked put prophets to death; prophets also put the wicked to death. The Jews scourged Christ; Christ also scourged the Jews. The apostles were given up by men to the civil powers; the apostles themselves gave men up to the power of Satan. In all these cases, it is important to attend to this: who were on the side of truth, and who on the side of iniquity; who acted from a desire to injure, and who from a desire to correct what was amiss?

You say that no example is found in the writings of evangelists and apostles, of any petition presented on behalf of the Church to the kings of the earth against her enemies. Who denies this? None such is found. But at that time the prophecy, "Be wise now, therefore, O you kings; be instructed, you judges of the earth: serve the Lord with fear," was not yet fulfilled. Up to that time the words which we find at the beginning of the same Psalm were receiving their fulfillment: "Why do the heathen rage, and the people imagine a vain thing? The kings of the earth set themselves, and the rulers take counsel together against the Lord, and against His Anointed" (Ps 2:1,2,10,11). Truly, if past events recorded in the prophetic books were figures of the future, there was given under King Nebuchadnezzar a figure both of the time which the Church had under the apostles, and of that which she has now. In the age of the apostles and martyrs, that was fulfilled which was prefigured when the aforementioned king compelled pious and just men to bow down to his image, and cast into the flames all who refused. Now, however, is fulfilled that which was prefigured soon after in the same king, when, being converted to the worship of the true God, he made a decree throughout his empire, that whosoever should speak against the God of Shadrach, Meshach, and Abednego, should suffer the penalty which their crime deserved. The earlier time of that king represented the former age of emperors who did not believe in Christ, at whose hands the Christians suffered because of the wicked; but the later time of that king represented the age of the successors to the imperial throne, now believing in Christ, at whose hands the wicked suffer because of the Christians.

It is manifest, however, that moderate severity, or rather clemency, is carefully observed towards those who, under the Christian name, have been led astray by perverse men, in the measures used to prevent them who are Christ's sheep from wandering, and to bring them back to the flock, when by punishments, such as exile and fines, they are admonished to consider what they suffer and why, and are taught to prefer the Scriptures which they read to human legends and calumnies...

93, 16-19.[25] You now see therefore, I suppose, that the thing to be considered when any one is coerced, is not the mere fact of the coercion, but the nature of that to which he is coerced, whether it be good or bad. Not that any one can be good in spite of his own will, but that, through fear of suffering what he does not desire, he either renounces his hostile prejudices, or is compelled to examine the truth of which he had been contentedly ignorant; and under the influence of this fear repudiates the error which he was wont to defend, or seeks the truth of which he formerly knew nothing, and now willingly holds what he formerly rejected. Perhaps it would be utterly useless to assert this in words, if it were not demonstrated by so many examples. We see not a few men here and there, but many cities, once Donatist, not Catholic, vehemently detesting the diabolical schism, and ardently loving the unity of the church; and these became Catholic under the influence of that fear which is to you so offensive by the laws of emperors, from Constantine, before whom your party of their own accord impeached Caecilianus, down to the emperors of our own time, who most justly decree that the decision of the judge whom your own party chose, and whom they preferred to a tribunal of bishops, should be maintained in force against you.

I have therefore yielded to the evidence afforded by these instances which my colleagues have laid before me. For originally my opinion was, that no one should be coerced into the unity of Christ, that we must act only by words, fight only by arguments, and prevail by force of reason, lest we should have those whom we knew as avowed heretics feigning themselves to be Catholics. But this opinion of mine was overcome not by the words of those who controverted it, but by the conclusive instances to which they could point. For, in the first place, there was set over against my opinion my own town, which, although it was once wholly on the side of Donatus, was brought over to the Catholic unity by fear of the imperial edicts, but which we now see

[25]Text: CSEL 34.461.

filled with such detestation of your ruinous perversity, that it would scarcely be believed that it had ever been involved in your error. There were so many others which were mentioned to me by name, that from facts themselves, I was made to own that to this matter the word of Scripture might be understood as applying: "Give opportunity to a wise man, and he will be yet wiser" (Prov 9:9). For how many were already, as we assuredly know, willing to be Catholics, being moved by the indisputable plainness of truth, but daily putting off their avowal of this through fear of offending their own party! How many were bound, not by truth—for you never pretended to that as yours—but by the heavy chains of inveterate custom, so that in them was fulfilled the divine saying: "A servant (who is hardened) will not be corrected by words; for though he understands, he will not answer" (Prov 29:19)! How many supposed the sect of Donatus to be the true Church, merely because ease had made them too listless, or conceited, or sluggish, to take pains to examine Catholic truth! How many would have entered earlier had not the calumnies of slanderers, who declared that we offered something else than we do upon the altar of God, shut them out! How many, believing that it mattered not to which party a Christian might belong, remained in the schism of Donatus only because they had been born in it, and no one was compelling them to forsake it and pass over into the Catholic Church!

To all these classes of persons the dread of those laws in the promulgation of which kings serve the Lord in fear has been so useful that now some say: We were willing for this some time ago; but thanks to God, who has given us occasion for doing it at once, and has cut off the hesitancy of procrastination! Others say: We already knew this to be true, but we were held prisoners by the force of old custom; but thanks be to the Lord, who has broken these bonds asunder, and has brought us into the bond of peace! Others say: We knew not that the truth was here, and we had no wish to learn it; fear, however, made us become earnest to examine it when we became alarmed, lest, without any gain in things eternal, we should be smitten with loss in temporal things, but thanks be to the Lord, who has by the stimulus of fear startled us from our negligence, that now being disquieted we might inquire into those things which, when at ease, we did not care to know! Others say: We were prevented from entering the Church by false reports, which we could not know to be false unless we entered it; and we would not enter unless we were compelled; but thanks be to the Lord, who by His scourge took away our timid hesitation, and taught us to find out for ourselves how vain and absurd were the lies which rumor had spread abroad against His Church; by this we are convinced that there is no truth in the accusations made by the authors of this heresy, since the more serious charges which their followers have invented are without foundation. Others say: We thought, indeed, that it mattered not in what communion we held the faith of Christ; but thanks to the Lord, who has gathered us in from a state of schism, and has taught us that it is fitting that the one God be worshipped in unity...

7

LATE LATIN CHRISTIAN FATHERS

We will conclude our survey of patristic social doctrine with two popes, Leo I and Gregory I. Both are called "Great" not only because of their holiness and administrative ability but also because of the importance of their teaching. In a real way they anticipated the more recent social teachings of their successors, from Leo XIII to John Paul II.

Part One: Leo the Great

Leo the Great (c. 390-461) is one of the greatest popes of antiquity. He distinguishes himself as a promoter of the unity of the church and a defender of Western civilization against the barbarian invaders.

Though Leo is mostly remembered in the history of dogma for his Letter to Flavian on the hypostatic union of Christ, his social teaching is no less influential. Thanks to his understanding of the Incarnation he has a high esteem for the dignity of human nature. Hence he urges respect and concern for the poor. In his sermons he strongly recommends fasting in view of almsgiving. "Let the abstinence of the faithful become the food of the poor" (Sermon 20). "Fasting without almsgiving is an an affliction of the flesh rather than a purging of the soul" (Sermon 15). He emphasizes the social purpose of riches and the strict duty of sharing them (Sermon 10). He also sternly condemns usury (Sermon 17).

SERMONS 10 AND 17

[Goods Are Given Us, Not as Our Own Possessions, but for Use in God's Service]

10.[1] Beloved: Keeping the ordinances of apostolic tradition, and with the shepherd's care for his flock, we exhort you to celebrate with the zeal of religious practice the day which our predecessors cleansed from pagan superstition and dedicated to works of mercy; let us show that the authority of our fathers lives amongst us and that their teaching is still preserved in our obedience. The holy purpose of this observance did not look only to times past, but to our age as well, and what served our forbears in the destruction of vanities was meant to profit us in the increase of virtues. For what can be so fitting to faith or so close a concern of piety as to assist the poverty of the needy, take up the care of the sick, relieve the wants of our brethren, and in the distress of others to call our own condition to mind? How much in this matter a person can or cannot do is a thing truly discerned only by him who knows his own gifts to each. For it is not only spiritual wealth and heavenly graces that are received from God's hands; earthly and material riches too flow from his bounty, and therefore it is with justice that he will ask an account of them, since he himself has not so much given them to be possessed as put them in trust to be administered. Justly and wisely, then, must we use the gifts of god, lest the means to good works should become a cause of sin. In their own nature, in their own kind, riches are good, and most

---

[1] Text: PL 54.164.

useful to human society; I mean when they are handled by men of good and generous heart, when they are not squandered by the prodigal or hidden by the miser, for by ill hoarding or foolish spending they are alike lost.

But though it is praiseworthy to shun intemperance and avoid the wastefulness of unworthy pleasures, and though again there are many persons given to magnificence who live lavishly, disdain to conceal their wealth, and shrink from petty and sordid meanness, yet there is no merit about such thrift and no happiness in such affluence if their riches serve themselves alone—if the poor are not helped by their money, if the sick are not cared for, if out of all the abundance of their prosperity the captive finds no ransom, the stranger no comfort, the exile no aid. Rich men such as these are poorer than all the poor. They lose the wealth which they might perpetuate; and while they cling to possessions which will not last long and which they cannot always freely enjoy, they are starved of the bread of justice and the sweetness of mercy; they are glittering without and dark within; they abound in things temporal but are poor in things eternal, for they afflict their own souls with hunger and shame them with nakedness, entrusting everything to their earthly barns and laying up nothing in the treasure-houses of heaven.

[The Duty of Mercy Outweighs All Other Virtues]

But perhaps there are some rich men who without assisting the Church's poor by alms nevertheless keep other commandments of God; having merits of faith and uprightness they think they will be pardoned for the lack of this one virtue. But this virtue is such that without it their other virtues—if indeed they have them—can be of no avail. For although a man be free of guilt, and chaste, and sober, and adorned with other still greater decorations, yet if he is not merciful, he cannot deserve mercy. Our Lord in fact says that the merciful are blessed because on them God will have mercy. And when the Son of Man comes in his majesty and sits on the throne of his glory; when all nations are assembled and division is made between good and bad, for what will they be praised who stand on the right? Only for the works of kindness and deeds of charity, which Jesus Christ will hold to be spent on himself; for he who made man's nature his own nature withdrew himself in nothing from human lowliness. And what will be the reproach to those on the left hand? Only the neglect of love, the harshness of inhumanity, the denial of mercy to the poor. It is as if the first had no other virtues, the second no other sins. But at the great and final day of judgment, such value will be set on the liberality of giving or the wickedness of avarice that they outweigh all other virtues and all other sins. Thus, it is by the path of that one good thing that men will gain entrance into the kingdom, and by the path of that one bad thing that men will be sent to everlasting fire.

[The Efficacy of Almsgiving in Forgiving Sins]
Therefore, beloved, let no man flatter himself on any merits of holy living if he lacks the works of charity, or be confident in the purity of his body when he is not cleansed by the purification of alms. Alms blot out sins, destroy death, and quench the punishment of eternal fire. But he who is without the fruit of them will be far from the mercy of the giver of a recompense, as Solomon says: "He who stops his ears that he may not hear the weak, he also shall call upon the Lord, and there shall be none to hear him" (Prov 21:13). And therefore Tobias also says, instructing his own son with the precepts of religion: "Give alms out of your substance, and turn not away your face from any poor person; and so it shall come to pass that the face of the Lord shall not be turned away from you" (Tob 4:7). This virtue makes all virtues profitable, since by its presence it quickens even faith, by which the just man lives and which without works is called dead; for as works find their principle in faith, so faith finds its strength in works. "Therefore," as the Apostle says, "while we have time, let us work good to all men, but especially to those of the household of faith. And let us not weary in doing good; for in due time we shall reap" (Gal 6:9-10). Thus our life now is the time of sowing, and the day of recompense is the time of harvest, when each man will reap the fruit of what he sowed, according to the quantity of

his sowing. Nor will hope be deceived at the harvest's yield; for it is the measure of will, not of spending, that will be reckoned, and the little increase from little will be as fruitful as great from great. Therefore, beloved, let the apostolic ordinances be fulfilled, Sunday is the day of the first Collection; prepare yourselves all for this act of free devotion, that each of you according to his powers may take his share in the sacred offering. The alms themselves, and those who benefit by your gifts, will alike make intercession for you, that you may be ready always for every good work, in Christ Jesus our Lord, who lives and reigns world without end. Amen.

[Fasting, Prayer, and Almsgiving in the Scripture]
17.[2] Beloved: The commands of the Gospel are much strengthened by the teaching of the Old Covenant when certain things from the Ancient Law are carried into the new Law, and when it is proved by the very observances of the Church how Jesus Christ our Lord came not to destroy the Law but to fulfill it (cf. Mt 5:17). There is indeed an end of the types by which our Savior's coming was heralded; the time of figures is past—they were abolished by the very presence of Truth. But things ordained by piety either for the rule of conduct or for the pure worship of God continue among us now in the very shape of their first founding, and ordinances fitting to either Testament have suffered no change. Among these is the solemn fast of the tenth month, which by yearly custom we are to celebrate now; for it is a thing full of justice and piety to give thanks to the divine bounty for the fruits which earth, under the guidance of Supreme Providence, has brought forth for the use of men. And to show that we make this thanksgiving with a ready will, we must take on ourselves not only the abstinence of fasting but the diligence of almsgiving, so that from the soil of our hearts too the shoots of justice and harvest of charity may spring forth. In this way we will deserve God's compassion by showing

[2]Text: PL 54.180.

compassion to his poor. For prayer to implore God is most powerful when it is seconded by the works of kindness; if a man does not turn away his will from the needy, he soon inclines to himself the hearing of the. Lord, as the Lord himself says: "Be merciful, even as your Father is merciful; forgive, and you shall be forgiven" (Lk 6:36-37). What could be more gracious than such justice or more merciful than such recompense, where the judge's sentence is put into the power of the man to be judged? "Give," he says, "and it shall be given you" (Lk 6:38). How quickly this cuts away the anxiety of the diffident, the miser's reluctance! Mercy may trustfully give away what truth itself promises to give back.

[Lending to the Lord Is a
Better Bargain than Lending to Man]
Be of good heart, then, Christian giver; give to receive, sow to reap, scatter to gather. Let there be no doubting over the outlay, no sighing over uncertainty in the yield. When your substance is rightly spent, it is increased. Let your desire be for mercy's righteous reward, let your trafficking be for everlasting gain. He who gives to you would have you a cheerful giver; he who bestows would have you distribute, saying, "Give, and it shall be given you." You are fortunate in the terms of that promise; embrace them; for though you have nothing that you have not received, you cannot but have what you have given away. If then any of you has a love of money, if he desires to multiply wealth with boundless increase, let him choose to ply this holy usury, let this be the method of interest that makes him rich—not the trading on wretched men's necessities, where specious benefit leads to the snare of irredeemable debts. Let him trust and lend his money to him who says: "Give, and it shall be given you; for with the same measure that you mete, it shall be measured to you again." A man is faithless and unjust to his own self if he refuses to keep for always what he thinks worthy of his affection. However much he may add to his wealth, however much he may store and heap up, he will go forth from this world poor and needy, as David the Prophet says: "For when he dies he shall take nothing with him" (Ps 48:18). If he

were kind to his own soul, he would lend his riches to him who is a faithful surety for the poor and who most bountifully renders interest. But unrighteous and shameless greed, pretending to benefit men while it deceives them, will not trust the truthful promise of God and yet trusts the bond of some fear-driven man; and thinking things present surer than things to come, often and rightly meets with such fortune that the lust for unrighteous gain is the cause of not unrighteous loss.

[Usury Is Evil in All Respects]

And therefore, whatever the outcome, the usurer's case is always evil, for whether he adds to his wealth or lessens it, he is equally evil—wretched if he loses what he has given, more wretched still if he gets what he has not given. This wickedness of usury ought to be shunned altogether—men should shrink from gain which is so inhuman. Their wealth is multiplied by unjust and ill-omened increase, but the wealth of their own selves withers away and the interest of money is the death of the soul. God's judgment of such is made plain by the holy Prophet David. "Who, Lord," he asks, "shall dwell in your holy tabernacle, or who shall rest in your holy mountain?" (Ps 14:1). The divine voice gives him answer and instruction; he learns that the man who wins everlasting rest is he "who," besides other rules of religious living, "has not put out his money to usury"; alien, it is revealed, alien from the tabernacle of God and far from his holy mountain is the man who seeks specious gain from usury on his money, and wishing to become rich by the loss of others, is found worthy to be punished by everlasting want.

[Avoid Avarice and Share God's Gift with Others]

You, therefore, beloved, who with all your hearts have believed the promises of the Lord, flee from the filthy leprosy of greed and use God's gifts with justice and wisdom; and since you justly rejoice at his bounty, busy yourselves to have sharers in your joy. Many lack what you have in plenty, and in some men's need you have been given the means of imitating the divine goodness, that through you

God's gifts might pass to others and that by right dispensing of good things temporal you might possess the good things eternal.

Part Two: Gregory the Great

Gregory (c. 540-604), of noble birth and wealthy family, abandoned his political career to lead a religious life. He sold his vast property and distributed the proceeds to the poor. During his pontificate (590-604), he strengthened the supremacy of the Roman see and established the temporal power of the papacy, especially in his dealings with the Lombards with whom he concluded a separate peace treaty in 592-3. In his administration of the vast estates of the Church, in which he spent huge sums for the relief of the poor, he showed conspicuous firmness and strength of character, gentleness and charity, skill and foresight. One of his claims to fame is also his success in converting England to Christianity.

Gregory is a very fertile author, and, like Leo I, is of a practical rather than speculative bent of mind. He is pre-eminently a moralist (the *Moralia*, the *Pastoral Rule*, and the *Dialogues*). His oratorical works include *Homilies on the Gospels* and *Homilies on Ezechiel*. As far as historical doctrine is concerned, Gregory re-affirms the teaching of the preceding Fathers regarding wealth and possessions: private property as administration, the social function of property, the strict duty in justice to share one's goods with others. The reason for the social function of property is that we have received all our goods from God not in order to possess them privately, but to use them for the common good. Gregory has preached a sermon on the Rich Man and Lazarus. It would be instructive to compare his commentary with those of John Chrysostom and Jerome.

THE PASTORAL RULE

[How to Admonish Those Who Do Not Give]
III, 21.[3] Different admonition should be given to those who neither desire what belongs to others nor give what is their own on the one hand, and to those who give of what they have, but do not desist from taking what belongs to others on the other. Those who neither desire what belongs to others nor give what is their own should be admonished to consider carefully that the earth of which they dispose is common to all men, and therefore brings forth nourishment for all in common. Wrongly, then, do those suppose themselves innocent who claim for their own private use the common gift of God; those who, by not sharing what they have received, are accomplices of the death of their neighbors, since they every day in a certain way kill as many as those who die of hunger whose subsidies they refuse to give. For, when we give necessities of any kind to the poor, we do not bestow our own, we give them back what is theirs; we rather pay a debt of justice than accomplish works of mercy.

[How to Admonish Those Who Give but also Rob]
On the other hand, those who both give what they have and do not desist from taking what belongs to others should be admonished not to desire to appear excessively generous, and so be made worse from the outward show of goodness. For these, giving what is their own without discretion, not only fall into the murmuring of impatience, but also, when necessity urges them, are swept along even to avarice. What, then, is more wretched than the mind of those in whom avarice is born of bountifulness, and a crop of sins is sown as it were from virtue? First, then, they are to be admonished to

³Text: PL 77.87; cf.ACW 11.158.

learn how to keep what is theirs reasonably, and then in the end not to go about getting what is another's. For, if the root of the fault is not burnt out in the profusion itself, the thorn of avarice, exuberant through the branches, is never dried up. So then, the occasion for robbing will be taken away if first the right to possess is properly exercised. Once they have learnt not to confound the good of mercy by throwing into it the wickedness of robbery, they will next be admonished how to give mercifully what they have. For they violently demand what they mercifully bestow. For it is one thing to show mercy on account of our sins; another thing to sin on account of showing mercy; which can no longer indeed by called mercy, since it cannot grow into sweet fruit, being embittered by the poison of its pestiferous root.

HOMILY

[The Rich Man's Sin Consists in Not Giving]
40.3.[4] "There was a certain rich man; he was clothed with purple and fine linen, and feasted sumptuously every day. And there was a certain beggar named Lazarus, who lay at the rich man's gate, covered with sores." There are those who think that the Old Testament has stricter commandments than the New, but they judge too hastily and deceive themselves. What is punished under the Law is not avarice but theft; the thing seized unlawfully is to be given back fourfold in restitution. But the rich man here is not blamed for stealing the goods of others, he is blamed for not parting with his own. Nor are we told that he cast down anyone by violence, only that in his wealth he exalted himself too high. Mark the inference; if a man is damned for not distributing goods of his own, what will be the penalty for plundering another's? Let no one then think to excuse himself by saying: "See, I commit no robbery, I do but enjoy my lawful portion." The cause of the rich man's doom was not that he took away anything from his neighbors, it was that through

[4]Text: PL 76.1304.

his riches he wilfully left behind him the care and the knowledge of himself. What sent him to hell was that he kept no misgivings in his prosperity, that he turned the good things given to him to the service of pride, that he did not regard feelings of pity, that he would not redeem his sins when he had in plenty the means of ransom...

[God Recognizes the Humble but Does Not Know the Proud]

Truth Itself is the speaker here; and we must closely mark how these two are spoken of in turn—the proud rich man, the humble poor man. The words are, first, "There was a certain rich man"; then, "There was a certain beggar named Lazarus." In common life the names of the rich are better known than those of the poor. How comes it then that when our Lord has to speak of both he names the poor man and not the rich? The answer is that God knows and approves the humble but does not know the proud. Hence, at the end of the world, there are some men proud of their mighty miracles to whom he will say: "I know not whence you are: depart from me, all you workers of iniquity." On the contrary it is said to Moses: "I know you by name" (Ex 33:12). Thus in our text he says of the rich man, "A certain man," and of the poor man, "A beggar named Lazarus." He means, that is: "I know the meek poor man, not the proud rich man; the one my acceptance knows, the other my judgment rejects and knows nothing of."

[A Twofold Judgment of God]

Consider, again, how skillful is our Creator's ordinance, and how one thing is made to serve more than one purpose. Here we have Lazarus the beggar, covered with sores, lying outside the rich man's gate. That is one thing, but in God's wisdom it accomplished a twofold judgment. The rich man might perhaps have had some excuse if Lazarus with his sores and poverty had not lain at his gate, if he had been further off, if his misery had not struck the eye. Again, had the rich man been far from the other's sight, the poor man's mind would have suffered less temptation. As it was, God placed the one at the other's gate—beggary and sores over against riches and luxury and abundance; the sight of the unpitied beggar filled up the rich man's measure of condemnation, the sight of the rich man was a daily trial and test to the beggar—each at the same time, each by God's providence. Here was the beggar, his body a mass of sores, lacking bread and lacking health; what temptations must have pressed upon him as he watched the other in health and wealth and luxury and enjoyment; as he looked at himself shot through with cold and pain and the other festive in purple and fine linen; himself all burdened with his afflicted flesh, the other at ease in his possessions; himself destitute, the other shutting his hand against him! Think, my brothers, what turmoil of temptations must have crowded then on the poor man's heart! His poverty would have been suffering enough had he been in health; his disease would have been suffering enough had he possessed the means of livelihood. Yet for his fuller testing he was wasted by poverty and disease at once. Then, too, he would watch how the rich man walked abroad with flatterers pressing at his side, while he in his want and wretchedness was visited by none—witness the dogs that were allowed to lick his sores. Thus in permitting one thing—the lying of Lazarus at the rich man's gate— Almighty God accomplished a twofold judgment— increased damnation for the rich man in his iniquity, increased reward for the beggar in his trial. The one saw daily an object for his mercilessness, the other means to his probation. Two hearts on earth, but one searcher of hearts in heaven, testing the one and training him to glory, bearing with the other and reserving him for requital.

[The Opposite Destiny of Lazarus and the Rich Man]
    The text goes on. "And it came to pass that the beggar died, and was carried by the angels into Abraham's bosom. And the rich man died also, and was buried in hell." The rich man in agony now seeks as his advocate the man whom on earth he had no pity for. Listen. "Lifting up his eyes when he was in torments, he saw Abraham afar off, and Lazarus in his bosom. And he cried out and said: Father Abraham,

have mercy on me, and send Lazarus to dip in water the tip of his finger to cool my tongue, for I am tormented in this flame." How scrupulous are the judgments of God, how searchingly he allots the recompense for good and for evil deeds! We were told before of Lazarus on earth that he craved for the crumbs from the rich man's table, and no man gave him them; we are told now of the rich man in hell that he yearned for water from Lazarus' finger-tip to be sprinkled upon his tongue.

[Consider the Riches of This World with Fear]

But Abraham's answer is to be marked, and marked with dread. "Son, remember that you in your lifetime did receive your good things, and Lazarus likewise his evil things. But now he is comforted and you are tormented." We need scarcely expound these words, my brothers, rather need we to tremble at them. Any of you who have received outward goods in this world should regard that outward gift with fear—fear that it may have been granted you as the sole recompense for some acts of yours, that the Judge who awards you outward blessings here may shut you out from the reward of inward blessing, that honor or riches here may prove to be not an aid to virtue but the final reward of your labor. In the words, "You in your lifetime did receive your good things," we are given to understand that the rich man had something good in him which called for a recompense of the good things in this life. Again, in the words of Lazarus, "He received his evil things," we are shown he had something evil in him which called for purging. But the evil in Lazarus was cleansed by the fire of destitution, the good in the rich man was recompensed by prosperity in this fleeting world. The one was afflicted and purified by poverty, the other rewarded and rejected by opulence. If then it is well with some of you in this world, when you recall good deeds of yours, view them with fear and trembling lest the prosperity you enjoy may be all the reward of those same deeds. And whenever you see poor folk doing some blameworthy things, do not despise them or give them up for lost; perhaps the light dross of evil in them is being purged in the furnace of poverty. Fear for yourselves in any case, for prosperous life has been known to follow on evil deeds. As for these others, scrupulously consider how poverty is their stern instructress, chastising their life and ways till she leads them to righteousness.

Then: "Besides all this, between us and you a great gulf is fixed, so that those who would cannot pass from here to you, nor come from there to here." We must ask ourselves what is meant by the words, "Those who would cannot pass from here to you." That those in hell should wish to pass to the lot of the blessed is manifest enough. But when men are received into bliss already, how can it be said of them that they wish to pass to the tortured in hell? Yet just as the reprobate seek to pass to the elect—to issue forth from the pains that harrow them—so too it is natural for the just to visit in thought those afflicted and tortured ones and wish to set them free. But they cannot do so, because the souls of the just, though their natural goodness inclines them to pity, are now conjoined to the justice of their Creator, and are themselves bound fast by such righteousness that compassion for the reprobate moves them no longer...

[Assist the Poor and the Afflicted]

So much, my brothers, in literal consideration of the story. Now for yourselves. You have learned of Lazarus' repose, you have learned of the rich man's torment. Act heedfully on this; seek out those who will plead for your sins and defend you in the day of judgment; these are the poor. You have many a Lazarus among you; many like him lie at your gates, in need of what falls from your tables when you have had your fill. The words of the sacred lesson should prompt us to do the commands of piety. Every day, if we will but search, we can find a Lazarus; every day we see a Lazarus although we make no search. The poor come unsought to crowd upon us and beg; and these are those who will one day be our intercessors. It is we who should do the asking, and yet they ask of us. Ought we to refuse the request when those who make it are our advocates? Do not waste the occasions for mercy, do not flout the means to salvation granted you. Think of doom before you come to it. When in this world you see outcast men, even though some things in them seem blameworthy, do not despise them. Poverty may be healing their blemishes. If some things in them really call for rebuke, you may and you should turn such things to your own reward, using these very faults to enrich your own piety. Give them bread and a word as well—the bread of refreshment, the word of correction; let them receive more food than they sought; nourish them with a spiritual as well as a bodily sustenance. If then the poor man you see is blameworthy, admonish him, but without despising him. If he has nothing to be reproached with, then give him your utmost veneration; he is one who will plead for you hereafter. But, you say, those we see are many, and we cannot apprize the deserts of each. Venerate them all, then; the greater your duty to humble yourself to all, since you do not know which poor man may be Christ.

Selected Bibliography

Baynes, *The Early Church and Social Life* (London, 1927)

Budde, G. J., "Christian Charity: The Fathers of the Church and Almsgiving," in *American Ecclesiastical Review* 85 (1931) 561-579.

Deane, H. A., *The Political and Social Ideas of St. Augustine* (Columbia University Press, New York and London 1963).

Gager, J. G., *Kingdom and Community: The Social World of Early Christianity* (Englewood Cliffs, New Jersey 1976).

Giordani, I., *The Social Message of the Early Church Fathers* (Paterson, New Jersey 1944).

Grant, R. M., *Early Christianity and Society* (Harper and Row, New York 1977).

Hengel, M., *Property and Riches in the Early Church* (Philadelphia 1974).

Huik, F. M., *The Philanthropic Motive in Christianity. An Analysis of the Relation Between Theology and Social Service* (Oxford 1938).

Parker, T. M., *Christianity and the State in the Light of History* (London 1945).

Ryan, J. A., *Alleged Socialism of the Church Fathers* (St. Louis 1913).

Shewring, W., *Rich and Poor in Christian Tradition* (London 1948).

Stead, F. H., *The Story of Social Christianity* (London 1924).

Wash, W. J. and Langan, J. P., "Patristic Social Conscious ness: The Church and the Poor," in J. C. Haughey (ed.), *The Faith that Does Justice*, Woodstock Studies 2 (Paulist Press, New York 1977) 113-151.